Running From A to Z

By the same author:
Cross Country & Road Running
Challenge of the Marathon

Running From A to Z

CLIFF TEMPLE

STANLEY PAUL
London Melbourne Auckland Johannesburg

Stanley Paul & Co. Ltd
An imprint of Century Hutchinson Ltd
62–65 Chandos Place, London WC2N 4NW

Century Hutchinson Australia (Pty) Ltd
PO Box 496, 16–22 Church Street, Hawthorn, Melbourne, Victoria 3122

Century Hutchinson New Zealand Limited
PO Box 40–086, Glenfield, Auckland 10

Century Hutchinson South Africa (Pty) Ltd
PO Box 337, Bergvlei 2012, South Africa

First published 1987

© Cliff Temple 1987

Set in 11/12 Ehrhardt

Printed and bound in Great Britain by
Butler & Tanner Ltd, Frome and London

British Library Cataloguing in Publication Data
Temple, Cliff
 Running from A to Z.
 1. Running – Dictionaries
 I. Title
 796.4'26   GV1061

ISBN 0 09 166410 1

This book is dedicated to my family, and in particular to my parents, William and Joan Temple, my wife Clare, and our children, Kristen, Kenza and William. All of them at some time or other during the previous three decades must have wondered where my long-time fascination with running would lead. This book is one result anyway!

Acknowledgements

The author and publishers would particularly like to thank Mark Shearman who supplied most of the photographs in this book. Thanks also to the BBC Hulton Picture Library, All-Sport, The Photo Source, Sport and General Press Agency, the National Film Archive and Dave Calderwood.

Contents

Acknowledgements	6
Introduction	9
AAA	11
Achilles tendon	11
Addiction	12
Adrenaline	12
AIMS	13
Alcohol	13
All-weather tracks	14
Altitude	14
Amenorrhoea	16
Anaemia	16
Ankle	17
Anorexia nervosa	18
Asthma	18
Bannister, Sir Roger	19
Barefoot running	21
BARR	22
Bay-to-Breakers	22
Bikila, Abebe	23
Bislett Stadium, Oslo	24
Black toenails	27
Blisters	27
Blood	28
Blood packing	29
Blood pressure	29
Body fat percentage	30
Bones	30
Boredom	31
Boston Marathon	31
Bowerman, Bill	34
Bras	35
Brasher, Chris	35
Breathing	37
Budd, Zola	37
Calf	41
Carbohydrate loading	41
Chafing	43
Chariots of Fire	44
Cheats	45
Chicago Marathon	47
Children	48
Cinque Mulini	50
Coaching	51
Coe, Sebastian	53
Coffee	58
Cold	58
Compartment syndrome	60
Course measurement	60
Cram, Steve	61
Cramp	65
Cross-country running	66
Decker-Slaney, Mary	76
Diary	78
Endorphins	79
Fantasy	79
Fartlek	80
Fibula	81
Fixx, James	81
Foot	83
Four-minute mile	84
Gasparilla Distance Classic	87
Gateshead	87
Gerschler, Woldemar	88
Glycogen	88
Gravity inversion	89
Great North Run	89
Hamstring	91
Heart	92
Heat	92
Hill training	94
Hip	95

Hitting the wall	96	Pronation	140
Holmér, Gösta	97	Pulse	141
Humidity	97		
Hypothermia	97	Quadriceps	141
IAAF	98	Resistance training	142
Ice	99	Rest	143
Injury	100	Restless leg syndrome	144
Insomnia	101	RRC	145
Interval training	102	Runner's high	145
Iron	103	Runner's knee	146
Jacuzzi	103	Sciatica	146
Jogger's nipple	103	Second wind	147
Jones counter	104	Sex	147
		Shin soreness	148
Knee	104	Shoes	148
Kristiansen, Ingrid	105	Sleep	155
		Smoking	155
Lactic acid	107	Snow	155
Lebow, Fred	108	Socks	156
Ligaments	109	Spikes	157
London Marathon	109	Sprinting	158
LSD	112	Staleness	160
Lungs	113	Starting blocks	161
Lydiard, Arthur	113	Steeplechase	162
		Stitch	163
Marathon	114	Stress fracture	163
Massage	117	Stride	164
Metatarsals	118	*Sunday Times* National Fun Run	165
		Supination	166
New York City Marathon	119	Sweating	166
Night running	121		
Nurmi, Paavo	121	Tibia	167
		Topless running	167
Orthotics	123	Track etiquette	168
Osgood Schlatter's disease	124	Tracksuit	168
Over-training	125		
Ovett, Steve	125	Ultramarathon: A tale of two races	170
Oxygen	129		
		Waffle-soled shoes	175
Pacemaker	130	Warming down	176
Peaking	131	Warming up	176
Penile frostbite	132	Wind chill factor	177
Pietri, Dorando	133	Wind gauge	178
Polytechnic Marathon	134	Women	179
Pregnancy	137		
Pre-race preparation	138	Zatopek, Emil	181

Introduction

In creating a book like *Running From A to Z*, my biggest problem was not what to put into it, but rather what to leave out. For my intention was to mix a running book cocktail which would reflect the long history of the sport and hint at the future, which would help you to run faster, identify and treat an injury, and yet still answer pub arguments about who won what, and when.

Most running books can be divided into groups. There are biographies, books on training, statistics, medical matters, and on history. This book is an attempt to be, uniquely I believe, all of these.

In its pages you will find some of the statistics which are such an integral part of the sport, plus lists of past champions, many compiled for the first time. If you want to know who won the 1976 New York Marathon, the 1899 National Cross Country title or the 1952 Cinque Mulini cross-country race, it's here.

If you want to know who invented the Jacuzzi (and why), which feuding brothers once jointly dominated the running shoe market, or how old Paavo Nurmi was when he died, it's here.

And if you are looking for some advice on training and health, on shoes and kit, on racing and recovering, I would like to think you will find what you are looking for here too.

So whether you are planning your training, settling a wager, or simply browsing and delving into some running trivia (what *is* a Jones counter?), I hope you enjoy our run from A to Z.

Cliff Temple
Hythe, Kent
August 1987

AUTHOR'S NOTE

The vast majority of practical topics in this book apply both to male and female runners, and where they do not it is usually self-evident. However, for the sake of simplicity in the text I have used the words he/him/his where she/her/hers could equally apply, and I trust the reasoning behind this apparently sexist approach will be understood.

A

AAA

The Amateur Athletic Association (AAA), the world's first governing body for track and field athletics, controls the men's section of the sport in England and Wales. It is the largest of the eight constituent bodies which represent the four home countries, and in turn form the British Amateur Athletic Board.

The AAA was founded on 24 April 1880 at a meeting in the banqueting hall of the Randolph Hotel, Oxford, where a plaque was unveiled exactly one hundred years later by Lord Burghley, the Olympic 400m hurdles champion of 1928, who was President of the AAA from 1936–76.

The annual AAA Championships were first held at Lillie Bridge, West Brompton, London, in 1880 and these open championships (now traditionally held at Crystal Palace in south London) remain one of the most prestigious championship events in the sport's calendar.

The AAA now has its offices at Francis House, Francis Street, London SW1P 1DL (Tel. 01-828 9326).

Achilles tendon

The Achilles tendon, which connects the calf to the heel bone, is frequently the site of pain among distance runners. Treatment with ice packs, and the temporary insertion of heel pads in the shoes to slightly reduce the range of movement of the tendons, is the most effective self-help, but tracing the cause of the pain is essential.

Often a sudden change in training, such as a switch to hill running or wearing spiked shoes after months in flat shoes, is enough to stretch the tendon a little further than it has recently been accustomed to working. In interval training, jogging the recovery in spikes can actually

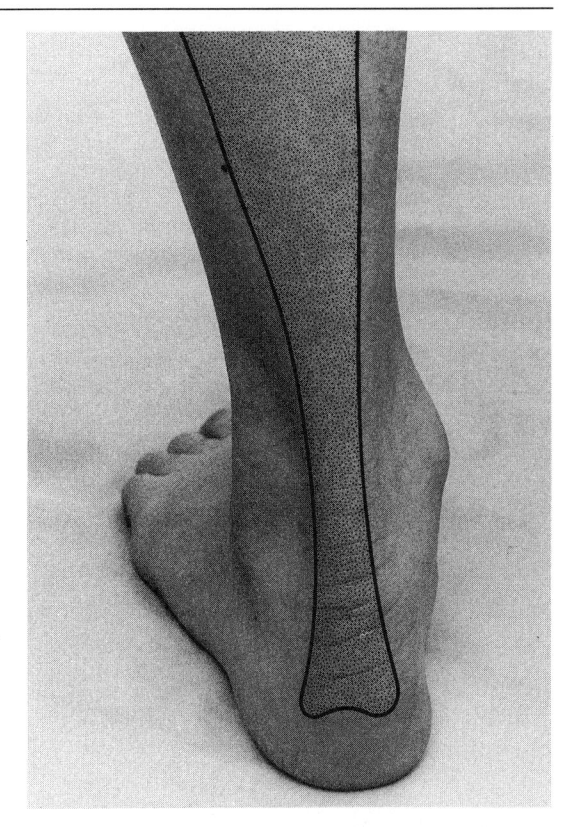

The Achilles tendon, connecting calf and heel bone, is often the cause of pain in distance runners

put more of a strain on the tendons than the actual running.

So a cautious approach to any such change is essential, and specific stretching exercises before and after training can help prevent Achilles tendon strain. These exercises can include standing on a step or kerb with the heels protruding some inches over the edge of the step, then gently lowering the heels, holding the position for 5–10 seconds, and repeating it a number of times. Alternatively, standing some 2–3 feet away from a wall, but leaning against it with the hands, and then bending the elbows but keeping the heels flat on the ground, can help to stretch the tendons.

In the case of Achilles tendon pain being caused by training shoes which have worn down excessively under the heels, nothing less than discarding them will prevent the problem recurring.

The potential for damage to the Achilles being caused by so-called Achilles tendon 'protectors' on running shoes has long been recognized by the medical profession. These are the raised sections of the shoe, behind the heel, which developed from being simply a convenient tab for pulling on the shoes into a frequently rigid design feature which can actually dig into the vulnerable tendon on every stride and cause damage. As a precaution, the cutting of two vertical slits, about three quarters of an inch in length, straight down each side of the offending tabs, can reduce the pressure being put on the tendons without adversely affecting the stability of the shoe. Gradually, shoe manufacturers are acknowledging this design blemish and adapting their new models accordingly.

Addiction

Although running regularly is widely accepted as an ideal means to maintain good health and fitness, as well as improving competitive performance, it may become, in extreme cases, addictive. Sometimes a runner may not even be able to properly relax and enjoy the rest of his activities until after his daily 'fix' of a run.

So caution and perspective have to be retained. If your need to run starts to infringe on the activities of others, particularly within the family circle, it can begin to become a sensitive area, and in extremes even create domestic tensions. At that point a re-examination of priorities may be required, because as a healthy recreational activity running should be seen as a way to expand, rather than restrict, the quality of life. But with some careful organization, and perhaps a little selfless restructuring of the daily routine, it should usually be possible for everyone to be satisfied.

Non-runners may find the slavish desire of others to get out and run somewhat mysterious. One explanation could come from the strong association now identified between exercise and a rise in the level of endorphins, which are brain chemicals produced by the pituitary gland. These have qualities similar to morphine in their pain-reducing effects, and may possibly also contribute towards a mild form of addiction for running. Certainly they are felt to be partly responsible for the euphoric feeling experienced by some runners during training and known as 'runner's high'. Runners therefore have to remain aware that their view of a training run as being indispensable may not necessarily be shared, or even understood, by non-runners. Diplomacy and negotiation may be required at times!

See also *Endorphins, Runner's High*.

Adrenaline

Adrenaline and noradrenaline are hormones which are released by the adrenal glands when the body is faced with a stressful situation. In athletic terms, they are associated with the nervous anticipation of a competition, or a strenuous challenge like a marathon, and the heart rate and blood pressure are involuntarily increased in readiness for hard physical effort.

More blood is consequently sent to the muscles at the expense of the supply to the skin and the gut, which is why the skin may go pale before a race, and why it would be difficult to digest heavy foodstuffs in the hours immediately prior to such an effort.

If the anticipation of this sporting equivalent of 'fight or flight' (Nature's original plan) is insufficient to set off this chain reaction, the athlete may complain of feeling flat, and subsequently perform below his normal level. But there is little doubt that to a reasonable degree such nervousness will actually heighten the ability of the body to perform well through the release of these hormones into the bloodstream.

But it may be the shorter-distance events which most benefit from adrenaline. To become too nervous before a long-distance event, such as a marathon, could result in setting off at an unreasonable pace, and regretting it later.

Other physical signs of nervousness are yawning before a race (subconsciously trying to drag in extra oxygen before the challenge ahead?), and an increased need to visit the toilets. In normal pre-race circumstances, neither is a cause for concern.

AIMS

The Association of International Marathons (AIMS) was founded in London in May 1982 'to foster and promote marathon running throughout the world. To work with the International Amateur Athletic Federation on all matters relating to international marathons. To exchange information, knowledge and expertise among the members of the association.'

Most of the world's leading marathons are members of AIMS, and its vigilance on such controversial matters as accuracy in course measurement has helped bring some form of self-governing standardization into an event which probably has more worldwide exposure than any other Olympic event.

At present records for marathon performances are not officially recognized because of the varying terrain on which such races are held, quite apart from the possibility of measurement error. But AIMS is hoping to be able to produce a formula acceptable to the IAAF with regard to allowable descent between start and finish, measurement stipulations, and even possible wind assistance, which will eventually see the recognition of marathon records alongside those set on the track.

Alcohol

Although many runners enjoy a drink or two in moderation, alcoholic drinking is best left until after a race or training run. While there are instances of people who claim to be able to run off the effects, alcohol does impair the runner's efficiency by decreasing the amount of blood the heart pumps with each beat, and increasing the heart's oxygen requirement.

Alcohol also has a diuretic effect, which includes making you sweat more easily, with the increased possibility of the runner becoming

International marathons, like the enormously popular London race, now work together through AIMS

dehydrated, particularly on a warm day. Around 100cc of water has to be excreted by the body for every 10gm of alcohol drunk; as an example of extremes, drinking whisky (approximately 40 per cent alcohol) in the desert would cause dehydration at such a rate that as a result of its effect as a diuretic, death could even occur. Wine (about 10 per cent alcohol) and beer (around 5 per cent) pose less of a threat, but half a pint of beer or a glass of wine still take an hour to be metabolized by the liver.

Running does enable you to combat the weight-gaining effects of drinking, and to enjoy a drink with a clear conscience. But it should always come in the order of running first, and drinking alcohol second.

Alternatively, there are a considerable number of runners who find that the exercise in itself is quite sufficient to induce the same type of relaxed and uninhibited feelings which alcohol can promote without drinking anything stronger than orange juice. It is also considerably cheaper.

All-weather tracks

Running tracks, traditionally constructed of cinder or grass, underwent a revolution in the sixties with the introduction of synthetic 'all-weather' surfaces which provided a reliable, weather-resistant track. The very first all-weather surface was a rubberized asphalt track laid at Buffalo, New York State, by the US Rubber Reclaiming Company in 1950.

But it was much later before such track surfaces became widely available. The first world record set on an all-weather surface was the 9.1-sec 100 yards run by American Bob Hayes (the 1964 Olympic champion) in winning the AAU National title of St Louis on 21 June 1963. The track consisted of a mixture of rubber, asphalt and crushed stone, laid on top of cinders and rolled to a thickness of $1\frac{1}{2}$ inches. The IAAF hesitated before ratifying the record, but finally did so. Also in 1963 the New Zealand runner Bill Baillie set world records for the 20km (59:28.6) and 1 hour run (20.190km/12 miles 960 yards) on a bitumen track in Auckland. The revolution had started, and the 1964 Tokyo Olympic Games was destined to be the last staged on a cinder track. Many all-weather tracks, today manufactured by a wide range of companies, and consisting of complex polymer compounds which are usually applied in liquid form and allowed to solidify, are often wrongly referred to as being 'tartan' tracks. This description has nothing to do with their colour, but stems instead from the great success of the particular type of all-weather track developed from 1963 by the Minnesota Mining and Manufacturing Company (3M), whose brand name 'Tartan' was already in use through products like adhesive and audio recording tapes, and was also applied to the new surface.

The first Tartan surfacing was actually produced for pony trotting, but an athletics track was later laid at Macalester College, St Paul, Minnesota. This type of rubberized surfacing proved so successful that Tartan tracks were used at a major Games for the first time at the Pan-American Games in Winnipeg in 1967, and later at the 1968 Mexico City Olympics and the 1969 European Championships in Athens.

The first complete Tartan track to be laid in Europe (field event run-ups had been laid elsewhere) was actually at Crystal Palace in May 1968, where it replaced an existing cinder track.

The considerable initial cost of laying all-weather tracks (usually somewhere in the region of £350,000) is offset by the low maintenance requirements and the reliability of the surface, which can be ready to stage another athletics meeting within moments of the last one finishing. The old cinder tracks normally required days of preparation and repair, and even then were still subject to weather conditions. The all-weather surfaces which replaced them at major venues can normally be in use twenty-four hours a day if necessary.

Altitude

When the 1968 Olympic Games were awarded to Mexico City, with its altitude of 7350 feet above sea level, a whole new area of athletics training was set into motion. In the short term, athletes from countries close to sea level tried to adapt before the Games to the reduced oxygen content of the high altitude in Mexico by acclimitization over some months at locations of similar heights.

But the need to train for long periods in unfamiliar and often unsuitable surroundings frequently proved counterproductive, and the fact that the Mexico Olympic endurance events were eventually dominated by athletes who had been born and raised in high-altitude countries like Ethiopia and Kenya, demonstrated that at those Games not everyone had an equal chance. Similarly, the host of records set there in the short, explosive events (which did not rely on oxygen intake, but actually benefited from the reduced air pressure) reiterated the unsuitability of Mexico City for such sporting events.

But an almost incidental benefit of altitude training and competition was noticed when the endurance athletes returned to sea level. Their bodies had, temporarily, adapted to altitude to some extent by increasing the red blood cell count and the haemoglobin content in the blood. Back at sea level, some of these athletes could perform as if with a supercharger for several weeks before the effects faded.

Thus a new era began, with athletes deliberately spending long periods at altitude before any major championships or Games in the hope of artificially inducing this supercharged effect. In the USA, for example, Boulder, Colorado (5430 feet) has developed into a second home for some of the world's leading distance runners in recent years.

However, not every athlete appears to benefit to the same extent from altitude training, and physiologists still tend to disagree about the optimal time for returning to sea level for the most advantageous results. In some athletes it could be four or five days, in others several weeks.

In 1972 the British Olympic team sent its endurance athletes to St Moritz, Switzerland, before the Munich Olympics, but the results at the Games were still generally disappointing.

A distance race competitor receiving oxygen at the 1968 Mexico City Olympics, where the 7350ft altitude was totally unsuitable

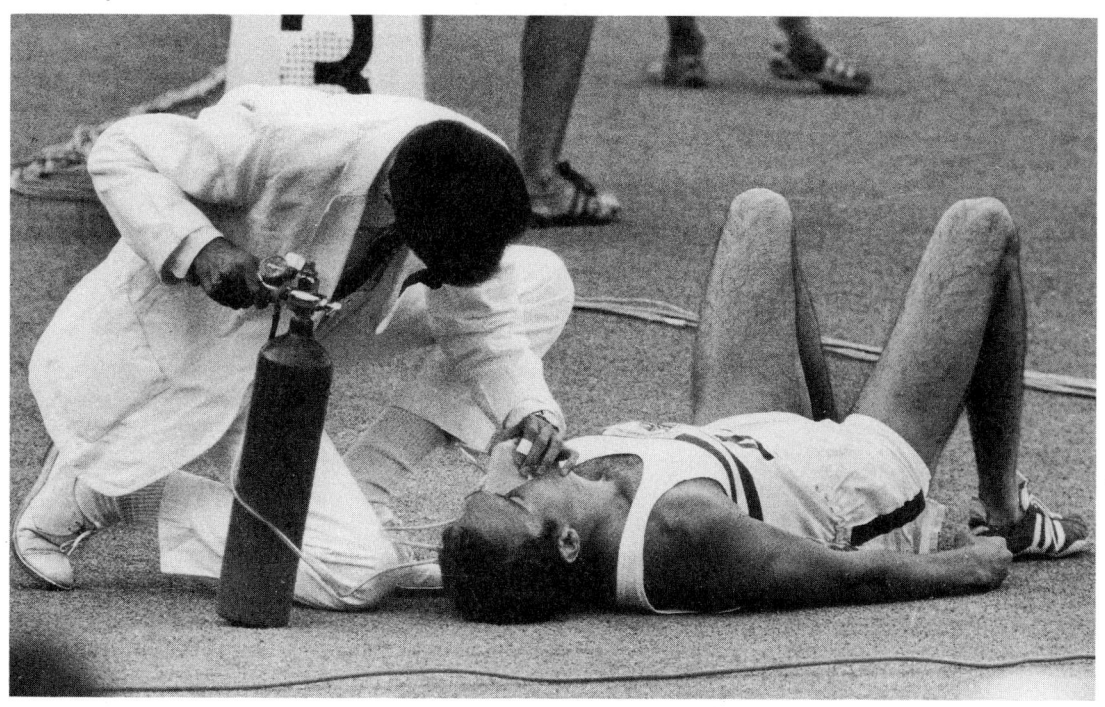

The main 'altitude' success was probably 1500m runner Sheila Carey, who came down from altitude into Munich well before the recommended time simply because of boredom, and then ran a brilliant fifth in the Games in a time which would have been a world record *before* the Games. Yet a number of other more fancied athletes were disappointments, and then ironically set personal best performances after the Games, suggesting that the method could work but that the timing differed among individuals.

But athletes who can afford the time, cost and disruption to personal life which sustained altitude training may cause, still employ it as a regular part of their preparation.

There is also growing evidence that the practice of 'blood doping', which is intended to achieve the same supercharging effect without athletes needing to live at altitude, is increasing.

Another shorter-lived approach to the subject of artificially inducing the effects of altitude came from California in 1981 with the introduction of the Inspirair P02 Aerobic Exerciser. This curious device incorporated a face mask attached to two canisters weighing four pounds, which were worn as a back pack. The runner, wearing the mask over his mouth and nose, actually breathed his own exhaled air from which the carbon dioxide content had been removed. The effect simulated running at 7500 feet, although the altitude could be adjusted. The devices, which cost $219, were uncomfortable to wear, and do not appear to have had the profound effect on training which their inventor, Dr Melvyn Henkin, had hoped.

See also *Blood, Blood Packing*.

Amenorrhoea

The regular strenuous exercise of the harder-training female runner may lead to amenorrhoea, which is a temporary cessation of the menstrual cycle, for precise reasons which are still unclear to physiologists. The high training mileage and the associated weight loss and fatigue are thought to be major factors, although runners weighing less than 110lb, or with less than 18 per cent body fat, or under the age of 24, are thought to be particularly susceptible.

Usually, a subsequent reduction in training load, or a rest taken voluntarily or enforced through injury, will cause the periods to return inside two months, and often sooner. Nor is it confined to runners by any means; swimmers, gymnasts and ballet dancers, who all put physical strains on their bodies, are among those affected too. But there is no evidence that amenorrhoeic runners suffer any reduction in their fertility when the menstrual cycle returns.

One medical problem so far noted, following an American study, indicated that amenorrhoeic runners do appear to suffer a higher incidence of stress fractures than other runners of otherwise similar backgrounds, but with normal menstrual cycles. This could in part be caused by a reduction in bone density, itself related (the study claimed) to a measured deficiency of oestrogen in amenorrhoeic runners. Oestrogen replacement, plus increased calcium intake, has been suggested by doctors as a precaution, but it should be remembered that stress fractures in the runner are primarily caused by too much running.

Anaemia

The most common type which affects distance runners is iron-deficiency anaemia. This occurs when there is a fall in the normal level of haemoglobin, the pigment in the red blood which combines with oxygen to carry it to the muscles, and itself comprises iron and protein. So if iron is deficient, perhaps through inadequate diet or excessive menstrual loss, or a combination of causes, the ability of the red cells to transport sufficient oxygen to the muscles will be impaired.

Symptoms include poor form in racing and training, shortage of breath, continual fatigue, and in extreme cases giddiness when rising. A simple blood test performed by a GP can confirm anaemia; and while there is no fixed level of haemoglobin, values in the region of 14–15g of haemoglobin per 100ml of blood for an adult male, and 12–14g/100ml for an adult female, are considered to be average healthy readings.

A course of iron supplements and an emphasis on an iron-rich diet, including plenty of liver, vegetables, and wholemeal cereal, is recommended as treatment. An average well-balanced diet should ensure there is normally no iron deficiency, but the most likely candidates for anaemia are pregnant women, feeding mothers, excessively weight-conscious youngsters, and students living away from home and catering for themselves.

Ankle

The ankle is the joint between the two lower leg bones (the tibia and fibula) and the uppermost of the complex bones in the foot, the talus. This joint operates only as a hinge, moving either downwards (plantarflexion) as when the toes are pointed, or upwards (dorsiflexion), with strong ligaments protecting the joint.

In the distance runner, the joint is used through its full range of movement in the normal heel-toe action, although sprinters running on their toes use a more limited range.

Ankle injury occurs when this basic up-and-down hinge receives undue force from one side or the other. In a physical contact sport, like soccer or rugby, it could be as the result of a direct kick or fall. But in distance running it is more likely to be caused by a gentle imbalance which has been repeated thousands of times in a run, and for a variety of reasons, such as favouring an existing injury (possibly in the opposite knee), trying to avoid aggravating a blister, or simply running in shoes which are worn out or contain too much (or too little) arch support.

Detecting and correcting the cause is the first step to recovery, and then restoring the joint to its natural movement. But more serious damage may occur if the injury is caused by a direct and violent force, as when the foot goes down an unseen hole and the joint is wrenched suddenly

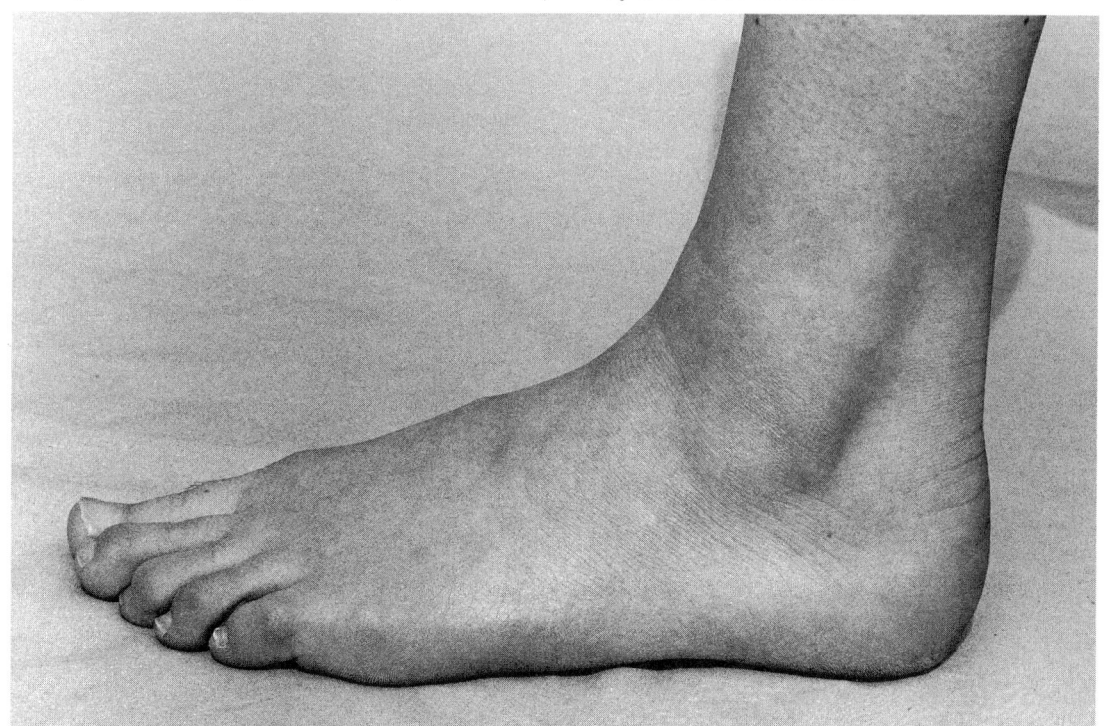

The up and down hinge of the ankle joint can be injured by unfamiliar movement

sideways. Attendance at a hospital casualty department for possible X-rays is advisable in such circumstances, while self-help treatment includes ice, elevation, support and rest.

Anorexia nervosa

Although the so-called slimmer's disease of anorexia nervosa has been identified for more than a century, its link with running has only recently been highlighted. The compulsive desire to lose weight, which mainly (but not exclusively) affects adolescent females, becomes an obsession which takes them well below their natural weight and can in extreme cases become life-threatening and even fatal.

It is usually triggered psychologically, but in the case of some female endurance runners starts with the linking of an initial weight loss with better racing performance. Oxygen uptake can be improved to some extent by the shedding of surplus pounds, but there is no reliable indicator as to when the optimum weight has been reached. A 10-stone female runner who slims down to 8 stones will almost certainly notice an upturn in performance. But if she continues losing weight down to, say, 6 stones, she will become weaker and slower and injuries will take longer to heal. At that point the obsession may be so strong that the very thought of putting on weight seems alien.

The success of ultra-thin female distance runners at international level often leads to other females trying to emulate their shape and weight, without giving sufficient regard to the fact that some runners are by nature thin. Indeed, those who are naturally thin but healthy do have an advantage in endurance events, in the same way that long-legged athletes have an advantage in high jumping. The physiological problems may continue if the athlete's body fat percentage drops below acceptable levels and she becomes amenorrhoeic, leading in turn to the possibility of adolescent osteoporosis (loss of bone density).

In addition to runners already in the sport who develop anorexia or other eating disorders, such as bulimia nervosa, there is an apparently increasing number of already anorectic females coming into running at modest levels (often non-competitively) because they see distance running as a further means of losing weight, of directing the hyperactivity which is often a symptom of anorexia, and above all as a camouflage for their continuing weight loss in a sport where female slimness is frequently seen and applauded. Indeed, coaches, parents and close friends of anorectic runners are often completely unaware of the existence of the problem. The anorectic may be ingenious and even devious in finding reasons for not eating in public situations, or pretending to do so, to the extent of possibly hiding food in their pockets or sleeves for later disposal.

Help is needed to assist anorectics to unravel the causes of their problem, and to understand the physical harm it may be doing them. Sometimes counselling by a trusted friend and simply talking it through can turn the tide. A surprising number of leading female international runners have suffered from eating disorders at some stage during their career and have successfully overcome them.

Happily, there have also been cases where anorectic youngsters of both sexes, who took up running simply as a means of becoming even thinner, found that the pleasure of running actually helped release the tensions and unhappiness which caused their condition in the first place. They were subsequently able to normalize their eating habits and return to a healthy weight, while also enjoying the sport.

See also *Amenorrhoea*, *Body Fat Percentage*.

Asthma

The lungs have extremely effective defence mechanisms, so that if an irritant like dust should get into the airways, the muscle fibres on the walls of the bronchioles (the smaller air passages) go into involuntary spasm, reducing their size and restricting the air flow to keep foreign bodies out. Sometimes, however, this effect is unnecessarily overachieved in response to a particular stimulus, causing an asthma attack as the airways constrict severely so that the sufferer is only able to breathe with great difficulty, usually accompanied by wheezing.

The exact cause of an attack may vary greatly between individuals. Pollen, pet hair, dust or feathers are just a few common triggers for attacks which may affect runners. But of particular concern to some runners is exercise-induced asthma (EIA), in which the very act of running hard for some minutes can cause an asthma attack, with the runner unable to breathe deeply, as gasping and wheezing replace the normal respiratory pattern.

Recovery may take from twenty minutes to several hours, and it can be difficult to pinpoint whether the cause was simply exercise-induced or set off by exercise in combination with another factor, such as temperature, an irritant, or even stress. Some purely psychological factors, including anxiety and nervousness, are thought to be among the precipitating causes. But, interestingly, an attack also brings about a refractory period afterwards in which further exercise does *not* cause another attack, and so before a race some sufferers have been known to induce an attack in early warm-up in the hope of guaranteeing an unaffected run afterwards.

Carefully prescribed medication can help to stabilize the airways and counter the attacks, but it is important that any doctor treating a competitive runner is informed in detail of the list of drugs banned in the sport. For some everyday treatments include the use of sympathomimetic drugs like ephedrine and isoprenaline, which are on the list of substances banned by the International Olympic Committee and International Amateur Athletic Federation because of their possible abuse as a stimulant. To a non-sportsman there would be no problem, but to a runner a trace of such substances found in a dope test could lead to a life ban from the sport. American swimmer Rick DeMont was disqualified after winning the 400m freestyle gold medal in the 1972 Munich Olympic Games after traces of ephedrine were detected from an anti-asthmatic drug he had even declared in advance. The same inadvertent error could happen in a running event too.

Asthma sufferers should still be able to enjoy the full benefits of exercise, and many doctors believe that regular running can actually help to control the condition. Certainly athletes like 1974 European and Commonwealth 400m hurdles champion Alan Pascoe and leading American sprinters Florence Griffith and Jeanette Bolden did not let asthma ruin their competitive careers. Asthma is not an illness; it is a condition, and as such it can be conquered.

See also *Lungs*.

B

Bannister, Sir Roger

Although forever linked with the first mile to be run in under four minutes, itself one of the most coveted achievements in sport, Roger Bannister was also an excellent competitor. In August 1954, three months after his historic 3:59.4 mile at Oxford, he beat Australian John Landy (who had subsequently reduced the world record to 3:57.9) to win the Empire (now Commonwealth) Games mile title.

That race was one of the most eagerly awaited confrontations in athletics history, as the first two men to have broken four minutes for the mile faced each other in Vancouver. After letting Landy build up an early lead, Bannister timed his finish to perfection, passing Landy on the final bend to win in 3:58.8. With Landy clocking 3:59.6, it was the first time two men had beaten four minutes in the same race.

Then, three weeks later in Berne, Bannister added the European 1500m title in what was his final major race. At the age of 25, his medical career took precedence, as he felt he was unable to devote sufficient training time to prepare for the 1956 Olympics.

Roger Gilbert Bannister was born in Harrow, Middlesex, on 23 March 1929. He showed such talent at the age of only 18, while studying at Oxford University, that he was invited to become a 1948 Olympic 'possible'. But he declined on the grounds of his youth, and had already decided to aim for the 1952 Olympics instead.

At the age of 20 he ran the mile in 4:11.1, a further sign of great promise, and finished a very close third in the 1950 European 800m final in 1:50.7. By the 1952 Olympics in Helsinki he was among the favourites for the 1500m title, following a three-quarter-mile time trial in 2:52.9, which was nearly four seconds faster than the unofficial world best.

Yet although he set a UK 1500m record of 3:46.0 in the Helsinki final, he could finish only a disappointed fourth behind the surprise winner, Josy Barthel of Luxembourg. Had Bannister won in Helsinki, he later admitted, he might well have retired there and then.

But, after mulling over the future, he decided to compete for two more years, 'to prove my attitude towards training had been the right one, and hence restore the faith in myself that had been shaken by my Olympic defeat'*.

Always wary of coaches, Bannister preferred

Sir Roger Bannister with an oil painting depicting his most famous athletic achievement

First Four Minutes, Roger Bannister (Putnam, 1955).

Bannister's Road to History

How Roger Bannister improved to reach a place in history:

Oct 1946	4:53.0	Oxford Univ. Freshmen's Sports, Oxford
22 Mar 1947	4:30.8	Oxford Univ. *v.* Cambridge Univ., White City
5 Jun 1947	4:24.6	AAA *v.* Oxford Univ., Oxford
20 Mar 1948	4:23.4	Oxford Univ. *v.* Cambridge Univ., White City
6 May 1948	4:22.8	AAA *v.* Oxford Univ., Oxford
19 Jun 1948	4:18.7	Kinnaird Trophy Meeting, Chiswick
3 Jul 1948	4:17.2	AAA Championships, White City
12 Mar 1949	4:16.2	Oxford Univ. *v.* Cambridge Univ., White City
11 Jun 1949	4:11.1	Oxford and Cambridge Univ. *v.* Cornell & Princeton, Princeton, USA
30 Dec 1949	4:09.9	Centennial Games, Christchurch, NZ
28 Apr 1951	4:08.3	Benjamin Franklin Mile, Philadelphia, USA
14 Jul 1951	4:07.8	AAA Championships, White City
2 May 1953	4:03.6	AAA *v.* Oxford Univ., Oxford
27 June 1953	4:02.0	Invitation race, Motspur Park
6 May 1954	3:59.4	AAA *v.* Oxford Univ., Oxford
7 Aug 1954	3:58.8	British Empire Games, Vancouver, Canada

to plan his own preparation, but trained regularly with Chris Chataway and Chris Brasher, fitting in lunchtime and evening sessions in between his medical studies at St Mary's Hospital, Paddington.

It was Brasher and Chataway, who were both to reach their own peaks at a later date, who were instrumental in the achievement of a sub-four-minute mile, as they undertook the pace-making at Oxford on 6 May 1954.

Bannister retired from the sport after his momentous 1954 campaign, and became a highly respected neurologist. But his links with sport were re-established from 1971–4 when he was Chairman of the Sports Council, and deeply involved in the launch of the Sport for All campaign.

He was knighted in 1975, but the same year was involved in a motor accident in Surrey in which he broke seven ribs and badly injured his foot. Firemen needed forty-five minutes to free him from his car, and his active recreational career came to an end. He and his Swiss-born wife Moyra, who were married in 1955, have four children and live in London.

See also *Chris Brasher, Four-minute mile*.

Barefoot running

Although the name of Zola Budd, the young South African-born runner who became a British citizen in 1984, may spring instantly to mind when thinking of barefooted runners, she was by no means the first to achieve international success without shoes. In 1985 she won the IAAF World cross-country title, the European Cup final 3000m and set a world record for 5000m in bare feet. But more than twenty years earlier Britain's Bruce Tulloh had won the 1962 European championship 5000m title in bare feet, and on a cinder track.

A number of Tulloh's contemporaries, including Tim Johnston, Ron Hill and Jim Hogan, also raced successfully without shoes. Hill, who finished seventh in the 1968 Olympic 10,000m in bare feet, even briefly contemplated running the 1972 Olympic marathon in bare

Barefooted Zola Budd, with toes protectively taped, on her way to a world 5000m record at Crystal Palace in 1985

feet, until the resurfacing of part of the course with stone chippings helped him change his mind.

In 1960 the Olympic marathon was won by a then unknown Ethiopian, Abebe Bikila, running barefoot across the cobblestones of Rome, and although by 1964 he was wearing shoes when he retained the title, that year witnessed the first sub-four-minute mile in bare feet: by South African DeVilliers Lamprechts, who ran 3:59.7 at Stellenbosch on 13 November 1964.

Even today, when modern technology has led to the design of some of the most comfortable (and uncomfortable) shoes possible, there are runners who prefer to train, and race if possible, in bare feet. But the chances to do so are limited.

For shoes are needed by any runner if the surface is too rough, stony or slippery. Heavily built runners in particular need the shock absorption of shoes to reduce the amount of impact (around three times the bodyweight) being felt in the unprotected foot and sent up the leg to the back.

The advantages of running barefooted are chiefly the feeling of lightness and freedom, as the feet land absolutely naturally, without any distortion from shoe interiors. But the disadvantages, apart from the loss of shock absorption, can include a reduced amount of grip compared to spiked shoes, and vulnerability not only to foreign bodies like sharp stones and broken glass, but also to changing weather conditions. A sudden rainstorm in the middle of a 5000 or 10,000m track race on a synthetic surface can leave the barefooted runner feeling the ground turn into a skating rink beneath him.

While barefooted running on roads or cinder tracks is not advised (although it has been done), barefoot running on most synthetic tracks is possible, and there are few more relaxing experiences than running barefoot on a well-kept grass surface on a summer evening.

Most runners who cover a reasonable mileage, even in shoes, will find that the soles of their feet are already quite tough and leathery. Surgical spirit, applied regularly to the soles of the feet, will also harden them. But before a track race, the individual taping up of the middle three toes, using long strips of zinc oxide tape wound four or five times round each toe, will help to protect the ball of the toe and reduce the possibility of friction burns or blisters on that small but important part of the foot which pushes off hard on every stride.

BARR

The British Association of Road Races (BARR) is a body formed in 1984 with the object of establishing a code of conduct for organizers of road-running events at all distances in the UK. It monitors organizational standards of races, and has introduced a grading system through which races are independently rated as a guide for intending participants. Races are awarded three levels of grading according to observations made by official BARR representatives and runners themselves. It also works in conjunction with the AAA and the London Road Runners Club in producing a comprehensive annual booklet of road-race fixtures.

Bay-to-Breakers

Claiming to be the world's largest race, with around 100,000 registered participants in 1986, this 12km event takes place each May in San Francisco. Dozens of race volunteers are needed to link arms and hold back the mass of runners while the 'elite' invited competitors start, before the huge tide of running humanity is unleashed through the San Franciscan streets.

The race has roots even before World War I, when the Californian city was still rebuilding after its disastrous earthquake of 1906. The first cross-city run was held there in 1912, with 186 runners, but it was renamed the 'Bay-to-Breakers' in 1963; that year only fifteen runners finished. But as the running boom took hold in the US, so the race grew dramatically. From 1966 it was sponsored by the city's *Examiner* newspaper, and in 1973 4000 runners finished. The numbers went up and up.

A new dimension was added in 1978 when the Aggies Running Club entered a team dressed as a centipede and set a historic precedent for the fancy dress which has now become one of the race's distinguishing characteristics. It is not unusual to see runners dressed as Minnie Mouse, the Easter Bunny, the *Mayflower*, Gandhi, and even a can of beer, jogging alongside each other. But the race has a serious side too, with men's and women's course records being set in 1986 by Ed Eyestone (34.33) and Grete Waitz (38.45)

Bay-to-Breakers: most recent winners

	MEN			WOMEN	
1973	Kenny Moore (USA)	37:15	1973	Cheryl Bridges (USA)	45:20
1974	Gary Tuttle (USA)	37:07	1974	Mary Etta Boitano (USA)	43:22 †
1975	Ric Rojas (USA)	37:18	1975	Mary Etta Boitano (USA)	46:04
1976	Chris Wardlaw (Aus)	37:28	1976	Mary Etta Boitano (USA)	49:33
1977	Paul Geis (USA)	37:03	1977	Ann Thrupp (USA)	46:00
1978	Gerard Barrett (Aus)	35:07*	1978	Skip Swannack (USA)	47:00*
1979	Bob Hodge (USA)	36:51	1979	Laurie Binder (USA)	43:08
1980	Craig Virgin (USA)	35.12	1980	Laurie Binder (USA)	42:20
1981	Craig Virgin (USA)	35:08	1981	Janice Oehm (USA)	41:47
1982	Rod Dixon (NZ)	35:08	1982	Laurie Binder (USA)	42:28
1983	Rod Dixon (NZ)	35:01	1983	Laurie Binder (USA)	41:24
1984	Ibrahim Hussein (Ken)	35:12	1984	Nancy Ditz (USA)	42:32
1985	Ibrahim Hussein (Ken)	34:54	1985	Joan Benoit (USA)	39:55
1986	Ed Eyestone (USA)	34:33	1986	Grete Waitz (Nor)	38:45
1987	Arturo Barrios (Mex)	34:45	1987	Rosa Mota (Por)	39:16

NB: Course became exactly 12km in 1983.
†Boitano was only 11 when she won the women's section in 1974.
*False start in 1978.

Bikila, Abebe

In his relatively short, spectacularly successful, but ill-fated running career, Abebe Bikila became, in 1964, the first man to successfully defend the Olympic marathon title. In winning both gold medals he set world best times, and in the thirteen marathons he completed between 1960–66, he lost only once.

He was born in the Ethiopian province of Mout on 7 August 1932, and as a boy tended his family's sheep. But he began school at the age of 13, and by 19 had become a member of Emperor Haile Selassie's Imperial Bodyguard in Addis Ababa. The accent on physical fitness within the bodyguard had led to the appointment of the Swedish athletics coach Onni Niskanen to supervise sports coaching, and he quickly noted the raw running potential of young Abebe.

Permission for Bikila to compete in the 1956 Olympics was withheld by the Bodyguard as Niskanen could not, at that point, guarantee a medal for him, and the pride of the Emperor demanded nothing less. But by the time of the 1960 Olympics in Rome, after Bikila had undergone four years of hard training, much of it at 6000 feet altitude, and including rugged twenty-mile runs over mountains, even Niskanen was prepared to almost guarantee gold.

Unknown and unconsidered before the Rome Olympics, the skinny Bikila, running barefooted, was dismissed by virtually everyone. But after a duel from halfway with Moroccan Rhadi ben Abdesselem, Bikila broke clear to win by twenty-five seconds in a world best time of 2hr 15min 16.2sec. Africa had made its presence felt in international long-distance running in the most dramatic way.

But before the next Olympics, in Tokyo, Bikila's chances appeared wrecked when he had

Abebe Bikila created history in Tokyo in 1964 as the first man to retain the Olympic marathon title

to undergo an emergency operation for appendicitis just six weeks before the Olympic race. Yet not only did he recover, he retained his title (this time wearing shoes), finishing over four minutes ahead of silver medallist Basil Heatley, and in another world best of 2hr 12min 11.2sec.

To demonstrate his freshness, Bikila even waved away a blanket at the finishing line and instead went through a series of mobility exercises on the grass infield, including lying on his back 'cycling'.

With the 1968 Olympics due to be held at high altitude in Mexico City, it seemed very probable that he could stretch his winning streak to three titles. But in 1967 he sustained a leg injury in Spain, and the same injury forced him to drop out of the 1968 Olympic race after only ten miles. Bikila's countryman, Mamo Wolde, kept the marathon title in Ethiopian hands, while Bikila nursed hopes of regaining it in 1972. Meanwhile, through his previous sporting achievements, he had been promoted to captain in the Imperial Bodyguard, in which he had started as a private.

But in March 1969 he was seriously injured in a car crash near Addis Ababa, and despite being flown to England for specialist treatment at Stoke Mandeville Hospital, he remained paralysed from the waist down and confined to a wheelchair for the rest of his life. He accepted his fate stoically, observing in 1971: 'It was laid down in my destiny that at a certain moment I would be a famous athlete and that at a certain moment I would be as you find me now. It is God's will. My satisfaction is in my memories and the results I obtained at my peak.'

Bikila attended the 1972 Munich Olympic Games in his wheelchair as an honoured guest of the organizers, and his courage was warmly applauded by the crowd. But within little more than a year he was dead, suffering a brain haemorrhage in Addis Ababa on 25 October 1973, at the age of just 41.

Bislett Stadium, Oslo

Regarded by many of the world's leading distance runners as the venue most suitable for a fast time, the aura of Bislett Stadium has grown over the years through a mixture of its rich history, atmosphere and an enthusiastic word-of-mouth reputation.

Since it opened on 8 October 1922, it has been reconstructed five times and, wedged tightly into a triangular site not far from the city centre, it is unlikely to expand further. But its very intimacy, with the crowd close to the athletes and lining the whole of the six-lane track, helps the adrenaline flow. When there are 10,000 spectators in Bislett, the Norwegians proudly boast, it looks like 30,000 and sounds like 40,000. Its capacity now is actually 23,000.

Nearly fifty world track and field world records have been set at Bislett, with the first in 1924, when Dutchman Adriaan Paulen (later President of the IAAF, 1976–81) ran the now-defunct 500m in 1:03.8 on its curiously shaped original track, which included two ninety degree turns. Understandably, many of the early world records were field events. But when the track was reshaped, more running records fell.

Today the number of tall buildings around the stadium help to keep any wind away from the track, although in July the weather is usually calm and warm for its annual Bislett Games meeting anyway. From the outside, the stadium appears disappointingly drab, with its dull brown walls sometimes sprinkled with graffiti. Even the world's greatest athletes have to warm up round a small car-park, or in the streets outside, because there is no room for proper facilities. But the electric atmosphere generated by the knowledgeable Oslo fans, and their chanting and barrier-drumming during the middle distance races, overcomes the initial misgivings most Bislett debutantes feel. Even the sweet smell from the adjacent Frydenlund brewery adds to the Bislett mystique.

The 1946 European Championships (in which Britain's gold medallists included Sydney Wooderson in the 5000m) were held at Bislett Stadium, and it was also the venue for the opening and closing ceremonies of the 1952 Winter Olympic Games. For Bislett has a second identity in the winter as a speed-skating circuit. The running track is flooded and frozen, and its reputation among speed skaters is as high as among athletes, probably for the same reasons; a large number of skating world records have been set there too.

The running-track surface has been changed a number of times. When Australian Ron Clarke achieved one of the greatest performances seen at Bislett when he knocked no less than thirty-five seconds from his own world 10,000m record with 27:39.4 in July 1965, it was still a cinder surface. It was changed to an all-weather track in the early seventies, but by the time Britain's Dave Moorcroft set his unexpected 5000m world record of 13:00.41 in 1982, that surface was patched and repaired.

The current surface was laid in the summer of 1985, and almost immediately provided an

Steve Cram (with Arne Haukvik behind) acknowledges the support of the closely-packed Bislett crowd

The forty-six World Records set at Bislett Stadium, Oslo
(as at 1 August 1987)

Date	Athlete	Event	Result
25 Jul 1924	Adriaan Paulen (Hol)	500m	1:03.8
13 Aug 1925	Charles Hoff (Nor)	Pole vault	4:23m
5 Aug 1934	Jack Torrance (USA)	Shot	17.40m
6 Aug 1934	Eulace Peacock (USA)	100m	10.3
6 Aug 1934	Percy Beard (USA)	120yd/110m hurdles	14.2
25 Aug 1934	Harald Andersson (Swe)	Discus	52.42m
2 Aug 1935	Al Moreau (USA)	120yd/110m hurdles	14.2
27 Aug 1936	Forrest Towns (USA)	120yd/110m hurdles	13.7
28 Jul 1949	Jim Fuchs (USA)	Shot	17.79m
31 Aug 1949	Richard Ault (USA)	440yd hurdles	52.2
14 Sep 1952	Sverre Strandli (Nor)	Hammer	61.25m
5 Sep 1953	Sverre Strandli (Nor)	Hammer	62.36m
17 Sep 1953	Audun Boysen (Nor)	1000m	2:20.4
15 Jul 1955	Pentti Karvonen (Fin)	3000m steeple	8:45.4
3 Aug 1955	Roger Moens (Belg)	800m	1:45.7
6 Sep 1955	Laszlo Tabori (Hun)	1500m	3:40.8
6 Sep 1955	Gunnar Nielsen (Den)	1500m	3:40.8
9 Aug 1957	Josh Culbreath (USA)	440yd hurdles	50.5
1 Jul 1964	Terje Pedersen (Nor)	Javelin	87.12m
2 Sep 1964	Terje Pedersen (Nor)	Javelin	91.72m
14 Jul 1965	Ron Clarke (Aus)	6 miles	26:47.0
14 Jul 1965	Ron Clarke (Aus)	10,000m	27:39.4
22 Aug 1973	Tony Polhill, John Walker, Rod Dixon and Dick Quaxs (NZ)	4 × 1500m Relay	14:40.4
30 Jul 1974	Rick Wohlhuter (USA)	1000m	2:13.9
24 Jun 1975	Grete Andersen (Nor)	3000m	8:46.6
25 Jun 1975	Anders Gaerderud (Swe)	3000m steeple	8:10.4
21 Jun 1976	Grete Waitz (Nor)	3000m	8:45.4
30 Jun 1976	John Walker (NZ)	2000m	4:51.4
27 Jun 1978	Henry Rono (Ken)	3000m	7:32.1
23 Sep 1978	Torill Gylder (Nor)	5000m walk	23:08.2
5 Jul 1979	Sebastian Coe (UK)	800m	1:42.4
17 Jul 1979	Sebastian Coe (UK)	1 mile	3:49.0
1 Jul 1980	Sebastian Coe (UK)	1000m	2:13.4
1 Jul 1980	Steve Ovett (UK)	1 mile	3:48.8
15 Jul 1980	Steve Ovett (UK)	1500m	3:32.1
11 Jul 1981	Ingrid Christensen (Nor)	5000m	15:28.43
11 Jul 1981	Sebastian Coe (UK)	1000m	2:12.18
7 Jul 1982	Dave Moorcroft (UK)	5000m	13:00.41
28 Jun 1984	Ingrid Kristiansen (Nor)	5000m	14:58.89
27 Jul 1985	Ingrid Kristiansen (Nor)	10,000m	30:59.42
27 Jul 1985	Said Aouita (Mor)	5000m	13:00.40
27 Jul 1985	Steve Cram (UK)	1 mile	3:46:32
5 Jul 1986	Ingrid Kristiansen (Nor)	10,000m	30:13.74

astonishing evening of athletics at the Bislett Games on 27 July 1985 when local Oslo resident Ingrid Kristiansen smashed the women's 10,000m world record by over fourteen seconds with 30:59.42, Morocco's Said Aouita broke Moorcroft's 5000m world record by one-hundredth of a second with 13:00.40, and a dramatic late-night Dream Mile clash between two Bislett favourites, Steve Cram and Seb Coe, resulted in Cram winning in a world record 3:46.32.

Those three performances took Bislett's world record tally up to 45, not quite as many as Stockholm's Olympic Stadium, but in recent years Oslo has become the Scandinavian capital of the big meetings. The Bislett Games is actually organized by an alliance of three separate Oslo clubs, Vidar, Tjalve and BUL, who form Bislett-Alliansen to stage the meeting. The profits from the widely televised event then go back to the clubs to help them operate the rest of the year.

The major force in building up the Bislett meetings has been promoter Arne Haukvik, a familiar figure at the stadium in his battered panama hat, as he tours the outside lane with a loud-hailer during major races, urging the crowd to make even more noise. For the athletes, a traditional part of the Bislett Games has been a barbecue and strawberry party in Haukvik's garden on the eve of the meeting.

Now, with Haukvik having undergone heart surgery, much of the Bislett organizational work-load is undertaken by his co-promoter, Oslo stamp-dealer Svein Arne Hansen.

Although the lack of many great Norwegian athletes has been a handicap in staging events at Bislett, local resident Grete Waitz has long been an enormously popular figure, and a statue of her now stands outside the stadium.

Black toenails

The blackening of a toenail is caused by bruising which occurs when that toe is repeatedly pressed upwards against the inner shoe surface, as in a marathon or long training run. The most painful instances are due to the build-up of pressure under the nail. To relieve this pressure heat up one end of a piece of paper clip wire until red hot, then use it to pierce a small hole in the centre of the nail, through which the blood will squirt to escape.

For the more squeamish, a simpler treatment is to cut a small hole in the upper of the shoe at the point where the particular toe makes contact, either in the hope of avoiding damage occurring in the first place, or if it is too late, still being able to continue training in the shoes until the bruising has cleared itself.

Blisters

Most runners suffer from blisters on their feet at some time, usually caused by friction between the skin and some rough or pressing inner part of the shoe. The outer layer of the skin (epidermis) separates from the layer below it (dermis) with a water component of the blood, called serum, filling the space in between to provide a makeshift cushion against the friction.

Occasionally, if the inner layer of skin is broken while the outer layer remains intact, the blister will fill with blood, giving it a dark brown appearance. Such blisters should not be punctured or drained, as the risk of infection is much greater than with ordinary blisters; instead, they should be padded and covered.

An ordinary clear blister can be drained quite simply, however, once the skin has been cleaned, by using a sterilized needle to pierce the outer layer of skin. The fluid is then squeezed out and mopped up with cotton wool, repeating the process several times if necessary. Covering the site with a protective plaster can help the healing process afterwards, and in some cases the skin may reattach.

Draining clear blisters not only reduces discomfort, it also allows continuation of training. Trying to train with painful blisters may worsen them, and can also cause the favouring of one leg, which in turn could lead to a muscle or ligament strain.

The origin of the blisters should also be considered. If they were caused by ill-fitting or tight shoes, these may need to be discarded. But if they were caused by heavy training or racing (perhaps even when the shoes were wet) then a precautionary covering of zinc oxide tape on the affected area would be advisable before continuing training in the same shoes.

The best preventive measure is to smear some petroleum jelly, such as Vaseline, on the toes, arches and around the heels before any runs of substantial length (or less if you are a new runner, just returned to running after a break, or are trying out new shoes). For while it does not guarantee to prevent the blisters, it will at least reduce a great deal of the dry friction which causes them in the first place.

Blood

The blood is a sea of supply: for a start, it provides the essential transport system which continually speeds oxygen to the muscles during exercise, to help create energy and keep the body in action. In fact, 7 per cent of the body is made up of plasma, a clear, pale yellow solution in which float red and white cells so tiny that in just one drop of blood there may be up to 250 million of the predominant red cells, and 400,000 white.

An adult male possesses about five litres (ten pints) of blood, and women about 15 per cent less, so the total number of blood cells in the human body is vast.

But it is the red cells which tend to primarily interest the runner because each round red cell (hollow on each side, and measuring approximately 0.008cm in diameter) contains a special pigment called haemoglobin, which is responsible for its colour. The haemoglobin, a mixture of protein (globin) and an iron-containing chemical grouping (haem), combines with freshly inhaled oxygen in the lungs and carries it to the muscles, where the oxygen is then released.

When this released oxygen is 'burned' with fuel to create energy, the waste product, carbon dioxide, is then removed by the circulating red cells back to the lungs, where it is exhaled, and the red cells in turn pick up further fresh oxygen to transport back to the muscles.

The red cells (known as erythrocytes) exist for around 120 days before being replaced by new cells produced from within the bone marrow. Such huge numbers of red cells are involved that approximately five million of them are being destroyed every second, even though the total number remains constant.

But hard training can lead to an increase in the number of red cells, and therefore produces an improvement in their oxygen-carrying capacity, while training at high altitude can also stimulate a natural increase in the red cells as a means of compensating for the decrease in available oxygen. On return to sea level the increase remains for several weeks, allowing a temporary supercharging in some athletes.

The system of sports medical malpractice known as 'blood packing' seeks to achieve the same result without the need to travel to altitude, yet still increasing the number of red cells. It is theoretically illegal, yet still impossible to prove at present.

A deficit of red cells in the blood, possibly caused by poor diet and in women perhaps aggravated by menstrual loss, can cause iron-deficiency anaemia, which in the runner may first become apparent in poor form, excessive fatigue, shortage of breath, and giddiness when rising. It is treated with iron supplements and an increase of iron-rich foods.

The white cells, known as leucocytes, are slightly bigger than the red cells and act as the body's defence against disease. They multiply and engulf invading bacteria.

In addition to its cells, blood also contains tiny fragments of bone marrow, known as platelets, which assist in the process of blood clotting and the repair of any damage, such as a cut or graze, subsequently becoming the components of a scab.

Blood also functions in the process of losing excess heat (or conserving heat if necessary), and carries nutrients, hormones and waste products to the parts of the body at which they are required.

See also *Altitude, Anaemia, Blood Packing, Breathing, Lungs.*

Blood packing

The practice known as blood packing, or blood boosting, or (misleadingly) blood doping, does not have a clear history, yet it poses one of the biggest ethical problems in competitive running.

It is simply a manipulation of the level of a runner's red blood cells which can in certain circumstances give him the same supercharged effect it is possible to achieve after training at altitude. Several Finnish runners have admitted using the system to improve performances, including the 1980 Olympic 10,000m silver and 5000m bronze medallist Kaarlo Maaninka and the 1972 Olympic steeplechase finalist Mikko Ala-Leppilampi.

Accusing fingers were also pointed at their compatriot Lasse Viren, the 5000/10,000m gold medallist at both the 1972 and 1976 Olympics in what has been hailed as a masterpiece of peaking by a man who achieved little outside those Games. Viren has always denied using blood packing, and no firm evidence has been offered.

More recently, some leading Italian distance runners, including 1984 Olympic 10,000m champion Alberto Cova, have been accused of using the system to obtain competitive success, and vigorously denied such accusations.

The method involves withdrawing a quantity of blood (up to two litres) from an athlete two or three months before a major event, then freezing and storing the red cell content, which is so vital in oxygen transportation. Just before the major competition, when the body has made up the deficit by natural means, the previously withdrawn red cells are re-injected, giving the athlete an additional supply of oxygen-carrying cells. Unlike drug taking, this process breaks no doping control rules, since the athlete is merely receiving his own blood. But the practice has now been banned by the International Olympic Committee and the IAAF, although being able to enforce the ban may be a more difficult matter.

The first clinical reports of blood packing came in 1971, when a well-respected 33-year-old Swedish physiologist, Bjorn Ekblom, conducted tests in the interest of research at the Institute of Sport in Stockholm. 'We took seven students from our school and let them run on our treadmill to get an indication of their capacity', he reported at the time. 'Then we drew twenty-seven ounces of blood (approximately equal to 20 per cent of a human's entire quantity). On the test next day, we saw a clear decrease in capacity. Then, day by day, as new blood was produced in their bodies, the values went up. After fourteen days, all were at their maximum again. Then, one month after the experiment began, we gave them back their own blood. The effect was stunning. Our test people increased their capacity by 20 per cent. The best was 23 per cent.

'It's easy to see the significance this could have on long-distance runners and cyclists. I have even been offered $20,000 for my exact method. Now, when I reflect on my laboratory tests, I feel scared. This is a method which is not against any rules and probably never could be. Even if I appeal to the sense of justice of all leaders and doctors in the world, I'm not sure someone will not make use of the results, say in the Olympics. And what will become of sport then?'

Although a long time later physiologists are able to point at potential problems which can arise with blood packing, such as making the blood too thick to be properly pumped by the heart, and the risk of reintroducing infection which might have existed when the blood was first taken out, the basic problem remains ethical. Is it a fair method of athletic preparation? Or is altitude training, which is widely accepted as legitimate, actually cheating in the same way?

Blood pressure

The pressure of the blood passing through the arteries with each beat of the heart can be measured with an instrument called a sphygmomanometer and a cuff which is wound firmly around the arm. Two readings are recorded from a column of mercury: the systolic, or highest pressure reached with each contraction of the heart, and the diastolic, the lowest pressure reached in between contractions.

A healthy adult will be somewhere in the region of 120mm (of mercury) systolic and 80mm diastolic, which is written as 120/80. Although there are individual variations, and anxiety in particular can lead to a temporary increase, a person may be said to have high blood pressure if the systolic pressure consistently exceeds 100 plus his age, or the diastolic exceeds 100.

Blood pressures are usually taken with the subject seated or lying down, because when standing there is a slight contraction of blood vessels in the legs.

Body fat percentage

Distance runners have among the lowest percentages of body fat among healthy people, and while physiologists estimate that in an average male there should be an ideal body fat percentage of 11–15 per cent, and anything over 20–25 per cent is considered to be too much, elite distance runners may sometimes be measured in the range of only 3–11 per cent. For females, the ideal percentage is estimated at 18–22 per cent, with readings in excess of 30–35 per cent considered too high, while elite female runners may be between 12–18 per cent.

For women, any measurement below 12 per cent (and 3 per cent for men) is considered to be under the requirements to maintain normal physiological functions, including athletic performance, and while percentages as low as 1.6 per cent for a male, and 7 per cent for a female, have been recorded among top distance runners, they were subsequently encouraged to try to increase their body fat levels to within a more acceptable range. In women, a low body fat percentage is thought to be one of the contributory causes of amenorrhoea.

Simple height and weight figures, even used in conjunction with one of the many charts listing 'ideal' weight for a certain height, can be a misleading way of assessing a runner's body composition. The actual percentage of body fat may still be quite high in a slim person, or low in a heavily built person, depending on the relative amounts of lean tissue and fat in their body.

Fat measurements are made either with skinfold calipers at a series of predetermined points of the body, or by hydrostatic weighing, which is a complex, but more accurate, method. It involves weighing the subject underwater, and comparing the result to a dry-land weighing. As fat floats, and lean tissue sinks, then the higher the percentage of body fat present, the less the subject will weigh underwater. By comparing the two weighings, the body fat percentage can be obtained.

See also *Amenorrhoea*.

Bones

The skeleton is a framework of bone and cartilage which supports the surrounding tissues, protects vital organs and assists in body movement by giving attachment to the muscles and providing leverage. The runner may only become aware of the skeleton through injury, such as a stress fracture or pressure from one of the vertebrae on a nerve, but he would be unable to function without it.

There are 206 bones in the human body, of which the thighbone, or femur, is the longest. Yet even below the femur in each leg alone there are twenty-nine other bones which help to support the running action: twenty-six of them are in the foot.

Bones have a complex internal structure, but they are light and strong (the femur can take vertical forces of one ton), retain a degree of elasticity, and are constantly regenerating. This process is partly regulated by the amount of strain on any particular bone. When confined to a plaster cast for any length of time, bones will tend to waste, along with the muscles around them, whereas bones in constant use will thicken and strengthen accordingly. The classic proof is the case of the cavalrymen who were found to have developed 'extra' bones in their thighs and buttocks as a result of their constant work on horses.

But a runner returning to training after weeks or months of inactivity must always beware the dangers of causing a stress fracture through trying to get back too quickly to a previous level of running. For during the lay-off the bones will have become softer and more vulnerable to fracture, and a carefully graduated training programme will be needed to build them up again to their former resilience.

In the adolescent, bone growth is achieved in the long bones through a thin cartilage plate, known as the epiphyseal plate, at one end of the bone. This comprises longitudinal columns of cartilage cells constantly reproducing themselves and turning into new bone, which is then pushed on to the main shaft, allowing it to grow in length.

This growing end occurs in the case of all three of the main leg bones (femur, tibia, fibula) at the knee end, and it is only around the ages of 18–20 in males and 16–18 in females that bone growth ceases. By then the bones will have usually completed what is known as ossification and this is one of the reasons behind the widely adopted rule of a minimum age of 18 for participants in a marathon race. Although runners of both sexes are probably capable of covering the distance at a considerably younger age, to subject the still-growing bones to such a prolonged effort on a hard surface (together with the requisite training) could actually interfere with the normal, healthy completion of the growth process.

Boredom

Variety is an important ingredient in any training programme, not only because it provides the opportunity to run over different distances at widely differing speeds, but also because it helps to keep the mind active, with the runner able to look forward to a contrasting training session. Usually a repeated weekly programme brings sufficient changes in pace.

So if the runner feels his training is becoming boring, he should examine its components, seeking out any sessions that are too similar and close together. Few runners, for example, would want to cover exactly the same course every day unless there was a very good reason for it, such as enabling them to run to and from work. In that case the additional free time gained might be considered worth the monotony. Yet even the routes used to run to work could be varied in some way, day by day, with additional loops added, or alternative paths followed.

Likewise, if a runner who trains from home *does* want to run six miles every single day, with no variation in distance, he could still adopt a series of different six-mile courses to suit his mood of the day. There could be a hilly route, a flat route, a sheltered route, an exposed route, and similar variations.

While progress in running inevitably involves a certain amount of repetition, few might feel like copying the training schedule of American Mark Nenow before he set a world 10km road best in 1984. His training schedule every day then was simply to run ten miles in the afternoon and seven miles at 11 p.m., with a fifteen-mile run on a Sunday.

It worked for him, but most ambitious runners would need to introduce a reasonable proportion of faster running, including some anaerobic interval work, to reach that level. For runners of all standards, ringing such changes is beneficial, especially in avoiding a state of staleness, a further extension of mental fatigue.

See also *Staleness*.

Boston Marathon

The Boston Marathon, the world's oldest annual marathon, was established in 1897, and is held each year on 19 April, or the nearest Monday to it. This is an official public holiday known as Patriots' Day in the state of Massachusetts, commemorating the battles of Lexington and Concord, which opened the American Revolution in 1775.

Although the start and finish lines of the marathon have been changed over the years, the route is virtually the same A–to–B course from the town of Hopkinton, through Ashland, Framingham, Natick, Wellesley and Newton,

Boston Marathon Winners

24 miles 1232 yards

Year	Winner	Time
1897	John J. McDermott (USA)	2:55.10
1898	Ronald J. McDonald (USA)	2:42.00
1899	Lawrence J. Brignolia (USA)	2:54.38
1900	James J. Caffrey (Can)	2:39.45
1901	James J. Caffrey (Can)	2:29.24
1902	Samuel A. Mellor, Jr. (USA)	2:43.12
1903	John C. Lorden (USA)	2:41.30
1904	Michael Spring (USA)	2:38.05
1905	Fred Lorz (USA)	2:38.26
1906	Timothy Ford (USA)	2:45.45
1907	Tom Longboat (Can)	2:24.24
1908	Thomas P. Morrissey (USA)	2:25.44
1909	Henri Renaud (USA)	2:53.37
1910	Frederick Cameron (Can)	2:28.53
1911	Clarence DeMar (USA)	2:21.40
1912	Michael Ryan (USA)	2:21.19
1913	Fritz Carlson (USA)	2:25.15
1914	James Duffy (Can)	2:25.02
1915	Edouard Fabre (Can)	2:31.42
1916	Arthur V. Roth (USA)	2:27.17
1917	William Kennedy (USA)	2:28.38
1918	Not held	
1919	Carl Linder (USA)	2:29.14
1920	Peter Trivoulidas (USA)	2:29.31
1921	Frank Zuna (USA)	2:18.58
1922	Clarence DeMar (USA)	2:18.10
1923	Clarence DeMar (USA)	2:23.38

26 miles 209 yards

Year	Winner	Time
1924	Clarence DeMar (USA)	2:29.41
1925	Charles Mellor (USA)	2:33.01
1926	John Miles (Can)	2:25.41

26 miles 385 yards

Year	Winner	Time
1927	Clarence DeMar (USA)	2:40.23
1928	Clarence DeMar (USA)	2:37.08
1929	John Miles (Can)	2:33.09
1930	Clarence DeMar (USA)	2:34.49
1931	James Henigan (USA)	2:46.46
1932	Paul de Bruyn (Ger)	2:33.37
1933	Leslie Pawson (USA)	2:31.02
1934	David Komonen (Can)	2:32.54
1935	John A. Kelley (USA)	2:32.08
1936	Ellison Brown (USA)	2:33.41
1937	Walter Young (Can)	2:33.20
1938	Leslie Pawson (USA)	2:35.35
1939	Ellison Brown (USA)	2:28.52
1940	Gerard Cote (Can)	2:38.29
1941	Leslie Pawson (USA)	2:30.38
1942	Bernard Smith (USA)	2:26.52
1943	Gerard Cote (Can)	2:28.26
1944	Gerard Cote (Can)	2:31.51
1945	John A. Kelley (Can)	2:30.41
1946	Stylianos Kyriakidis (Greece)	2:29.27
1947	Yun Bok Suh (Kor)	2:25.39
1948	Gerard Cote (Can)	2:31.02
1949	Karl Gosta Leandersson (Swe)	2:31.51

to the finish in the city of Boston. The first race over 24 miles 1232 yards, was won by American John McDermott in 2hr 55min 10sec.

From 1927 the course was lengthened to the standard 26 miles 385 yards, although between 1953 and 1956 it accidentally dropped to 25 miles 938 yards due to road works. The error was only discovered when Finn Antti Viskari won the 1956 race in 2hr 14min 14sec, which seemed just *too* fast at the time. From 1957 it was restored to its full distance, with the runners still enjoying the benefit of the estimated 480 feet drop from the start to the finish.

The biggest challenge on the course is the notorious Heartbreak Hill, just after twenty miles, which is actually the last of a series of four climbs. Heartbreak Hill itself rises only ninety feet, but takes a mile to do so, and for runners at that stage of the race it is particularly tough. But, once it has been negotiated, the course then drops some 200 feet over the next four miles.

The Boston Marathon has thrown up its own characters over the years, including John Adelbert Kelley, who won the race twice (in 1935 and 1945), finished second seven times, and in 1984 actually completed the race for the fifty-third time at the age of 76!

Another American, Clarence DeMar, was warned by doctors not to compete when they

Year	Winner	Time
1950	Kee Yong Ham (Kor)	2:32.39
1951	Shigeki Tanaka (Jap)	2:27.45
1952	Doroteo Flores (Guatemala)	2:31.53

25 miles 938 yards

1953	Keizo Yamada (Jap)	2:18.51
1954	Veikko Karvonen (Fin)	2:20.39
1955	Hideo Hamamura (Jap)	2:18.22
1956	Antti Viskari (Jap)	2:14.14

26 miles 385 yards

1957	John J. Kelley (USA)	2:20.05
1958	Franjo Mihalic (Yug)	2:25.54
1959	Eino Oksanen (Fin)	2:23.39
1960	Paavo Kotila (Fin)	2:20.54
1961	Eino Oksanen (Fin)	2:23.39
1962	Eino Oksanen (Fin)	2:23.48
1963	Aurele Vandendriessche (Bel)	2:18.58
1964	Aurele Vandendriessche (Bel)	2:19.59
1965	Morio Shigematsu (Jap)	2:16.33
1966	Kenji Kimihara (Jap)	2:17.11
1967	Dave McKenzie (NZ)	2:15.45
1968	Amby Burfoot (USA)	2:22.17
1969	Yoshiaki Unetani (Jap)	2:13.49
1970	Ron Hill (UK)	2:10.30
1971	Alvaro Mejia (Colombia)	2:18.45
1972	Olavi Suomalainen (Fin)	2:15.39
1973	Jon Anderson (USA)	2:16.03
1974	Neil Cusack (Eire)	2:13.39
1975	Bill Rodgers (USA)	2:09.55
1976	Jack Fultz (USA)	2:20.19
1977	Jerome Drayton (Can)	2:14.46
1978	Bill Rodgers (USA)	2:10.13
1979	Bill Rodgers (USA)	2:09.27
1980	Bill Rodgers (USA)	2:12.11
1981	Toshihiko Seko (Jap)	2:09.26
1982	Alberto Salazar (USA)	2:08.51
1983	Greg Meyer (USA)	2:09.01
1984	Geoff Smith (UK)	2:10.34
1985	Geoff Smith (UK)	2:14.05
1986	Rob de Castella (Aus)	2:07.51
1987	Toshihiko Seko (Jap)	2:11.50

WOMEN

1972	Nina Kuscsik (USA)	3:10.26
1973	Jackie Hansen (USA)	3:05.59
1974	Miki Gorman (USA)	2:47.11
1975	Liane Winter (W. Ger)	2:42.24
1976	Kim Merritt (USA)	2:47.10
1977	Miki Gorman (USA)	2:48.33
1978	Gayle Barron (USA)	2:44.52
1979	Joan Benoit (USA)	2:35.15
1980	Jacqueline Gareau (Can)	2:34.28
1981	Allison Roe (NZ)	2:26.45
1982	Charlotte Teske (W. Ger)	2:29.33
1983	Joan Benoit (USA)	2:22.43
1984	Lorraine Moller (NZ)	2:29.28
1985	Lisa Weidenbach (USA)	2:34.06
1986	Ingrid Kristiansen (Nor)	2:24.55
1987	Rosa Mota (Por)	2:25.21

detected a heart murmur before the 1911 race. But DeMar, who had finished second in 1910, ran anyway, broke the course record by three minutes, and scored the first of seven victories in the race which spanned a period of nineteen years.

More recently, in 1970, Ron Hill became the first Briton to win the race, setting a course record of 2hr 10min 30sec, while local resident Bill Rodgers took the first of his four victories in 1975 with a US record of 2hr 9min 55sec. He became known as 'Boston Billy'.

Women runners were officially recognized by the Boston Marathon from 1972, but had been taking part unofficially since Canadian Roberta Bingay ran the course in 1966. But the best-known female pioneer at Boston was Kathrine Switzer, who survived an attempt by a race official to physically remove her from the race in 1967.

In 1980 an unknown Cuban-born runner named Rosie Ruiz ran through the Boston finish line, claiming victory in the women's race in 2hr 31min 56sec. But she was later exposed as a fraud (see page 46).

In 1983 the undoubtedly genuine Joan Benoit (who was destined to become Olympic champion in 1984) set a world women's best of 2hr 22min 43sec in winning at Boston. But the race was already becoming starved of other big

The finish of the Boston Marathon, established in 1897 and, despite changes, still going strong

names by the refusal of the organizing Boston Athletic Association to offer cash prizes, appearance money, or even expenses for leading runners. In the changing climate of distance running, the leading marathoners preferred to run in London, New York or Chicago where their efforts were well rewarded financially. But after holding out for the traditions of the race (including its Monday date, which made it unattractive for US network television as it was a public holiday only in Massachusetts), the Boston AA finally agreed to offer cash incentives from 1986 in order to keep pace with the rest of the marathon world. It made all the difference, and that year top names Rob de Castella and Ingrid Kristiansen were the race winners, with De Castella's victory in 2hr 7min 51sec earning him $60,000 including bonuses, plus a Mercedes-Benz car. The pioneers may have shuddered, but it seemed the only way to retain Boston's prestige as a major international event.

Bowerman, Bill

In the USA, a country whose athletic development has long been built on its highly-competitive inter-collegiate system, the name of Bill Bowerman is revered as the outstandingly successful coach – not only for his leadership of the University of Oregon track team as Head Coach from 1949 to 1972, but also for his example to other American middle-distance coaches.

Of all the training principles on which he worked, he became particularly associated with the 'hard–easy' aspect of his system. This did not necessarily mean that an athlete would train hard one day, and easy the next; it could mean 2–3 days of hard work, followed by 2–3 easy days. But the results he produced were consistently good, and helped develop some of America's top middle-distance stars including Dyrol Burleson, Jim Grelle, Kenny Moore, Bill Dellinger (later Bowerman's successor as Oregon coach) and the late Steve Prefontaine. In 1962 his University of Oregon team of Archie San Romani, Vic Reeve, Keith Forman and Dyrol Burleson set a world 4×1 miles relay record of 16:09.0.

Bowerman took this team to compete in New Zealand early in 1963, where he first met Arthur Lydiard, coach to most of New Zealand's leading distance runners. He was influenced by Lydiard in a number of ways, notably by the jogging programme which he had developed there, and on returning to the USA, Bowerman co-authored a book entitled *Jogging*, which explained how gentle, non-competitive running could help men and women of all ages stay fit and healthy. It was published in 1967, and sold over a million copies in six languages.

In 1972, the year of his retirement from the University of Oregon, he was appointed Head Coach to the US Olympic track team in Munich, and the same year co-founded the Nike running shoe company with one of his former milers, Phil Knight. The company was to become one of the biggest in the USA. William Jay Bowerman was born in Portland, Oregon, on 19 February 1911.

See also *Waffle-soled shoes*.

Bras

Even women who normally choose not to wear a bra are well advised to do so when running, because research has shown that the muscles and ligaments in the breasts can easily become damaged if they are not sufficiently supported. They will begin to sag and not regain their shape again.

But the choice of a bra is a personal decision, which a woman can make only through trial and error as to which type and make is best suited to her shape and running action. There are now a number of specifically designed sports bras on the market, which most average-busted women would find suitable for running, although many standard style bras are also quite adequate as long as certain considerations are observed. The bra should have no seams across the cups, as they might rub or irritate the nipples, nor should there be any trimmings or metal fastenings which could cause chafing. There should be a broad band around the base, under the cups, to ensure it does not ride up during exercise and a cotton or cotton mixture lining to the cups helps absorb moisture.

Some large-breasted ladies, even though they already have a comfortable, supporting bra, still find the problem of a bouncing chest somewhat embarrassing. Apart from wearing a loose-fitting top so as not to draw too much attention, the bounce has been effectively reduced by some lady runners through wearing two bras. Other runners report that wearing a leotard as well as a bra under their running kit helps them feel more in control and less self-conscious. A bra designed for a mother-to-be probably provides the best support, but care must be taken to avoid any potential chafing hazards.

Recently a new style of bra, designed for 'minimal bounce', has been developed. It is manufactured from cotton and lycra in the style of a vest which finishes at the midriff, and is worn instead of a bra, holding the bust snugly and flatteringly against the chest. It has no cups, hooks, clips, wires or darts, or any other fastening, thus greatly reducing the risk of chafing.

Bra straps are often a problem for runners because they tend to slip down, or simply show and look untidy. Some sports bras are joined at the back by a central panel, to prevent the straps slipping off the shoulders, but a disadvantage of a few models is that while being comfortable, supportive and non-slip, they are also non-adjustable, which can be a disadvantage for those who suffer from pre-menstrual swelling.

Several British international runners have adapted the straps of their own favourite bras in the past by snipping the straps at the back, then resewing them in a crossover style to prevent slipping. But bras with detachable straps now mean this can be done more simply while offering a variety of combinations.

The accurate fitting of a bra is more important for a runner than a non-sporting woman, and the ideal method of obtaining an accurate measurement is in the corsetry section of a department store. As a rough guide, a bra size is normally the measurement immediately under the bust plus five inches, which would be an 'A' cup; for example, a 31-inch under-bust measurement would normally mean a 36-inch bra with an 'A' cup. If the difference is six inches, a 'B' cup would be required, eight inches would mean a 'C' cup, nine inches a 'D' cup, and ten inches a 'DD'.

Brasher, Chris

Known primarily these days as the driving force behind the London Marathon (along with John Disley, his long-time friend and racing rival), Chris Brasher can also lay claim to two particularly outstanding achievements in the closing years of the Oxbridge domination of the British athletics scene during the mid-fifties.

It was Brasher, then a regular training partner of Roger Bannister, who made the pace for the opening two and a half laps of the first four-minute mile at Oxford on 6 May 1954 and, far less predictably, it was Brasher who won the Olympic gold medal for the 3000m steeplechase at the 1956 Games in Melbourne. Born in Georgetown, British Guiana (now

Chris Brasher (second left) behind the scenes at the London Marathon, which he created with John Disley (second right)

Guyana), on 21 August 1928, Christopher William Brasher was a middle-distance runner of good, but not outstanding ability, yet prepared to punish himself very hard in pursuit of a goal. He ran his first-ever steeplechase in 1950, while on tour with the Achilles Club in Greece, simply to earn some points in a two-day match held, appropriately, in the stadium built for the 1896 Olympic Games.

But he began to take the event more seriously afterwards, and by 1952 was good enough to join the British number one, John Disley, in the Olympic final at Helsinki. Disley took the bronze medal, and Brasher was eleventh out of twelve. But his regular training with Bannister and Chris Chataway paid dividends, and at the Melbourne Olympics he finally came out of their shadow to score an upset win in 8:41.2. He even survived an initial disqualification after judges ruled he had obstructed bronze medallist Ernst Larsen of Norway on the last lap. But the jury of appeal ruled it had been an accidental clash of elbows and reinstated him.

Disley, ill before the Games, finished sixth.

Brasher retired from running and pursued a career which included being sports editor of the *Observer* newspaper from 1957 (and for whom he is still athletics correspondent), and later a BBC TV reporter, working for programmes like 'Tonight', 'Time Out' and 'Man Alive', and rising to the post of head of features for BBC-2.

He returned to running in the seventies through helping Disley publicize the sport of orienteering in Britain, and particularly the 1976 World Championships at Aviemore in Scotland. Both Brasher and Disley joined Ranelagh Harriers, and decided to finally attempt a marathon by taking part in the 1979 New York City race. It made such an impression on both of them that the idea of a similar race in London was born in the following weeks, and held for the first time in 1981.

See also *Sir Roger Bannister, Four-minute Mile, London Marathon.*

Breathing

When the rate at which oxygen is required by the muscles increases during running, so the breathing rate becomes more rapid, from 12–15 breaths per minute at rest up to 50 breaths a minute or more at hard effort.

Breathing in through the nose and mouth, as the lungs expand to their maximum volume, and then exhaling as the lungs are squeezed, the runner draws in the fuel for his engine with the oxygen in the air, then getting rid of the carbon dioxide, or exhaust.

The inhaled oxygen is picked up by the red blood cells at the alveolar wall of the lungs, through a thin membrane, and taken off to the muscles where it combusts with the body's fuel stores to make energy. Then the resulting carbon dioxide is taken back to the lungs by the red blood cells for expulsion from the body through expiration, and the whole process is repeated.

The blood itself is pumped from the heart to the lungs for oxygenation, and returns to the heart to be pumped to the body's tissues. Then it returns to the heart to be pumped back to the lungs for a new supply of oxygen, which has been breathed in from the air.

At high altitude, where the oxygen content of the air is much thinner than at sea level, breathing becomes much more difficult, and the red cells in the blood multiply to compensate for the smaller amount of oxygen each is able to take to the muscles.

See also *Altitude, Blood, Heart, Lungs, Oxygen.*

Budd, Zola

Few athletes can have said so little, yet created so many front-page headlines and as much controversy as Zola Budd following her arrival in Britain from her native South Africa in 1984. Born in Bloemfontein on 26 May 1966, the quiet, shy Zola had already made a name for herself in athletics with a series of unofficial world junior records at the age of 17, plus a 5000m time of 15:01.83 which was nearly seven seconds inside Mary Decker's world senior best.

But living and racing in South Africa, a country suspended from both the International Olympic Committee and the International Amateur Athletic Federation, meant that Zola could not compete outside it.

Then early in 1984 the Budd family realized that although Zola's father, Frank, was also South African-born, his own father had been born in Hackney, London, in 1886, and had emigrated to South Africa early this century. By claiming UK citizenship through his own father, Frank Budd thus became 'British' and it proved a short step for Zola herself to follow suit.

The Budd family travelled to England in strict secrecy on 23 March 1984, assisted by the *Daily Mail* which had signed up the family for exclusivity to the end of the year. To the intense annoyance of immigrant welfare groups, who were used to long waits for UK citizenship decisions, on 6 April 1984, just thirteen days after its submission, it was announced that Zola's application for a British passport had been approved, hastened by the intervention of the then Home Secretary, Leon Brittan. It was admitted that her application had been speeded up to allow her the chance to compete in the Los Angeles Olympics, and that if her application had been filed after her eighteenth birthday on 26 May 1984 she would have had to serve a five-year residency qualification period.

In Parliament accusations flew from the Labour opposition benches that the Home Office had been manipulated by the commercial interests of the Tory-sympathetic *Daily Mail*, which was making enormous capital out of the public interest in Zola. Sports officials argued that it was a back door to eligibility based on a very slender British connection. But Zola had a British passport.

Within eight days she had also joined a British club, Aldershot, Farnham and District AC, and made her debut in their colours at Central Park, Dartford, on 14 April 1984, running in the 3000m at the Southern Women's League fixture. There was never a Southern League fixture like it, with BBC TV 'Grandstand' covering the race live, and thousands of spectators standing around the open track. Wearing spikes, she did not disappoint, breaking Yvonne Murray's UK junior record by five seconds with 9:2.6.

It was the first of a whole series of events where the relaxed family sport found itself in the middle of espionage-like proceedings, with heavy security everywhere Zola was due to run, while *Daily Mail* representatives tried to make sure their 'property' was protected, and anti-apartheid demonstrators seized any opportunity to remind everyone of what was happening in South Africa.

Settled in rented accommodation in Guildford, Surrey, with her parents, and coach Pieter Labuschagne, it was a curious existence for Zola. She mixed little with other athletes, partly through circumstances and partly through shyness. She had to withdraw from her second race in Britain, a 1500m at Crawley, where the town's Labour-controlled council made it clear that she would not be welcome at their brand-new £300,000 arena.

But Zola had no trouble qualifying for the British Olympic team for Los Angeles, where her 3000m race against an athlete she had always idolized, Mary Decker of the USA, was seen as one of the potential highlights of the Games, especially as most of the Eastern Europeans were boycotting. The diminutive Zola, who usually ran barefooted and was frequently the smallest competitor in her races, had quickly become very popular with the British public, although arguments about her still raged among politicians and sports officials.

But in Los Angeles her new-found world collapsed in the 3000m final. Around the 1730m point, Zola was leading when Decker apparently tried to move up to her shoulder, but on the inside. Decker's feet briefly caught Budd's ankle, and the American fell on the grass infield, twisting her hip and being unable to continue. Some of the partisan US crowd began to boo Zola, who perhaps was not quite ready for the Olympics anyway, and she drifted back, totally demoralized, to finish seventh. Rumanian Maricica Puica, always a potential winner, took the gold and Britain's Wendy Sly the silver.

To make matters worse for Zola, she was also disqualified after the race for obstruction, but this decision was reversed after an appeal by the British team management.

The emotional strain of the year was vast, and by November 1984 Zola had announced that she had decided to return permanently to South Africa, where she would feel much happier, even though she would not be able to compete internationally again.

But after a period of contemplation and discussion with athletics officials from Britain and South Africa she changed her mind, and returned to England in the New Year to race indoors and at cross country. In her first appearance in the National Women's Cross-country Championships, at Birkenhead in February 1985, a long-anticipated incident occurred. Two demonstrators (both female) jumped in front of the leaders after a mile and forced Zola out of the race, although she was unhurt and they were both quickly arrested. But it was a reminder that controversy would never be far away. She was still selected for England's team for the World Cross-country Championships in Lisbon, and responded by running away, barefooted, with the individual title.

But she was not in such devastating form when she took part in an over-hyped 3000m race during the Peugeot-Talbot Games at Crystal Palace in July. Billed as 'the Olympic re-match, Zola Budd v. Mary Decker', it was really a non-starter because Zola had been in poor form early in the 1985 track season, while Decker – with a lot to prove in a race being beamed live to the USA – was in excellent form. Predictably, Decker ran right away with the race, leaving Zola a lacklustre fourth, a

---

Facing page

Top: Zola Budd training in Bloemfontein, South Africa, before her move to England which created such controversy

Below: Zola Budd (151) and Mary Decker-Slaney (373) lead the 1984 Olympic 3000m final before the fateful collision

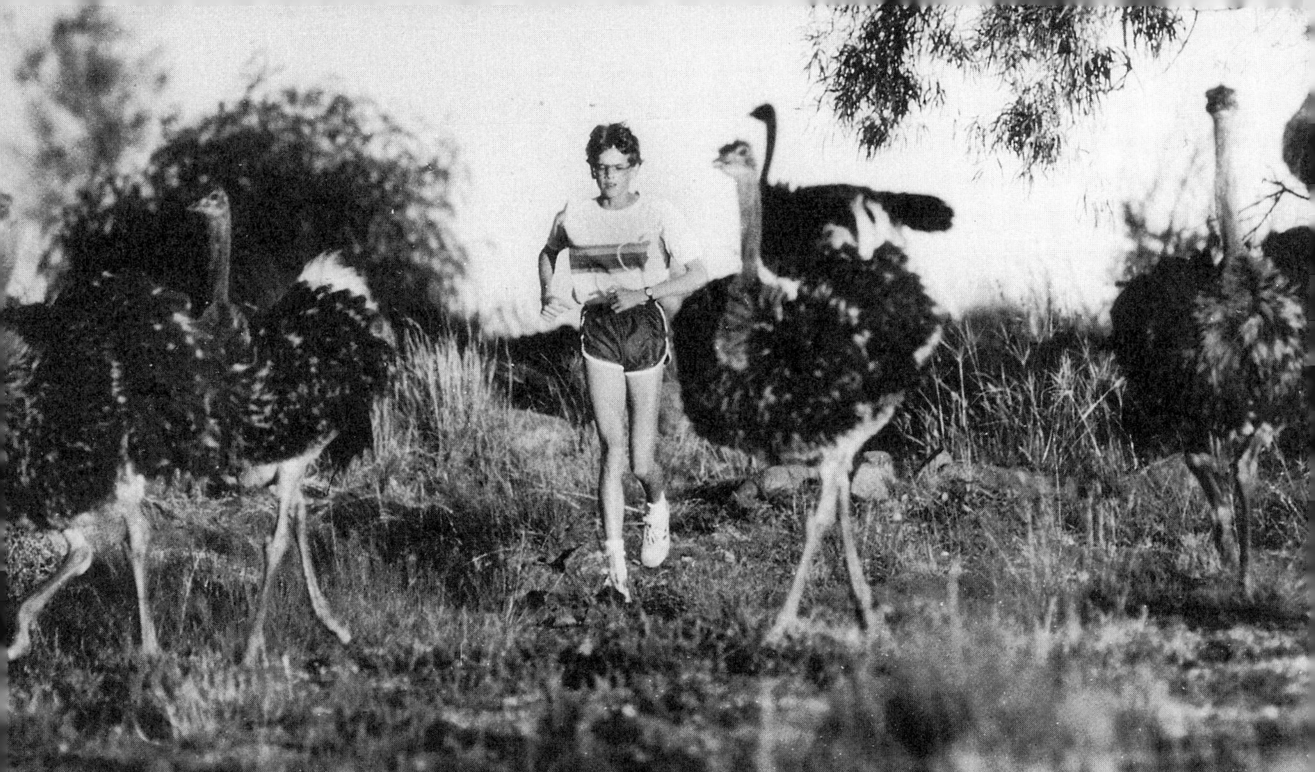

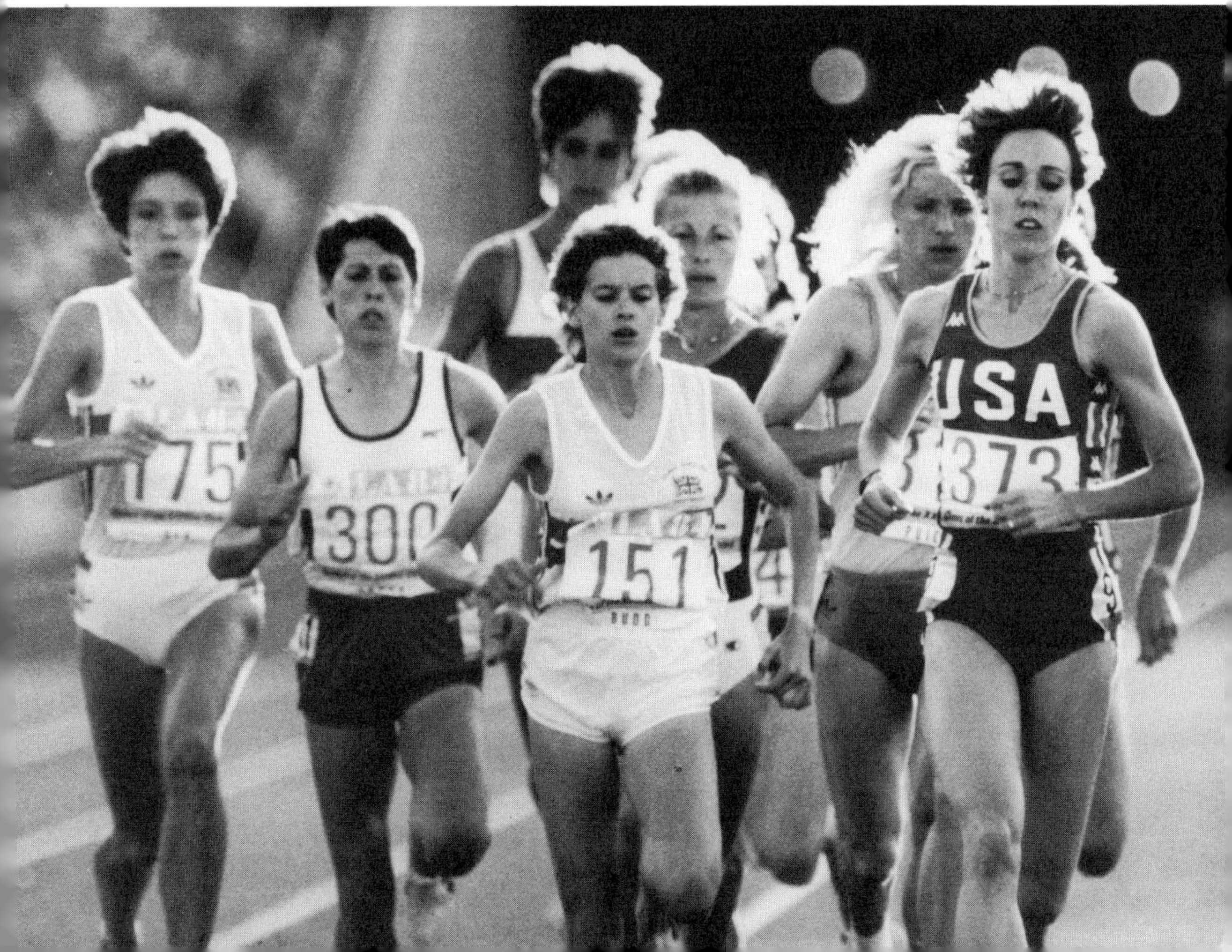
175
300
151
BUDD
USA
373

Track progress

Born 26 May 1966.

Year	800m	1500m	Mile	2000m	3000m	5000m
1980		4:24.3			10:06.5	
1981	2:07.4	4:19.0				
1982	2:06.5	4:09.1			8:59.2	
1983	2:05.4	4:06.87			8:39.0	15.10.65
1984	2:00.9	4:01.81	4:30.7	5:33.15	8:37.5	15:01.83
1985		3:59.96	4:17.57		8:28.83	14:48.07
1986	2:00.55	4:01.93	4:27.5	5:30.19	8:34.43	

dozen seconds behind. The reverberations went on for months, particularly when it was revealed that while Decker had received $50,000 appearance money, plus $25,000 bonus for winning, Budd had been paid a staggering $125,000, easily the biggest appearance fee ever paid on the track, and for a race she always seemed destined to lose.

Yet with that traumatic, if financially rewarding, experience behind her, Zola quickly found a new level of form. Running in the European Cup final in Moscow just a month after the Crystal Palace debacle, she led all the way in the 3000m and held off the experienced Zamira Zaitseva of the USSR and Ulrike Bruns of the GDR all the way down the home straight to record Britain's first European Cup final women's track win for eighteen years. Her time of 8:35.32 was a Commonwealth record, and before the track season was over she had reduced it to 8:28.83 in the IAAF Grand Prix final in Rome (placing third behind Decker and Puica), as well as becoming the first female UK runner to break four minutes for 1500m (with 3:59.96 in Brussels), had set a Commonwealth mile record of 4:17.57 in Zurich, and broken the world 5000m record with 14:48.07 at Crystal Palace. She lost more big races than she won, but she learned a great deal, and proved she really was a world-class runner.

But 1986 was a less happy year, even though it started well. She set a Commonwealth indoor 1500m record of 4:6.87, a world indoor 3000m record of 8:39.79, and then retained her World Cross-country title in Neuchatel, Switzerland, in March.

Just before the Commonwealth Games in Edinburgh, however, Zola was declared ineligible to compete for England by the Commonwealth Games Federation on the grounds that she had spent relatively little time actually living in the country, despite her British passport. It was not a complete surprise, although the lateness of the decision made it more disappointing for Zola.

Then in the European Championships in Stuttgart a month later, she was edged out of a bronze medal by teammate Yvonne Murray in the 3000m final, and finished only ninth in the 1500m final. A hamstring injury, the first serious injury of her career, had affected her, and through the winter of 1986–87 her winter preparation was badly disrupted.

Having raced three summer seasons for Britain, she announced at the end of 1986 that she intended to live more permanently in England, to study at an English university, and to work with an English coach, although still being guided by her former schoolteacher and original coach Pieter Labuschagne, who had returned to his teaching career in South Africa. The story is by no means over yet.

C

Calf

The calf is formed by two muscles. The gastrocnemius is the wide, dual muscle extending from the rear of the knee to midway down the lower leg, while the soleus lies beneath it, but more towards the outer side of the leg. These muscles, known jointly as the triceps, merge into the Achilles tendon halfway down the leg, and when the triceps is contracted the heel is pulled back and up by the Achilles tendon (which is also known as the heel cord).

See also *Achilles Tendon*.

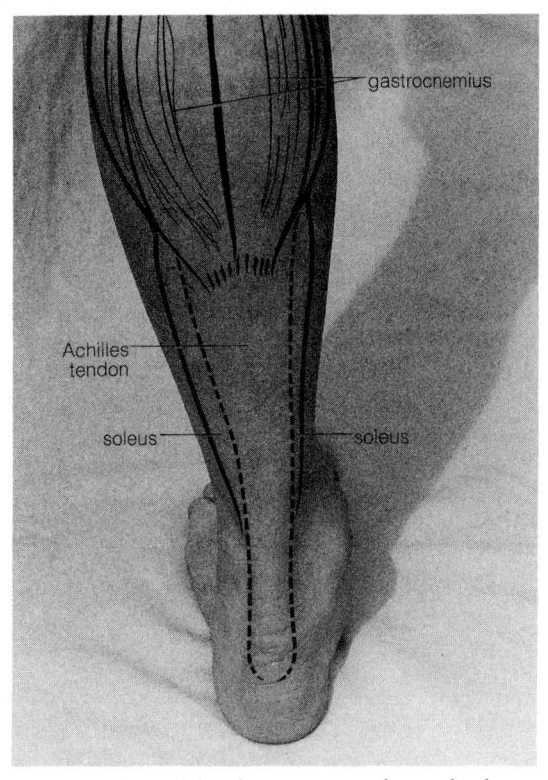

The calf, formed by the gastrocnemius and soleus muscles, known jointly as the triceps

Carbohydrate loading

So much has been written about the dietary manipulation known as carbohydrate loading and its apparent benefits to marathon performance, that it has been wrongly regarded in some circles as an alternative to hard training.

Its historical background is therefore important. As long ago as 1939 it had been demonstrated in a classic study (*Christensen & Hansen*) that while reducing the normal carbohydrate levels in an endurance competitor's diet lowered his endurance capacity, increasing the carbohydrate significantly prolonged it. In 1966 further laboratory tests were performed in Sweden (*Bergström, Hultman, Hermansen and Saltin*) using long distance cyclists riding bicycle ergometers. They showed not only that additional carbohydrates could prolong endurance, but that if this 'loading' followed a hard session of exercise (sufficient to deplete the body's supply of the energy fuel, known as glycogen) and several days of abstention from the carbohydrates which would normally have replenished the glycogen supplies, then it was possible to actually super-load glycogen to levels higher than existed before the exercise.

What happens is that during the post-exercise period, in which the expected replenishment of glycogen is not forthcoming, the body is instead stimulated into producing extra glycogen-storing enzymes to try to compensate, and when the glycogen levels finally *are* replaced through the reintroduction of carbohydrates several days later, more of it can be stored.

So a successful formula for dietary manipulation seemed to be:

1. Hard exercise to deplete the glycogen stores.
2. Ignore the temptation to replace them immediately.
3. Allow the body to produce extra glycogen-storing enzymes.
4. Re-introduce carbohydrates, which can then be stored as glycogen at a higher volume than before.

In an event like the marathon, where the natural exhaustion of the body's glycogen stores (known as hitting the wall) usually takes place around the 18 to 22 miles mark, to be able to delay that point until later in the race or even postpone it altogether by manipulating the body's chemistry seemed to be a process – like altitude training or blood doping – which might change its whole aspect.

News of the Swedish experiment was sent by a friend to British marathon runner Ron Hill, whose sharp, analytical mind was always searching for ways of trying to improve performance. He developed his own version of the diet in time for the 1969 AAA Marathon championship in Manchester, and in that race beat the holder of the world best, Derek Clayton, by two minutes. Hill took the lead at fifteen miles and went on to record his then best time of 2hr 13min 42sec, the second fastest ever by a British runner.

Two months later the same dietary preparation brought Hill his first major international honour when he won the European Marathon title in Athens. And, significantly, he won the race only in the closing stages. At nineteen miles he was third and had mentally settled for the bronze medal. But he then steadily turned a deficit of $1\frac{1}{2}$ minutes into a lead of $\frac{3}{4}$ minute over Belgium's Gaston Roelants by the finish, ending the race almost as strongly as he had started.

Ecstatic after the race, Hill revealed details of the diet in a newspaper interview, and later progressed through a series of other racing successes, including victory in the Fukuoka classic marathon in Japan in December 1969 (2:11.54), in the Boston Marathon in a course record of 2:10.30 in April 1970, and in the Commonwealth Games three months later in a European record of 2:09.28.

His new-found level of ability and consistency really gave the carbohydrate-loading diet the public stamp of approval and recognition, and everywhere marathon runners were trying it out, often with mixed fortunes. The popular version of 'The Diet' (as it became colloquially known) at that time consisted of three phases: Firstly, the 'bleed-out' of existing glycogen stores, which could be achieved by a long run of 20–22 miles six or seven days before the marathon (and the severity of which has since been questioned); secondly, after the run and for the following three days, the diet should consist of a high protein and fat content, with very few carbohydrates; training is continued only lightly; thirdly, from the Wednesday lunchtime before a Saturday marathon, a switch is made to a high percentage carbohydrate diet (such as bread, cereals, cake, doughnuts and chocolate), but still taking in fats, protein, vitamins and minerals, and training lightly.

The disadvantages soon began to become apparent. Not everyone noticed the same beneficial effects, and for each one who did, there seemed to be someone else who had suffered from major digestive problems before and during the race. Some of these related to overdoing the third, or 'loading', phase. For at a time when training is being reduced anyway, the extra food can sometimes cause a weight increase of 3–4lbs during the final week of preparation, as well as a bloated feeling in the athlete which may even undermine his confidence. To feel sluggish, full and heavy is not always the best preparation for a long road race. So the emphasis should really be on a higher percentage of carbohydrate in the diet rather than an enormously increased volume.

Also, during that second phase, when an iron-will is needed to resist the temptation to eat sweet foods, the body may be weak and vulnerable to any germ or virus which may be around; its natural defences are lessened, and there is a higher risk of contracting a cold or flu.

Ron Hill, with the hindsight now of many more marathons and experiments using high and low carbohydrate diets behind him, has modified his own views on the diet. He was never in favour of a run as long as twenty miles to deplete the glycogen stores in the first place, feeling that several shorter, harder runs would achieve the same 'bleed-out' effect during the first two days of the week-long regime, with just an easy run on the third day.

During these first three days he still eats food like bacon, cheese, eggs, ham, cooked meats (boiled ham or tongue), butter, fish and other meats (chicken, steak, chops), together with green salads, tomatoes and other vegetables, such as carrots, turnips, cabbage, cauliflower, peas and beans (but no potatoes). In avoiding sweet and starchy foods in this time, he allows himself four Ryvita biscuits (rather than bread), an apple, an orange and a yoghurt each day. He emphasizes that he reduces but does not omit carbohydrates totally during this phase as he did in the earliest days, because he has come to realize that some are needed just to sustain the vital life processes. From midway through the fourth day, his emphasis switches to a much higher concentration of carbohydrates, but with care not to overdo the total quantity of consumed food, which should remain about normal.

As the man who bridged the gap between the research scientist's laboratory and the road racing world, Hill is still, nearly twenty years later, having to explain and illustrate his dietary experiences. Often the biggest demand is from runners who hope they may be able to discover from him a short cut to success.

There is none. By 1969, when his diet-aided races started, Hill had already competed in two Olympic Games and was one of the world's top distance runners, training regularly in excess of 100 miles a week. The diet did not turn him into a world-class runner. He was there already, and his experiments were those of a man simply trying to find another 0.1% which might make the difference between a gold and silver medal, not someone expecting to knock off 20 or 30% of the effort needed to train and race.

The carbohydrate loading diet can help, but cannot necessarily help everybody. It is certainly not recommended for first-time marathon runners, who will benefit far more from staying with their familiar eating habits. For those who do want to try the diet, it is worth undertaking a trial version before a minor event first rather than risk spoiling a good performance in a major race in case it does not work for you.

Above all, though, nothing can replace training. There is little point in going to considerable extremes of dietary manipulation intended to help you over the last miles of the marathon if you are not basically fit enough to get that far in the first place!

See also *Glycogen*, *Hitting the Wall*.

Chafing

The repetitive action in long-distance running, with many thousands of identical strides in every race or training run, sometimes leads to painful chafing, where the runner's clothing may cause extreme friction of the skin.

The most vulnerable areas include the upper thighs, where the shorts may rub, (or where in overweight runners the thighs themselves may rub together), the shoulders and the chest, particularly across the nipples, where the constant rubbing of a damp vest may cause the condition known as 'jogger's nipple', in which they may even bleed.

Sometimes the cause of chafing may be clothing that is too tight, or becomes an irritant when sweat-soaked, or has an inner seam which, when wet, may take on saw-like properties.

Prevention is of paramount importance, since races for which the runner has conscientiously prepared may otherwise be spoiled by a small but painful oversight. All running kit should be tried and tested on long training runs, and new kit should never be worn for the first time in a race. Petroleum jelly (like Vaseline) should be smeared generously on any areas which are prone to chafing (such as the groin and armpits), to reduce the possibility of friction, and tight clothing avoided altogether. Some runners cover their nipples with Elastoplast or Band-Aid before a marathon to prevent chafing.

If you do suffer in a race, an unofficial stop by a first-aid post may provide some petroleum jelly, and in some long races the organizers even provide Vaseline alongside the drinks and sponges at the later refreshment stations. Strictly speaking, it would probably count as 'illegal assistance'; but at that stage you are probably past caring!

Chariots of Fire

Chosen for the Royal Film Performance of 1981, *Chariots of Fire* has been the most successful attempt so far by the cinema to portray the tensions of athletic performance. It followed the build-up of two contrasting British sprinters, Harold Abrahams and Eric Liddell, to their eventual gold medal successes in the 1924 Paris Olympics.

There Abrahams, spurred on by his experiences of anti-semitism at Cambridge University, won the 100m while his great Scottish rival Liddell, whose strong Christian beliefs would not allow him to run the 100m which was held on a Sunday, unexpectedly won the 400m.

Director Hugh Hudson and producer David Puttnam created a film which was spellbinding even to non-sporting audiences, and while the excellent screenplay by Colin Welland took a fair number of dramatic liberties in terms of fact, it did not spoil the production, even for the most pedantic athletics historian.

For example, in the film, when Liddell (played by Ian Charleson) discovers that the 100m heats will be held on a Sunday, he is just about to board the boat for Paris; in fact, he knew a year before and his intentions to run the 400m instead were well known. And the romance between Abrahams (played by Ben Cross) and his eventual wife Sybil (played by

Harold Abrahams (played by Ben Cross, left) and Lord 'Lindsey' (Nigel Havers, right) bent history slightly in 'Chariots of Fire'

Alice Krige) did not actually happen until some time after the Paris Olympics. For legitimate dramatic purposes, though, time was somewhat twisted.

Nor does the film acknowledge that the two men raced each other at the Paris Olympics in the 200m (which took place after the 100m, but before the 400m). Liddell took the bronze medal, with Abrahams a tired last. But certain changes in history were forced upon the production when several of the surviving athletes declined to be portrayed in the film. This led to the introduction of the fictional Lord Andrew Lindsey (played by Nigel Havers), an aristocratic 400m hurdler, who is very clearly based on Lord David Burghley, the 1928 Olympic 400m hurdles champion, who was brought forward in time for the plot.

Burghley, who became President of the AAA from 1936 to 1976, and of the IAAF from 1946 to 1976, was actually robbed of one of his achievements in the production. In an early sequence, Harold Abrahams is depicted as successfully running round the 370 yards of uneven flagstones of the Great Court at Trinity College, Cambridge, including three right-angled turns, before the clock finishes striking noon (which takes 44.9 seconds). In fact, the feat was achieved not by Abrahams, but by Lord Burghley, during his last term at Cambridge in 1927, and he is the only man on record as having successfully completed the run.

But Lord Burghley, who died shortly after the film's release in 1981, was undismayed about this change in history for the film, insisting that he only did the run for a bit of fun anyway. He also denied the long-accepted embroidery to the story that he was wearing a dinner jacket when he ran! One irony was that the film makers could not get permission to film this sequence at Trinity College itself, and so it was actually staged around the quad at Eton instead.

The sequences of the 1924 Paris Olympics (for which the actors had been specially coached by former British Olympic coach Tom McNab) were staged at Bebington Oval, near Liverpool, which was cosmetically transformed into Colombes Stadium.

The film, which also brought plaudits to actor Ian Holm for his portrayal of Sam Mussabini, the professional coach to Abrahams, is likely to remain a classic for many aspects, not least of them the haunting and evocative theme music composed and performed by Vangelis.

The film ends with the homecoming of the Olympic champions, before cutting to a re-creation of the 1978 memorial service for Abrahams. His own competitive career had actually lasted less than another season after his Olympic success, for Abrahams had to retire prematurely at the age of 26 in 1925 following a serious leg injury sustained while long jumping. He went on to become a ubiquitous figure as an athletics administrator (elected to the AAA general committee in 1926, half a century later he was its president), journalist (as athletics correspondent to the *Sunday Times* from 1925 to 1967), and broadcaster on BBC radio. He died on 14 January 1978, at the age of 78, fifteen years after his wife.

Liddell, who had been born of Scottish parents in China in 1902, did not compete again seriously after 1925 either. He devoted the rest of his life to missionary work in China, and married his wife, Florence McKenzie, the daughter of Canadian missionaries, in Tientsin in 1934. They had three daughters, though he never saw the youngest of them, and had to spend a great deal of time apart from them in China. He died of a massive brain haemorrhage at the age of 43 while in a Japanese internment camp at Weihsien in Shantung Province, just south of Peking, on 21 February 1945. His last words were: 'It's complete surrender.'

Cheats

When American Fred Lorz ran into the Olympic Stadium at St Louis in 1904 he was acclaimed as the marathon winner. He even waved to the crowd, and was about to be presented with his laurel wreath by the daughter of President Roosevelt as his fellow American, Tom Hicks, staggered into the arena, the real winner. Only then did it transpire that Lorz had actually covered part of the course by car!

Lorz, from New York City, had been a genuine starter, but after ten miles on the hot dusty roads, sustained cramp, and was picked up by an official vehicle. Most of his rivals saw him pass by them in it. But after twenty miles, the car itself broke down, and Lorz decided to run the rest of the way back to the stadium. As he neared it, however, spectators began acclaiming him as the race leader and in a moment of weakness he decided to carry the charade through. He owned up immediately afterwards, saying it had simply been a joke, but his national federation could find little humour in it, and suspended him from competition. (Full of remorse, Lorz redeemed himself the following year by genuinely pushing himself into a state of exhaustion to win the 1905 Boston Marathon.)

At least his actions were not premeditated, unlike those of Rosie Ruiz in the 1980 Boston Marathon. The unknown Miss Ruiz, a 26-year-old Cuban-born resident of Miami, amazed the running world by crossing the finish line of the women's race first in 2hr 31min 56sec, which six months earlier would have been a world best. It was an apparent improvement of more than twenty-five minutes over her previous declared best (of 2hr 56min 29sec in the 1979 New York Marathon). But she had been running so fast that no one around the course saw her, other than two Harvard students who reported to officials afterwards that they had seen a woman answering the description of Ruiz joining in the race about half a mile from the finish.

Ruiz was allowed to receive the victor's wreath and medal, but suspicions began almost immediately. She looked just a little too heavy and a little too fresh to have run so fast on a hot day. When finally challenged, she insisted she had done, but further investigation by officials showed she had not. She had not been recorded as passing any point on the course, other than the finish.

In interviews she showed only superficial knowledge of training, and detective work by the New York Road Runners Club revealed that her qualifying time for Boston of 2hr 56min 29sec in the New York Marathon was also fraudulent. (A witness recalled travelling with Ruiz part of the way in New York by underground, and how Ruiz then managed to have the barcode on her number read at the finish by claiming she was injured. She thus ensured herself of a place in the results even though video tapes of her supposed finishing position did not show her at all.)

Ruiz was disqualified from both the Boston and New York races, and the real 1980 Boston women's winner, Canadian Jacqueline Gareau (2hr 34min 28sec), finally received her awards nearly eight days after crossing the line. Ruiz still maintained her innocence, and promised to prove her ability by running another race. But she has not done so yet. At the time of the 1980 race it also transpired that she was already due to face legal proceedings over ten fraudulent cheques, and two years later was arrested on charges of stealing $25,000 from her employers.

The London Marathon has had a number of disqualifications for apparent course cutting. In 1986 48-year-old Brian Lockyer was disqualified from his eighty-third place in the race (second in the Veterans 45–49 age category) in 2hr 23min 28sec after officials alleged that he did not run the section between twelve and twenty-five miles and so did not appear on the judges' sheets or video tapes between those points. Lockyer maintains he did, but has been unable to produce any satisfactory explanation for his apparent absence between those points.

Later in 1986, the originally proclaimed winner of the Veterans section of the New York City Marathon, 43-year-old John Bell from Indiana, was disqualified from the race (and forfeited his $3000 prize) when he and twenty-three other runners were ruled to have cheated after missing video checks.

In the same event, Poland's surprise overall second-place finisher Antoni Niemczak was disqualified for failing a dope test after the race. Niemczak protested that he had been given an injection for a tooth problem before leaving Poland, and had been unaware that it contained any illegal substances.

Deliberate drug-use is still the most serious and sinister form of cheating, and although it is still associated primarily with the 'explosive' events in athletics, it was actually a marathon runner who was the first athlete to be banned for drug use. In August 1968 Belgian runner Joseph Rombaux was disqualified for life after a positive dope test following his victory in his national marathon championship.

A number of track runners have subsequently been banned for failing drug tests, most notably the Finn Martti Vainio, the 1978 European 10,000m champion, who in 1984 became the first-ever athlete to be stripped of an Olympic medal for a doping offence. Vainio showed traces of anabolic steroids in his test after taking a silver medal in the Los Angeles Olympic 10,000m. The test results were confirmed quickly enough for him to be prevented from taking part in the 5000m final later in the Games but, incredibly at a time when the sport needed to crack down on such offenders, he was reinstated for international competition by the IAAF early in 1986 after having served just the eighteen-month minimum disqualification period.

The Chicago Marathon, which boosted itself into a race as prestigious as the New York and Boston events

Chicago Marathon

From a modest beginning, the America's Marathon/Chicago (to give its proper name) grew rapidly in status to threaten the New York City Marathon for prestige if not quantity. It was first held in September 1977 as the Mayor Daley Marathon and became, briefly, the world's largest-ever marathon when 4000 people took part. But New York bettered that figure a month later, and then for several years the Chicago event drifted along as just another US marathon. Internal wrangling, and public controversy over the race, threatened its very future.

But the appointment of an ambitious ex-marine, Bob Bright, as race director in 1982 made a significant difference, and so did the result of the 1983 race, in which Kenyan Joseph Nzau and Britain's Hugh Jones sprinted together dramatically for the finish line (and the eye-opening $20,000 first prize), seizing the attention of the running public. Nzau was judged the winner, though both men shared the same time of 2hr 9min 45sec. Then in the women's race New Zealander Anne Audain, leading at twenty-five miles but slowing, turned to check on her rivals and fell, twisting her ankle. So her own $20,000 first prize shrunk to a $4000 fourth place as three other runners passed her in the final mile.

Another drama followed in 1984 when Welshman Steve Jones shocked everyone by winning in a world best time of 2hr 8min 5sec, which gave the event a new aura. And although Jones subsequently lost the record to Carlos Lopes (who ran 2hr 7min 12sec in Rotterdam seven months later) the following year in Chicago Jones again produced an astonishing performance with 2hr 7min 13sec. Yet despite

America's Marathon/Chicago

Year	Finishers	Men's winner	Women's winner
1977	2131	Dan Cloeter (US) 2:17.52	Marilyn Bevans (US) 2:54.56
1978	4069	Mark Stanforth (US) 2:19.20	Lynae Larson (US) 2:59.25
1979		Dan Cloeter (US) 2:23.30	Laura Michalek (US) 3:15.45
1980	3624	Frank Richardson (US) 2:14.04	Sue Petersen (US) 2:45.03
1981	4252	Phil Coppess (US) 2:16.13	Tina Gandy (US) 2:49.39
1982	4642	Greg Meyer (US) 2:10.59	Nancy Conz (US) 2:33.23
1983	5237	Joseph Nzau (Ken) 2:09.45	Rosa Mota (Por) 2:31.12
1984	5844	Steve Jones (UK) 2:08.05	Rosa Mota (Por) 2:26.01
1985	7687	Steve Jones (UK) 2:07.13	Joan Benoit-Samuelson (US) 2:21.21
1986	8173	Toshihiko Seko (Jap) 2:08.27	Ingrid Kristiansen (Nor) 2:27.08

bettering his old record by nearly a minute, he fell just one frustrating second short of the new world best (and a $50,000 bonus!) by running the second fastest-ever marathon. In the same race the Olympic women's champion, Joan Benoit-Samuelson, gained revenge over Ingrid Kristiansen, the Norwegian who had taken her world record in London six months earlier. After a terrific struggle, Benoit-Samuelson broke away just before twenty miles to win in 2hr 21min 21sec, just fifteen seconds outside Kristiansen's world best. So the race was a total of just sixteen seconds away from two world bests, and on a course which had been confirmed by AIMS as accurately measured.

Despite the 1985 frustrations for Bob Bright and his fellow organizers, this series of dramatic incidents helped to establish the America's Marathon/Chicago as a truly elite race, with large amounts of prize and sponsorship money, which in 1986 amounted to $285,000 split among the top finishers.

Children

Running as a form of recreation, and an outlet for natural competitiveness, can be a healthy addition to the life of the average child. At a time when there are long-term dangers ahead for the child allowed too many sweets, too much TV and chauffeured transport everywhere, a diversion towards sport in general in its many facets is to be welcomed.

But if exercise in moderation can help the natural growth and development of the young boy or girl, there are two major areas of hazard, one physical and one psychological, which have to be appreciated by each new wave of parents and coaches.

Firstly, the running boom, and particularly the interest in the marathon, brought forth a number of 'wonder kids' in different countries who were encouraged by adults (who should have known better) to run marathons as young as five years of age. One American 9-year-old was claiming under-20 age records for performances in 50-mile and 100km races in 1979, while in 1981 11-year-old Jennifer Amyx of the USA clocked a prodigious 3hr 2min 57sec marathon. Her preparation included frightening training loads of up to 115 miles a week. In sports medicine centres everywhere, alarm bells were sounding.

For there are very good physiological reasons why children should not be covering this sort of mileage, or even attempting marathons. The minimum marathon age limit in the UK is 18 years old, and unlikely to drop any lower. And although in some ways a child is equipped with a good 'endurance quotient' (a figure devised by the German coach Ernst van Aaken, and reached by dividing heart volume in cubic centimetres by body weight in kilograms), as

While reasonable amounts of exercise help growth and development in children, excessive training may lead to physical problems

the child grows and the body weight increases, so the figure diminishes. More importantly, the child's bones are still growing, and the three long bones in the leg (the tibia, fibula and femur) all grow from the knee end of the bone. Consequently, continual strain on the knee through long-distance running can adversely affect the growth process. A condition known as Osgood Schlatter's disease is often seen in over-training youngsters, where the bony lump below the knee (the tibial tuberosity) becomes very painful, and a long period of rest is the only cure. Similarly, Sever's disease, in which pain is felt under the heel bone (the calcaneum) is often caused in adolescence by bruising from too much training before the bone growth process has been completed. Bones do not usually finish growing and complete the ossification process until around the ages of 18–20 in males and 16–18 in females.

Athletic competition for children in all events should be encouraged, and specialization in only one event before their late teens discouraged. But the predominant cause of avoidable injuries among young athletes is too much distance running and participation in long-distance races before their physical maturity.

The second problem area for young athletes, and less in their control, is that of parents and coaches being too pushy for success, or unable to cope with defeat or their perception of 'failure'. The real reason some of the most promising young athletes never reach the heights as seniors often has less to do with lack of facilities as a lack of patience among those around them.

The youngster whose parents become obsessed with the idea of their son or daughter becoming a champion, even if he has insufficient talent, truly carries a millstone around his neck. Encouragement, sympathy and a readiness to keep everything in true perspective are far more valuable in helping a young athlete improve than aggressive instruction and threats.

So often the element of sport is lost, and by the mid-teens, when sometimes the temporarily disrupting effects of puberty are causing inconsistency or even loss of athletic form in the youngster, the tension between athlete and parent or coach can be at its height, with the very high risk of drop-out from the sport. The coach who recognizes this situation developing often has to help both athlete and parent through this black patch.

The young runner who tries hard and has an understanding back-up team around him or her is sometimes destined for greater long-term achievements than the runner who is consistently made to feel that even a silver medal in a national junior championship is failure.

See also *Osgood Schlatter's Disease*.

Cinque Mulini

The Cinque Mulini, or Five Mills, is a unique cross-country event held each spring in the otherwise quiet Italian farm town of San Vittore Olona (population 6000), situated to the north of Milan. Some of the world's greatest runners (a few of them particularly unsuited to it!) have taken part since the event began in 1933.

Its testing circuit takes the runners literally in and out of 200-year-old flour mills (hence the race title), up and down flights of steps, through barnyards inhabited by bewildered goats, chicken and sheep, while watched in a carnival-like atmosphere by large, excitable crowds.

The constantly weaving and varied route in the men's four-lap (9.5km) and women's two-lap (4.7km) races make it a test of concentration as much as fitness. The men's event, which was held throughout the war years too, became an international race in 1953, while the women's race began in 1971.

Grete Waitz, six-times winner of the women's event, leads Agnese Possamai in the unique Cinque Mulini cross-country race in 1981

Cinque Mulini: past winners

MEN
- 1933 Mario Fiocchi (Ita)
- 1934 Luigi Pellin (Ita)
- 1935 Luigi Pellin (Ita)
- 1936 Luigi Pellin (Ita)
- 1937 Romano Maffeis (Ita)
- 1938 Umberto De Florentis (Ita)
- 1939 Vittorio Avila (Ita)
- 1940 Antonio Vitali (Ita)
- 1941 Romano Maffeis (Ita)
- 1942 Salvatore Costantino (Ita)
- 1943 Salvatore Costantino (Ita)
- 1944 Giuseppe Bevilacqua (Ita)
- 1945 Armando Cesarato (Ita)
- 1946 Aldo Rossi (Ita)
- 1947 Cristoforo Sestini (Ita)
- 1948 Giuseppe Italia (Ita)
- 1949 Giuseppe Bevilacqua (Ita)
- 1950 Giuseppe Italia (Ita)
- 1951 Luigi Pellicioli (Ita)
- 1952 Luigi Pellicioli (Ita)
- 1953 Agostino Conti (Ita)
- 1954 Hahmed Labidi (Tun)
- 1955 Giacomo Pepicelli (Ita)
- 1956 Rino Lavelli (Ita)
- 1957 Franjio Mihalic (Yug)
- 1958 Franjio Mihalic (Yug)
- 1959 Francesco Perrone (Ita)
- 1960 Gian Franco Baraldi (Ita)
- 1961 Franjio Mihalic (Yug)
- 1962 Michel Jazy (Fra)
- 1963 Michel Jazy (Fra)
- 1964 Antonio Ambu (Ita)
- 1965 Billy Mills (USA)
- 1966 Mike Turner (UK)
- 1967 Nikolai Dutov (USSR)
- 1968 Gaston Roelants (Bel)
- 1969 Kipchoge Keino (Ken)
- 1970 Naftali Temu (Ken)
- 1971 Daniel Korica (Yug)
- 1972 Dave Bedford (UK)
- 1973 Frank Shorter (USA)
- 1974 Emiel Puttemans (Bel)
- 1975 Filbert Bayi (Tan)
- 1976 Filbert Bayi (Tan)
- 1977 Yohannes Mohammed (Eth)
- 1978 Willy Polleunis (Bel)
- 1979 Leon Schots (Bel)
- 1980 Leon Schots (Bel)
- 1981 Mohammed Kedir (Eth)
- 1982 Eshetu Tura (Eth)
- 1983 Rob de Castella (Aus)
- 1984 Bekele Debele (Eth)
- 1985 Fiseha Abebe (Eth)
- 1986 Alberto Cova (Ita)
- 1987 Paul Kipkoech (Ken)

WOMEN
- 1971 Rita Ridley (UK)
- 1972 Rita Ridley (UK)
- 1973 Paola Cacchi (Ita)
- 1974 Rita Ridley (UK)
- 1975 Gabriella Dorio (Ita)
- 1976 Renata Pentlinowska (Pol)
- 1977 Bronislawa Ludwichowska (Pol)
- 1978 Grete Waitz (Nor)
- 1979 Grete Waitz (Nor)
- 1980 Grete Waitz (Nor)
- 1981 Grete Waitz (Nor)
- 1982 Grete Waitz (Nor)
- 1983 Margaret Groos (USA)
- 1984 Grete Waitz (Nor)
- 1985 Betty Springs (USA)
- 1986 Lynn Jennings (USA)
- 1987 Lynn Jennings (USA)

Coaching

Although the stereotype of a coach is usually portrayed as a loud extrovert figure, with a whistle and stopwatch hanging round his neck, there are a great many other types of coaches, and coaching requirements. Indeed, the National Coaching Foundation, which is concerned with all sports, defines a coach (perhaps somewhat tongue in cheek) as someone capable of filling the roles of instructor, teacher, motivator, disciplinarian, manager, administrator, publicity agent, social worker, friend, scientist and student.

In very broad terms, a runner progressing from pre-teen novice level to Olympic champion would probably learn the basic essentials about warming up, training, stretching and warming down in a large group of youngsters at a local club. They might then progress to a specialist group of athletes who all took part in the same type of event, where they would learn from a more specialized coach (and also from the more experienced athletes with whom they trained).

A step which fewer make is to then have considerable personal attention from a very experienced coach, not necessarily attached to their club, but who would help them refine the ideal training programme for their talents and competitive requirements, and support them into the territory of international competition. And the final stage is where the athlete, having become by then so experienced in major games and international meetings, primarily needs the coach more as a partner with whom to discuss ideas rather than as someone to dogmatically lay down the law about what they should or should not do.

Some larger athletics clubs have complete coverage of coaching in all events and at all levels; some small clubs may just have one or two interested parents trying to help out. But in such circumstances, especially with younger athletes, enthusiasm and encouragement can often compensate for a lack of formal qualifications, as long as the training is kept within the grounds of common sense.

Most athletics coaches, qualified and unqualified, are amateurs, working in their spare time and often at considerable personal expense. This is sometimes not understood by the athletes they coach (and their parents), who may assume that the coaches are paid by the club, as does happen in some other sports. It is a rarity in athletics, however, although the sport is moving towards greater professionalism.

If an athlete wishes to change coaches, the correct procedure would be to approach the existing coach, explain the problems or reasons behind the wish to change, and if it is not possible to solve them through further discussion, to thank the coach for the time spent on him in the past. Every effort should be made to retain friendship and to accentuate that the decision is for sporting, rather than personal, reasons (unless it isn't!). An understanding coach will always see reason, and wish the athlete well for the future.

Before this stage is reached, an informal approach should have been made to the other coach to ensure that he would be willing to take on the athlete, for there is no point in leaving one coach, and only then trying to find another. The procedure for the new coach, if agreeable, should be to insist that the athlete explains and thanks his previous coach first, and not to start work with the athlete until that has been satisfactorily accomplished. The biggest insult to a coach is for an athlete to surreptitiously switch to another coach without telling him, and for the original coach to only find out by chance, or through a third party.

But many runners, particularly long-distance runners, manage to work out their own training without the help of a coach, often relying instead on advice from the considerable number of books and magazines on the subject. A pole vaulter or hammer thrower would find it much more difficult to operate with similar independence, because of the complex technical nature of their events.

It is always helpful, though, for the distance runner to have a chance to chat to a coach on occasions, or at least to a more experienced runner who may be able to offer advice without entering into a long-term coaching relationship. A great deal of distance runners' training knowledge is picked up informally while training or travelling with other runners.

Even the greatest runners need reassurance; Ingrid Kristiansen consults her coach, Johan Kaggestad

But there is a network of national, regional and county coaches in all events to provide general guidance to individual athletes and help them, if they wish, to find a coach in their area. For assistance, contact in the first instance the headquarters of the UK Athletics Coaching Scheme, Francis House, Francis Street, London SW1P 1DL (Tel. 01-828 9326). They also oversee nationwide courses for potential coaches in all events, and can supply details of forthcoming courses in each area of the UK.

A separate range of courses, booklets and video-cassettes dealing with topics like nutrition, physiology, sports injuries and coaching, and all complementing each other, has been established by the National Coaching Foundation with a view to encouraging more people to become coaches, and to increase the knowledge of those who already are, in the whole range of sports. Details of these can be obtained from the National Coaching Foundation, 4 College Close, Beckett Park, Leeds LS6 3QH (Tel. 0532-744802).

Coe, Sebastian

When Sebastian Coe became the first man ever to retain the Olympic 1500m title, at Los Angeles in 1984, it helped to reduce the painful memories of the intervening four years since he had first won the title in Moscow. The injury, illness and frustration he suffered in that time meant that he could scarcely be said to have totally dominated world 1500m running in between. But on the days of those two Olympic 1500m finals, the days which really do matter to the athletes more than any other, he was ready.

After Coe's decade in the top strata of international middle distance running, with a host of world records and big victories, it is still somewhat surprising to realize that up to the end of 1986 his tally of gold medals in major championships was just three: the two Olympic gold medals, and the 1986 European 800m title.

Yet he had shown the world new levels of 800m and mile running, and hinted at untapped potential at longer distances. His 'rivalry' with Steve Ovett, constantly if unconvincingly denied, helped to promote public awareness of the sport in the UK and elsewhere. And while still competitively successful at the highest levels, he also developed a keen interest and presence in the world of sports politics, an area not previously noted for the athleticism of its practitioners.

Sebastian Newbold Coe was born in Chiswick, West London, on 29 September 1956, but went to secondary school in Sheffield, where his father, Peter, had been appointed production manager in a cutlery factory. Sebastian joined the Sheffield club Hallamshire Harriers at the age of 12 after showing some early ability as a runner, even though there was little athletic background in the family. His father had been a club level cyclist, and his mother, Angela, had a strong arts tradition on her side.

His father decided to put his engineer's training to use in helping Sebastian develop a suitable training programme, even though he knew nothing about the sport at that time. But Peter methodically studied books and magazines, and attended coaching courses, to learn all he could to devise a training schedule suitable for his son.

At the age of 14, Sebastian was Yorkshire Schools junior cross-country champion, but on his first appearance in the English Schools track championships that summer (at Crystal Palace) he failed to even reach the final of the Junior 1500m! Gradually, though, with refinement and development of his training and approach to races, he climbed the ladder. In 1973 he became English Schools Intermediate 3000m champion, and in 1975 he had improved sufficiently to become the European Junior Championships bronze medallist at 1500m.

Far from becoming a 1500/3000m specialist, Sebastian decided with his father that his competitive career should be moving down in distance rather than up. You cannot, they realized, hide from speed forever. Sebastian also managed to successfully merge his academic and sporting lives, and from the autumn of 1975 attended Loughborough University to study economics and social history amid the athletically-enthusiastic atmosphere of the Loughborough campus.

It was while studying at Loughborough that Sebastian made his first international impact. In early 1977, as part of his moving-down policy, he twice broke the UK indoor best for 800m, and capped that by surprisingly winning the European Indoor title in, appropriately, San Sebastian. Outdoors, he finished fourth for the UK in the Europa Cup final 800m after being blatantly pushed by the West German Willi Wulbeck, but ended the season by setting a UK 800m outdoor record of 1:44.95.

His training, which now included a great deal of sprinting and mobility work, was clearly paying off, and by 1978 it was certain that Coe would be a force at that year's European Championships in Prague, especially when he improved his own UK record to 1:44.25 just before the championships. It would also be intriguing to see how he fared against Britain's already established leading 800m competitor, Steve Ovett, who had been European silver medallist in 1974 but had now successfully moved up to 1500m as well. Apart from an almost insignificant meeting in the English Schools cross-country championships in 1972 (when Ovett was 2nd and Coe 10th) the pair had not actually raced each other since. At Prague they were even kept apart in the European 800m heats and semi-finals, but in the final, for the first time ever on the track, it was Coe v. Ovett.

Coe stormed through the first lap in under 50 seconds, with Ovett right on his shoulder. But it was simply too fast, and both men suffered. In the home straight, as Coe faded and Ovett moved past him, apparently for victory, a little known East German, Olaf Beyer, passed them both to snatch the gold, with Ovett second and Coe third. It was disappointing for both Britons, but while Ovett came back to win the 1500m later that week, Coe just had to put it down to experience.

But in 1979 it took just one vivid 41-day period during the summer to establish Coe as more than just another good runner. It started on 5 July in Oslo where, quite unexpectedly, he set a world 800m record of 1:42.33, becoming the first British athlete to hold the record since before the war. Then just twelve days later, on the same Oslo track, he beat nearly all of the world's top milers in the IAAF Golden Mile in another world record, 3:48.95. Missing the race, however, was Ovett, the previous winner, who had declined an invitation to run.

On 5 August Coe won the European Cup 800m final for Britain (beating old rivals Wulbeck and Beyer) in a tactical 1:47.3, and on 15 August in Zurich Coe set an unprecedented third world record in 41 days by running 1500m in 3:32.03, despite a lack of pacing over the final 750m. Coe had really arrived as a runner of the highest stature, despite his lean and misleadingly frail appearance.

Ovett, meanwhile, had been moving into top form himself but had been rejected from a place in the Zurich 1500m race by the organizers, who apparently felt that his appearance with Coe would turn into a cat-and-mouse dawdle, rather than a record attempt. But shortly afterwards Coe was injured and had to sit out the rest of the season, as Ovett uncharacteristically attacked his 1500m and mile records. He missed both, very narrowly, but the rapidly increasing public anticipation of seeing the two apparently unassailable Britons racing each other rather than the clock would have to wait until 1980 to be satisfied.

They finally met for only the second time on the track at the Moscow Olympics, where both ran the 800 and 1500m, despite not having raced each other during the selection process. Yet on the eve of the Games, in Oslo, both had set world records within an hour. Coe ran 2:13.4 for 1000m, while Ovett sliced one-fifth of a second off Coe's world mile record with 3:48.8. Both were clearly in brilliant form for the Games.

In Moscow the 800m, for which Coe was favoured, came first. But Coe ran a strangely lethargic race, hanging too far back off the pace, and when the race began in earnest on the second lap he had left himself too much to do.

Facing page
Sebastian Coe leads Steve Ovett in the 1980 Moscow Olympic 1500m final

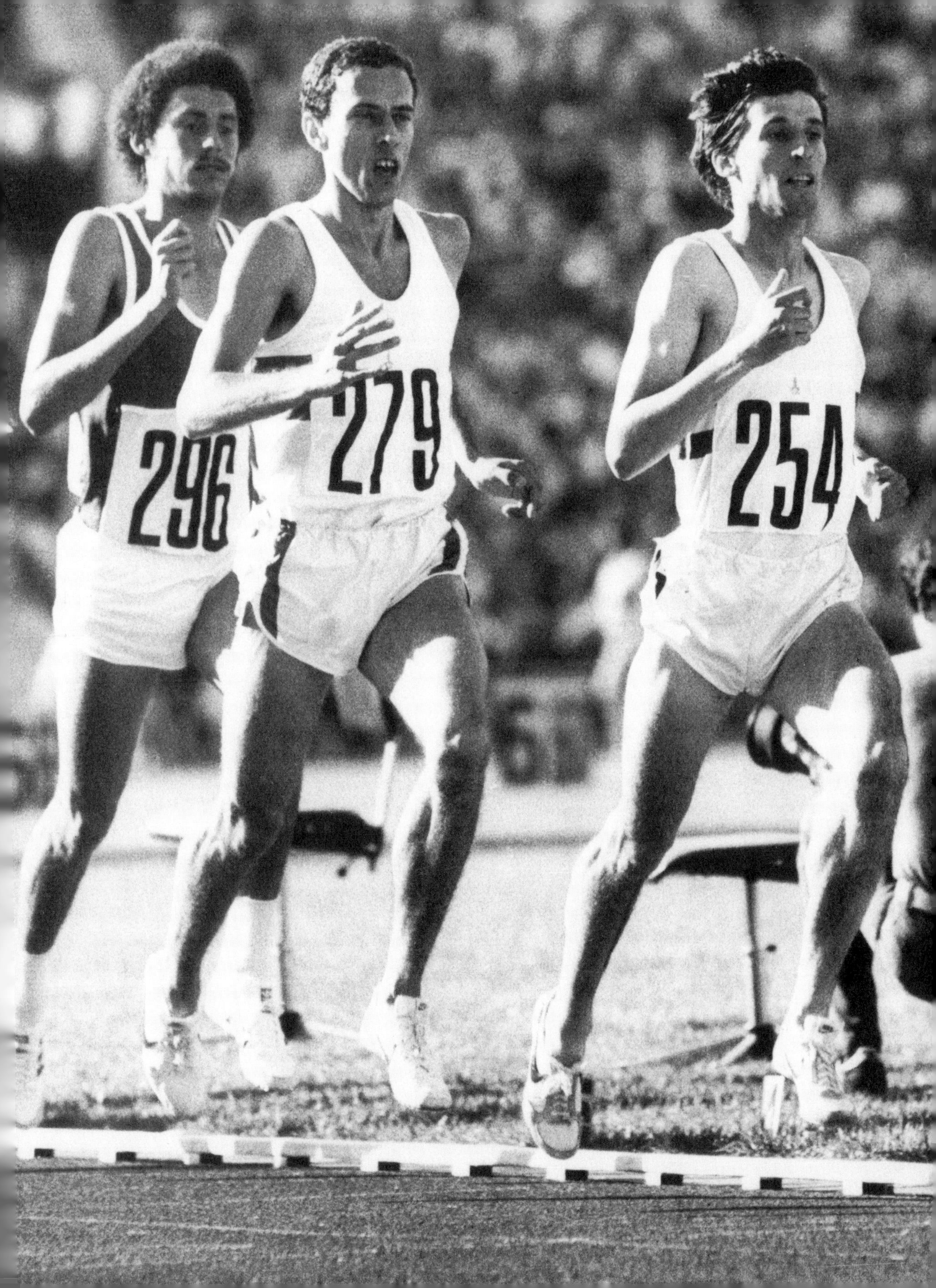
296
279
254

Track progress

Born 29 September 1956

Year	400m	800m	1000m	1500m	Mile	3000m	5000m
1970	—	—	—	4:31.8	—	—	—
1971		2:08.4	—	4:18.0	—	—	—
1972		1:59.9	—	4:05.9		8:50.0	—
1973		1:56.0	—	3:55.0		8:34.6	—
1974	Injured						
1975		1:53.8	—	3:45.2	—	8:14.8	—
1976		1:47.7	—	3:42.7	3:58.4	—	—
1977	48.9	1:45.0	—	—	3:57.7	—	—
1978	47.7	1:43.97	—	—	4:02.17	—	—
1979	46.87	1:42.33	2:20.8	3:32.03	3:48.95	7:59.8i	—
1980	47.10	1:44.7	2:13.40	3:32.19	—	7:57.4	14:06.2
1981	46.9	1:41.73	2:12.18	3:31.95	3:47.33	7:55.2i	—
1982		1:44.48	—	3:39.1	—	—	—
1983		1:43.80	2:18.58i	3:35.17	3:52.93	—	—
1984		1:43.64	—	3:32.39	3:54.6	—	—
1985		1:43.07	—	3:32.13	3:49.22	—	—
1986		1:44.10	2:14.90	3:29.77	—	7:54.32i	—

Ovett, scarcely able to believe how easy it was, won in 1:45.4, with Coe an unavailing second in 1:45.9. 'He ran like an idiot,' commented his father/coach Peter Coe, with the bluntness for which he had become known.

But six days later, in the 1500m final, the tables were turned. Coe, desperate to make amends for his disappointment in the 800m, turned in a last lap of 52.2 to win in 3:38.4. Ovett, unable to mount a real challenge, was third in 3:39.0. So it had ended one-all. Yet Ovett had the final word that year, breaking Coe's world 1500m record, with 3:31.36 in Koblenz, West Germany, after the Games. During 1981, both men were in outstanding form, but again did not meet in competition. Yet their rivalry had, if anything, intensified.

As early as 10 June 1981, Coe produced a phenomenal world 800m record of 1:41.73 in Florence, and was so dominant on the stopwatch that the average of his five fastest 800m races at that moment (1:43.27) was faster than any other runner had achieved even once. Ovett, content with his Olympic gold medal at the 800m, left the shorter distance records to Coe. But at the mile, he was prepared to cross swords, or at least stopwatches.

In one astonishing nine-day spell in August they swapped the world mile record three times, as though it was a ping-pong ball. First, Coe recaptured it from Ovett with 3:48.53 in Zurich on 19 August; then Ovett took it back with 3:48.40 in Koblenz on 26 August; but Coe had the final say with 3:47.33 in Brussels on 28 August. The world marvelled, but still wanted to see them meet in competition. They seemed in no hurry. Yet, with hindsight, the peak of public interest in their rivalry at 1500m seems to have been reached then. Injury and illness (and the emergence of Steve Cram as the third Musketeer) would mean that it would never be quite the same again.

The 1982 season offered chances of gold medals at both the European Championships in Athens and the Commonwealth Games in Brisbane. But for Coe it was to prove a dismal year. Following a stress fracture in his foot, he managed to get back to fitness in time for the European Championships, only to suffer an unexpected defeat in the home straight of the 800m to the little rated Hans-Peter Ferner of West Germany. Coe then withdrew from the 1500m, and returned to England for hospital tests, which indicated possible glandular fever. He pulled out of the Commonwealth Games.

In 1983 he struggled back to fitness, only to suffer a series of losses in the run-up to the inaugural World Championships, to be held that summer in Helsinki. After the last, in which he was pushed back into fourth place by Steve Cram, Willi Wuycke of Venezuela and Peter Elliott over 800m at Gateshead, he suspected there was a physical problem, and again withdrew from a major Games for medical tests.

These eventually proved he was suffering from an infection known as toxoplasmosis, which is passed on from cats. Its exact cause was never discovered, but it is likely to have been the root of Coe's poor form in both 1982 and 1983. But once discovered and cured, it was possible for Coe to begin a serious winter build-up to the 1984 Olympics where he would again be trying to win the elusive 800m title, as well as defending his 1500m crown. Steve Ovett, who had his own medical problems in 1982 and 1983, was getting back to peak form, while Steve Cram, who had won the Commonwealth, European and World 1500m titles in the previous two seasons, was looking to complete a clean sweep in Los Angeles.

Coe, who by then had finished two years of post-graduate research at Loughborough, was living full-time in London and decided to join Haringey AC in North London for club competition and training companionship. His 1500m selection for Los Angeles was not without controversy, however. With Cram and Ovett already selected, and only one place left, Coe was surprisingly beaten in the AAA Championships by the dogged Yorkshireman Peter Elliott. Although better known as an 800m

World Records

800m
1:42.33 Oslo   5 July 1979
1:41.73 Florence   10 June 1981

1000m
2:13.40 Oslo   1 July 1980
2:12.18 Oslo   11 July 1981

1500m
3:32.03 Zurich   15 August 1979

Mile
3:48.95 Oslo   17 July 1979
3:48.53 Zurich   19 August 1981
3:47.33 Brussels   28 August 1981

runner, Elliott felt, like many other people, that this victory would automatically bring him the third 1500m place for Los Angeles, where he was already running the 800m. But the selectors had greater faith in Coe and, despite that AAA defeat, still named him as their third choice. They felt that the five weeks remaining before the Games would allow him the chance to get to peak form.

Their confidence proved justified. In LA, although he was once again pushed into a silver medal position in the 800m (this time by the young Brazilian Joaquim Cruz) and admitted he believed he would never win a major title at the distance, in the 1500m Coe was back to his best. Running his last 800m in an almost frightening 1:50, he kicked into the lead with 200m left to hold off Cram down the home straight, and win in an Olympic record of 3:32.53. Ovett, suffering from a viral problem dropped out at 1150m.

In 1985, which was very much Steve Cram's year, a Dream Mile clash in Oslo saw Cram beat Coe and take his world record. But in 1986, with the Commonwealth Games (in Edinburgh) and European Championships (in Stuttgart) Cram and Coe were due to meet each other in four championship events: 800 and 1500m at both. However, once again the jinx on Coe and major championships struck, and on the eve of the Commonwealth Games he went down with flu, missing them completely, while Cram won both convincingly.

By the time of the European Championships, Coe had recovered, and in a glorious moment for British athletics, he, Cram, and the young Scot Tom McKean battled out the 800m medals down the home straight. This time, at last, Coe was the winner in 1:44.50, but a few days later, attempting the double, he had to give best to the determined Cram in the 1500m, losing in a furious last 800m run in 1:46.0.

With plans to move up to 5000m from 1987, thus following Steve Ovett who had made the same elevation with mixed fortunes in 1986, Coe was ready to explore a new chapter of his career, while combining his running with a part-time post as vice-chairman of the Sports Council. He was made an MBE in 1982.

See also *Steve Cram* and *Steve Ovett*.

Coffee

The sight of marathon runners drinking coffee an hour or so before their race has become a regular one in recent years, since the American physiologist Dr David Costill reported that his laboratory studies had shown that the ingestion of caffeine through coffee could assist long-distance runners to perform faster and more efficiently.

The theory was that the caffeine in two cups of coffee (or one double-strength cup) an hour before endurance exercise could artificially increase the amounts of free fatty acids in the blood, which would be used by the exercising muscles in favour of the natural stores of glycogen early in the run. Thus the stores of the energy-giving glycogen would be preserved longer, and delay the onset of 'the wall', the point at which the glycogen is exhausted. One of Costill's laboratory studies using caffeine showed an increase of 19 per cent exercise time to exhaustion, while another study showed a 7 per cent increase in the amount of work which could be performed in a two-hour exercise period.

But Costill himself admits that there are significant variations between individuals in their sensitivity to caffeine, and that the runner should try four or five ten-mile training runs with and without taking a double-strength cup of caffeinated coffee one hour beforehand in order to assess their own personal reaction.

Another potential setback is that caffeine increases the rate of urine production, and that even if dehydration is not a problem, the need to go off the course for a pit-stop in mid-race can be frustrating and actually wipe out any time gain from the caffeine.

The morality of taking even a humble cup of coffee may offend some runners, of course, if it was purely to artificially enhance performance. Caffeine was actually on the list of substances banned as a psychomotor stimulant drug by the International Amateur Athletic Federation for some years, before being removed in 1986 because there was no evidence of it ever having been used as a stimulant in athletics. In the terms of the IAAF Medical Committee, they were looking for the caffeine equivalent of something like twenty cups of coffee, used in its pure form, rather than the relatively tiny dose contained in a single cup. But they are keeping the situation under review.

Cold

In normal circumstances, a cold day presents the runner with fewer problems than a hot one. For, although muscles work less efficiently when cold, the runner can at least take temperature-controlling precautions to keep the muscles sufficiently loose by wearing appropriate clothing. Close-fitting tracksuit trousers and several layers of thin, long-sleeved tops are among the most popular combinations. But any belief that there is some form of heroic Spartan value in training in vest and shorts on a freezing day is misplaced, and could be dangerous.

In the coldest conditions, many runners also don a woollen hat, since a third of all body heat is lost through the head. The hands may also become very cold, but while every runner has his personal preference, a problem with normal gloves is that the hands may soon become overheated. One compromise is to use fingerless gloves, mittens or even woollen socks worn over the hands, as the subsequent build-up of heat is not quite so extreme and the fingers can be spread if necessary.

The heart, well protected inside the body, actually works more efficiently in cold weather because it does not have to continually pump blood to the skin surface to assist cooling. Research in the USA also indicates that an increase of energy-utilization of 2–5 per cent when running in cold weather was caused solely by the effect of wearing extra clothing (though not in itself a sufficient reason *not* to wear the layers!), whereas in exceptionally hot weather there was a relatively higher demand on energy to help control the temperature as well as that used purely to fuel the running action.

Within certain limitations, the convection of cool air also helps regulate the runner's temperature. But in extremes, this can become a threat not only to his well-being, but to life itself. For, when running well, the body is generating enough heat to maintain its core temperature, even in very cold conditions. But if the heat production is then severely reduced, through such circumstances as extreme fatigue, or the runner becoming injured or lost in an isolated area (especially if only lightly dressed), there will be a strong threat of hypothermia, a dramatic chilling of the body. Runners in the closing stages of marathons are particularly at risk, because after several hours of running, they may be reduced to a shuffle or walk, and if weather conditions are bad, their body temperature may drop rapidly.

At first, the body tries to retain its heat by contracting the blood vessels near the skin surface and reducing the conducting capacity of the nerves, causing the exposed skin to become numb. On the skin surface, goose pimples form, which is another body mechanism to reduce heat loss, by trapping still air in the spaces formed next to the skin. Shivering, too, is an involuntary attempt by the body to raise its heat production.

But if the body temperature still falls below 35°C (95°F), as opposed to its normal range of 36–37.2°C (97–99°F), a state of hypothermia

The startling effects of training in the bitter Finnish winter, shown on the beard of quadruple Olympic winner Lasse Viren

is said to exist. Mental confusion may be a symptom, and drowsiness may follow, and if the dropping temperature is not reversed by getting the runner to warmth and shelter, death from exposure could eventually result.

Prevention is the best policy, through wearing sufficient clothing, and adapting it if necessary (e.g., sleeves rolled up, gloves tucked in shorts waistband) rather than jettisoning kit early in endurance races, in case there is a need later.

Every runner has to find, through trial and error, the right amount and type of clothing to suit his running needs. Practicality is more important than appearance, which is why the sight of runners wearing disposable dustbin liners, or with old newspapers wrapped around their middle, or runners of both sexes wearing ladies' tights beneath their shorts, is not considered eccentric in the running world these days. Additionally, on any areas of skin which have to be exposed to the cold, a smearing of olive oil, petroleum jelly, or one of the warming massage creams, can help to retain body heat.

Fears about the effects on the lungs of breathing in bitterly cold air appear to be unfounded. The air, however cold, is naturally warmed up before it reaches the lungs, and so actual freezing is virtually impossible. Experiments conducted at the US Air Force School of Aerospace Medicine had subjects cycling hard in controlled conditions at temperatures of −35°C (−95°F), far colder than anyone in Britain is likely to encounter.

Yet the only changes noted in the subjects related to an elevation of their diastolic blood pressure and a lower temperature of their expired air. Their oxygen uptake (which reached 60–70 per cent), respiratory rate and core temperature were all unaffected. So while breathing cold air deeply may irritate any existing bronchial infection, it should not in itself create any lung problem, even at minus 35.

Running in the cold is actually less of a physical threat than running in hot weather, as long as you prepare for it in the right way.

See also *Hypothermia, Penile Frostbite*.

Compartment syndrome

When mistaken for shin soreness, the condition of compartment syndrome causes pain during and after running in the muscles on the upper and outer part of the shin ('anterior compartment syndrome'). The problem occurs when the muscle expands during exercise and becomes too bulky for its rather inelastic restraining sheath, creating pressure and pain.

If you had a semi-inflated balloon, wrapped it up in paper, and were then able to further inflate it, you would expect some pressure on the wrapping paper, as the size of its contents became too big. Similarly, in compartment syndrome the muscle becomes too big for the sheath, and its blood supply may even become restricted, causing numbness and pins and needles. The ultimate treatment is usually a relatively simple operation in which the restraining muscle sheath is slit with an incision about five inches long, and the edges kept as far apart as possible so they do not join back. Instead, the sheath repairs itself by growing a pseudo-membrane, which allows the muscle more room to expand.

It is not a common injury, but of its type the anterior compartment syndrome is the most usual, with Mary Decker among the leading athletes who have successfully undergone the operation.

The 'posterior compartment syndrome', in which the same de-restricting operation is performed on the calf muscles, was suffered by Dave Moorcroft for several years up to 1981, but the success of the operation was such that he was able to break the world 5000m record just ten months afterwards.

Course measurement

In order to receive a certificate of accuracy from AIMS (Association of International Marathons) a road race has to comply with strict measurement procedures. The course is measured by an independent and accredited AIMS measurer, whose apparently quaint but in fact highly accurate method of measurement is now recognized universally.

The measurer rides the course on a pedal-bicycle, on which a device known as a Jones Counter is attached to the front axle. This records twenty counts for every revolution of the wheel, which has already been ridden at least four times along an accurately measured kilometre on a straight, smooth-surfaced road with the tyres on the twenty-seven-inch wheels being kept at a constant high pressure of 60–80 psi.

Thus, knowing the number of counts for an accurate kilometre, and ensuring the tyre pressures remains the same, it is possible to assess with accuracy the length of a road race, by riding the bike along the shortest possible route the runners could take. The previous method of measuring the route one metre from the kerb edge was flawed because runners would often swing across the road to take advantage of a bend, and thus save considerable distance. The current measuring method means that it is, in the opinion of the measurer, impossible to run less than the stipulated distance, even taking the sharpest route at bends. Allowing an additional one metre per kilometre for possible error, a certificate of accuracy is then issued to the race organizers.

The IAAF rules for road races stipulate that 'the course shall be measured along the ideal line of running or walking, i.e., the shortest possible path' and that 'the course must not measure less than the official distance for the event, and the variation must not exceed 0.1 per cent (i.e., forty-metres for the marathon)'.

A great deal of pioneering work in this area was done by the Road Runners Club in both the UK and USA, and AIMS have subsequently taken up the torch for greater accuracy. Seminars are now held for prospective course measurers to learn both the art and science of measurement.

Cram, Steve

It seemed unlikely, at a time around 1980, when British athletics was still marvelling at its good fortune in simultaneously having two such brilliant 1500m runners as Steve Ovett and Sebastian Coe, that a third runner of similar stature could emerge.

Yet Steve Cram was just that. He followed both his countrymen as a holder of the world 1500m and mile records, won the 1983 World 1500m title and 1500m gold medals at the Commonwealth Games and European Championships in both 1982 and 1986.

But to reach that position, he passed through a number of obstacles which could have sidetracked him. First was his abiding passion for soccer, which still exists today in his fervent support of Sunderland FC, and the irresistibility of a kick-about whenever it is offered. His uncle, Bobby Cram, played more than 150 times for West Bromwich Albion, and later for Colchester.

But as Steve showed his talent as young runner in his native northeast, gradually his attention became focused more on running. He was encouraged as a 12-year-old by Jimmy Hedley, coach to Jarrow and Hebburn Athletic Club, which Cram joined. His first track race in their colours was a Colts mile at the Vaux meeting on a five-laps-to-the-mile track at South Shields on 1 July 1973, where he finished second of five.

Some encouraging performances in 1975, notably in the English Schools junior championships, where he was third in the cross country and fourth in the 1500m, helped reassure Cram that he had made the right choice of sport, and guided by Hedley he soon made his mark as one of Britain's leading young middle-distance prospects.

But there were so many other good prospects that at several points during his teens he had seriously considered whether he should adopt a West German nationality for international athletics, as he felt he was sometimes overlooked for inclusion in British junior squads. This possible German eligibility came about through the nationality of his mother, Maria. Although his father, Bill Cram, was a Geordie, he had been stationed in Germany at RAF Gutesloh, where he met Maria, who had come to work at the camp. But when his son's possible defection was publicized in a newspaper, Steve was quickly invited to join an England squad.

Steve himself was born in Gateshead on 14 October 1960, when his parents came to live in nearby Hebburn. Athletically, Gateshead Harriers was the fashionable local club of the seventies, with Brendan Foster as its competitive figurehead, but Cram has always remained loyal to the relatively small Jarrow and Hebburn club, whose yellow vest with its blue diagonal stripe he has worn in so many of his greatest races. The club is naturally now much bigger than when he first joined it.

In May 1977 Cram surprised the athletics world by running a UK age 16 best of 3:47.7 for 1500m at Gateshead, and the following year, with nine GCE 'O' levels under his belt, he suddenly improved again with a 3:42.7 run during the Durham Schools Championships in June, passing 400m in 58 seconds during a self-made run in a race which he won by over 15 seconds. His time was 2.2 seconds faster than the UK 17-year-old best set by Steve Ovett some years earlier, although in Scotland another equally promising 17-year-old, Graham Williamson, had just run 3:42.1.

Both were invited to run in the prestigious Emsley Carr Mile at Crystal Palace in July 1978, where Williamson finished second to fellow Scot John Robson in a UK Junior record of 3:56.4, while Cram was fourth, just edged by his boyhood hero Brendan Foster, as both recorded 3:57.4. With Williamson having just turned 18, Cram's time constituted a world age record for a 17-year-old.

Surprisingly, with the Commonwealth Games approaching a month later in Edmonton, Canada, the Scottish selectors did not send Williamson. But Cram was picked for England (with Dave Moorcroft and Tim Hutchings), and although he did not get through his heat, it was the start of an international apprenticeship which was to continue for some years, but then pay valuable dividends.

Williamson continued to have the edge over Cram in most of their meetings in 1978–79, to the extent that at the European Junior Championships at Bydgoszcz, Poland, in August 1979 Cram opted for the unfamiliar 3000m because he could not see himself beating Williamson at 1500. Both men came home happy; Williamson did win the 1500, but Cram took the 3000m gold medal.

Around this time neither seemed a real threat to either Steve Ovett or Sebastian Coe, who between them were engaged in the build-up to a duel at a much higher level. Coe, with three world records during 1979, had successfully moved up from the 800m. But a third runner was needed for the 1500m in Britain's Moscow Olympic team. At the UK Championships in June, the main trial, disaster struck Cram, who tripped and fell just after the bell, and jogged home a dejected last, while Williamson finished second to Dave Moorcroft.

But with Moorcroft opting for the 5000m in Moscow instead, and Cram a few days later in Norway running the fastest time by a British athlete in 1980 with a 3:37.3 to ease his frustration, the selectors asked Williamson and Cram to race again, during a Dream Mile in Oslo in July. The race was won in a world record 3:48.8 by Ovett, but Cram finished second in 3:53.8, 2.6 seconds ahead of Williamson, and the coveted third place in Moscow was his.

In Moscow Cram reached the 1500m final, placing eighth, as Seb Coe reversed his own earlier upset (when he lost the 800m title to Ovett) by beating Ovett to the gold. But for Cram, just being in Moscow was an extremely valuable experience: he looked, listened and learned.

In 1981 he continued to be rather overshadowed by the Big Two, but he was getting closer. When Coe set a world mile record of 3:48.53 in Zurich, for instance, Cram dipped under 3:50 for the first time with 3:49.95. But if, in 1982, he was able to step out of the shadow a little, he still did not feel he was fully accepted. Although he won both the European and Commonwealth 1500m titles that year, and established himself as a top-class racer, he was constantly being reminded that in neither event did he have to face either Coe (who was ill) or Ovett (who was injured).

A year later, at the inaugural World Championships in Helsinki, he added another gold medal to his collection, this time with Ovett in the 1500m final (although Coe was again absent with illness). But Ovett had run an uncharacteristically poor tactical race, and several weeks later showed his best form by breaking the world 1500m record in Rieti with a time of 3:30.77; the same day, but in worse conditions, Cram himself had tried and failed to break the same record in Knarvik, clocking 3:33.6.

But probably the most memorable race for British fans that season came in the IAC Coca-Cola Floodlit event at Crystal Palace on 9 September. At the end of a long season, Cram was due to run the mile. A few days beforehand, Ovett announced that he, too, would run the

---

Facing page
No medals, no records, but a marvellous race as Steve Cram holds off Steve Ovett at the 1983 IAC/Coca-Cola Floodlit meeting

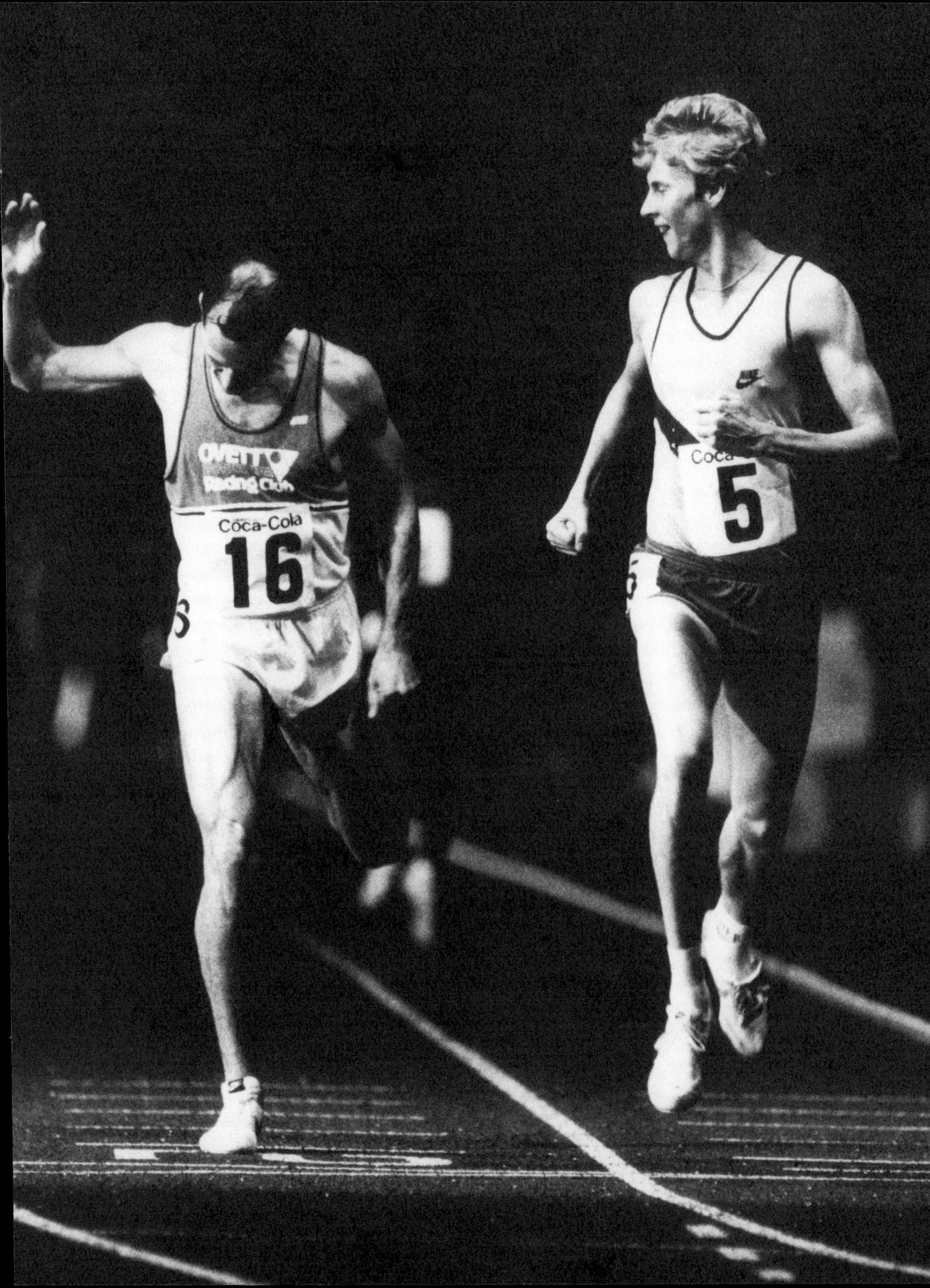
OVETT
Coca-Cola
16
5

mile. Initially it seemed likely to produce another round of musical chairs, with athletes chasing or dodging each other, as Ovett himself had done with Coe for years. But he wanted another crack at Cram before the end of the year. Ovett had lost the World title, but he wanted to even the score, especially as his world 1500m record had shown him he was in terrific form.

Cram, with apparently nothing to gain by taking on the hungry Ovett, earned the undying admiration of athletics fans everywhere by standing his ground, instead of ducking into another event. 'If I'm going to believe I'm the best in the world, which I'm supposed to be as World champion, then I shouldn't be frightened of anybody. And if I'm frightened of Steve Ovett, then I don't really believe I can beat him,' he said.

Crystal Palace was sold out, and the race lived up to expectations. After following the early pacemakers, Cram made the first move from 350m out, and Ovett chased him all the way to the finish, just a stride behind. In the home straight, he could not get on terms, and Cram remained just in front, to win in 3:52.56 to 3:52.71.

Although Cram was to win more gold medals and set world records later in his career, that single race against Ovett sums up his attitude best of all. He enjoys collecting gold medals and setting records, but above all he loves winning races. And for a British public suffering from a surfeit of staged record attempts and of stars avoiding each other, that race was, literally, a 'mile' stone.

The year ended with two other major events off the track for Cram. He was able to collect his BA degree in Sports Studies, and on 17 December 1983 he married his long-time fiancée Karen Waters.

In the run-in to the 1984 Olympics, when Cram had hoped to complete his set of gold medals, he was reduced to the role of TV viewer as main rivals Coe and Ovett advanced their preparations, winning 800 and 1500m events respectively at Oslo. Meanwhile, Cram was being treated for an injury to his right calf, which had seriously interrupted his Los Angeles preparation. And although he made a miraculous recovery, to actually finish second to Coe in Los Angeles, the defect subsequently irritated him intensely; not because he had lost, but because he had lost when he was less than 100 per cent fit, and chances of Olympic titles come only once in four years.

So in 1985, with no major championships on the fixture list, Cram set out to improve his best times, but in racing situations. He set his first world record of 3:29.67 for 1500m in narrowly beating Olympic 5000m champion Said Aouita of Morocco in Nice on 16 July, and gained revenge over Seb Coe by beating him in Oslo and taking his world mile record away with 3:46.32 on 27 July. Then on 4 August he shaved a fraction off the world 2000m record in a much less competitive situation in Budapest.

He even narrowly missed setting a world 1000m record in poor weather conditions at his native Gateshead on 9 August, and, while he was still getting faster in training, beat Olympic 800m champion Joaquim Cruz in Zurich in his fastest-ever 800m time of 1:42.88. But a hamstring injury, frustratingly, ended his phenomenal season.

For 1986 he decided to go for a 'double double', aiming for both the 800m and 1500m titles at the Commonwealth Games in Edinburgh, and at the European Championships in Stuttgart. In excellent early season form, he made light work of both titles in Edinburgh, aided by the illness of Seb Coe, who had to withdraw from the Games with flu. But a month later, at Stuttgart, Cram was again trying to come back from injury.

The 800m final proved a proud moment for Britain, as the recovered Coe, Scotsman Tom McKean, and Cram fought out the medals well clear of the rest of Europe. But in a close finish, a bitterly disappointed Cram took only third place, as Coe won from McKean. A few days later, though, Cram turned the tables again on Coe, outsprinting him on the final lap of the 1500m final, to end the championship season on a high note, with at least three of his four gold medals.

In some ways, not winning the 1984 Olympic

title may have been a godsend to Cram. Trying to win the one 1500m title to have eluded him keeps him motivated. 'I've got to try to win it in Seoul, otherwise when I'm 50 people will still come up to me and say: "Ah, but you weren't as good as Coe because you never won the Olympics." I want to be the best ever.'

World Records

1500m		
3:29.67	Nice	16 July 1985
Mile		
3:46.32	Oslo	27 July 1985
2000m		
4:51.39	Budapest	4 August 1985

Track progress

Born 14 October 1960.

	800m	1000m	1500m	Mile
1973			4:31.5	
1974	2:11.0		4:22.3	
1975	2:07.1		4:13.9	
1976	1:59.7		4:07.2	
1977	1:56.5		3:47.7	
1978	1:53.5		3:40.09	3:57.43
1979	1:48.5		3:42.5	3:57.03
1980	1:48.41	2:24.5	3:34.74	3:53.8
1981	1:46.29	2:18.5	3:34.81	3:49.95
1982	1:44.45	2:15.12	3:33.66	3:49.90
1983	1:43.61		3:31.66	3:52.56
1984	1:46.0	2:15.98	3:33.13	3:49.65
1985	1:42.88	2:12.88	3:29.67	3:46.32
1986	1:43.19	2:15.77	3:30.15	3:48.31

Cramp

The involuntary and painful contraction of muscles in the spasm known as cramp is experienced by most distance runners at some time. Usually it is associated with prolonged exercise, as in a single long run, or a particularly intensive period of training. Sometimes the spasm will occur during running, when it will be essential to stop and relieve the spasm by gently stretching the affected muscle, reversing the painful sensation of contraction. If a calf muscle cramps, for example, then lifting the front of the foot upwards will help to stretch the calf. Removing the shoe on the affected leg may also

Cramp is painful and unpredictable, and running has to be halted before the condition can be relieved

assist recovery, especially if it has been tied too tightly, perhaps contributing to the cause.

Sometimes the cramp attack will occur in bed at night, when an inadvertent overstretch may set off a spasm in the calf, foot, hamstring or quadricep areas. Again, stretching the afflicted muscle, and gentle massage, should relieve the condition.

Cramp is still somewhat unpredictable, and its precise mechanism unknown, although a number of leading sports physiologists now disregard the popular view of salt-loss as a cause. But they do take seriously the dehydration also associated with prolonged exercise, especially in hot, humid conditions. Thus taking in plenty of liquids at a time of extended exercise can act as a preventive measure, as can a relaxing massage of the susceptible muscles.

If cramp remains a problem, and a cause such as extended or intensive exercise or use of an unfamiliar muscle group cannot be clearly associated with it, then medical advice (which may include dietary evaluation) should be sought.

Cross-country running

Although the public face of cross-country running tends to be races held on relatively short laps or on horse-race courses, mainly for the convenience of television coverage, to many traditionalists cross country still means long, tough events, such as the annual Orion Harriers invitation race, consisting of a single fifteen-mile lap in Epping Forest.

It was in England that the organized section of the sport began, primarily as a winter pursuit for members of the Thames Rowing Club, which met at Roehampton in Surrey. They organized paperchases on Wimbledon Common from 1868 to keep fit, with 'hares' laying trails of pieces of paper and the other runners trying to track them down as 'hounds'. From this, the club's running section became known as the Thames Hare and Hounds, a title which they still keep today.

The first English Cross-country Championships as such were staged in Epping Forest in 1876, but all thirty-two competitors went off course and the race was declared void. The inaugural National Championship is therefore considered to have been the 1877 race, held over eleven and a quarter miles at Roehampton and won by Percy Stenning from thirty-two other starters on 24 February 1877.

The English Cross-country Union (ECCU) was founded in 1883, and the first International Cross-country Championship was held at Hamilton Park, Glasgow, in 1903, with just the four home countries taking part. France joined in 1907, the event grew, and in 1973 it came under the wing of the world's governing body, the International Amateur Athletic Federation, which has subsequently helped expand it into a more representative annual World Championship. In 1986 runners from sixty-one countries took part. The Junior Men's race in these championships was first held in 1961.

Women's cross-country running dates back to the twenties, and France held a Women's National Championship in 1923. The first English Women's National Championship was held at Luton in 1927 with Anne Williams of Littlehampton beating 107 rivals.

The first international women's match was in 1931 at Douai, in France, but international women's championships were not held regularly until 1967. From 1973 they became a part of the IAAF World Cross-country Championships.

For a short time, men's cross country was included in the Olympic Games programme, but the occurrences at the 1924 Games in Paris led to its removal thereafter. The 10km race was held on a scorching hot July day with the temperature as high as 45°C (113°F). Many of the competitors suffered heat stroke, dehydration, and ran themselves into an advanced and dangerous state of collapse, with only fifteen of the original thirty-nine starters finishing.

Of these, a number were in a very poor state, reeling insensibly around the track at Colombes Stadium, where the race finished, and one competitor actually slumped on the track just fifty yards from the line.

Only the legendary Finn Paavo Nurmi, who won the race by nearly one and a quarter minutes and took a total of four gold medals at those Games, appeared unaffected by the weather. Late into the evening, officials were still searching the course for runners who were missing. Sadly, the freak weather conditions which, rather than the severity of the course, caused the collapses, cost cross-country running its own place in the Games, even though it exists today as part of the Modern Pentathlon competition.

What exactly constitutes 'cross country' has been open to many different interpretations over the years. Even the IAAF admits in its own rule book that 'owing to the extremely varying circumstances in which cross-country running is practised throughout the world, especially in regard to different seasons, climatic conditions and distances, it is impossible to lay down any rigid legislation for international standardization of this sport'.

Its own definition of a course for championship and international events reads: 'The race shall be run over a course confined, as far as possible, to open country, fields, heathland, commons and grasslands. A limited amount of ploughed land may be included. If the course passes through woodland without any clearly defined path or track, it must be clearly marked for the runners. The traversing of roads of any description should be limited to the minimum.'

There are no record times in cross-country racing, because the exact distance even on the same course may vary from year to year, according to where the course marshals place the flags, and it is much more difficult to measure distances as accurately as on the road.

Generally, times would be slower (were comparison possible) because of the braking effect of mud, uneven ground, and long grass. Spiked or studded shoes are usually necessary to retain grip on some courses. But some runners find they have a special knack for cross country, while faster athletes on the firm surfaces of road and track may be left struggling. And for all runners there is a beneficial training effect in stamina and strength, regardless of where they finish competitively. It is a branch of the sport which every distance runner should at least experience.

The world of cross-country running offers its own challenges, and races take place in all conditions!

World Cross Country Champions

Year	Venue	Winner and Nationality	Team Champions
SENIOR MEN			
1903	(Glasgow)	Alf Shrubb (Eng)	England
1904	(St Helens)	Alf Shrubb (Eng)	England
1905	(Dublin)	Albert Aldridge (Eng)	England
1906	(Caerleon)	Charles Straw (Eng)	England
1907	(Glasgow)	Alfred Underwood (Eng)	England
1908	(Paris)	Arthur Robertson (Eng)	England
1909	(Derby)	Edward Wood (Eng)	England
1910	(Belfast)	Edward Wood (Eng)	England
1911	(Caerleon)	Jean Bouin (Fra)	England
1912	(Edinburgh)	Jean Bouin (Fra)	England
1913	(Paris)	Jean Bouin (Fra)	England
1914	(Chesham)	Arthur Nichols (Eng)	England
1915–19 Not held			
1920	(Belfast)	James Wilson (Sco)	England
1921	(Newport)	Walter Freeman (Eng)	England
1922	(Glasgow)	Joseph Guillemot (Fra)	France
1923	(Paris)	Charles Blewitt (Eng)	France
1924	(Gosforth)	William Cotterell (Eng)	England
1925	(Dublin)	Jack Webster (Eng)	England
1926	(Brussels)	Ernest Harper (Eng)	France
1927	(Caerleon)	Lewis Payne (Eng)	France
1928	(Ayr)	Harold Eckersley (Eng)	France
1929	(Paris)	William Cotterell (Eng)	France
1930	(Leamington)	Tom Evenson (Eng)	England
1931	(Dublin)	Tim Smythe (Ire)	England
1932	(Brussels)	Tom Evenson (Eng)	England
1933	(Caerleon)	Jack Holden (Eng)	England
1934	(Ayr)	Jack Holden (Eng)	England
1935	(Paris)	Jack Holden (Eng)	England
1936	(Blackpool)	William Eaton (Eng)	England
1937	(Brussels)	James Flockhart (Scot)	England
1938	(Belfast)	Jack Emery (Eng)	England
1939	(Cardiff)	Jack Holden (Eng)	England
1940–45 Not Held			
1946	(Ayr)	Raphael Pujazon (Fra)	France
1947	(Paris)	Raphael Pujazon (Fra)	France
1948	(Reading)	John Doms (Bel)	Belgium
1949	(Dublin)	Alain Mimoun (Fra)	France
1950	(Brussels)	Lucien Theys (Bel)	France
1951	(Caerleon)	Geoff Saunders (Eng)	England
1952	(Hamilton)	Alain Mimoun (Fra)	France
1953	(Paris)	Franjo Mihalic (Yug)	England
1954	(Birmingham)	Alain Mimoun (Fra)	England

1955	(San Sebastian)	Frank Sando (Eng)	England
1956	(Belfast)	Alain Mimoun (Fra)	France
1957	(Waregem)	Frank Sando (Eng)	Belgium
1958	(Cardiff)	Stan Eldon (Eng)	England
1959	(Lisbon)	Fred Norris (Eng)	England
1960	(Glasgow)	Abdesselem Rhadi (Mor)	England
1961	(Nantes)	Basil Heatley (Eng)	Belgium
1962	(Sheffield)	Gaston Roelants (Bel)	England
1963	(San Sebastian)	Roy Fowler (Eng)	Belgium
1964	(Dublin)	Francisco Arizmendi (Spa)	England
1965	(Ostend)	Jean Fayolle (Fra)	England
1966	(Rabat)	Assou El Ghazi (Mor)	England
1967	(Barry)	Gaston Roelants (Bel)	England
1968	(Tunis)	Mohammed Gammoudi (Tun)	England
1969	(Clydebank)	Gaston Roelants (Bel)	England
1970	(Vichy)	Mike Tagg (Eng)	England
1971	(San Sebastian)	Dave Bedford (Eng)	England
1972	(Cambridge)	Gaston Roelants (Bel)	England
1973	(Waregem)	Pekka Paivarinta (Fin)	Belgium
1974	(Monza)	Erik de Beck (Bel)	Belgium
1975	(Rabat)	Ian Stewart (Sco)	New Zealand
1976	(Chepstow)	Carlos Lopes (Por)	England
1977	(Dusseldorf)	Leon Schots (Bel)	Belgium
1978	(Glasgow)	John Treacy (Ire)	France
1979	(Limerick)	John Treacy (Ire)	England
1980	(Paris)	Craig Virgin (USA)	England
1981	(Madrid)	Craig Virgin (USA)	Ethiopia
1982	(Rome)	Mohamed Kedir (Eth)	Ethiopia
1983	(Gateshead)	Bekele Debele (Eth)	Ethiopia
1984	(New York)	Carlos Lopes (Por)	Ethiopia
1985	(Lisbon)	Carlos Lopes (Por)	Ethiopia
1986	(Neuchatel)	John Ngugi (Ken)	Kenya
1987	(Warsaw)	John Ngugi (Ken)	Kenya
1988	(Auckland)		
1989	(Stavanger)		

JUNIOR MEN

(Under IAAF Rules, Junior Men are those who remain under twenty years of age throughout the calendar year of competition)

1961	(Nantes)	Colin Robinson (Eng)	England
1962	(Sheffield)	Abdesselem Bouchta (Mor)	England
1963	(San Sebastian)*	Declared null and void	
1964	(Dublin)	Ian McCafferty (Sco)	England
1965	(Ostend)	Johnny Dumon (Bel)	Belgium
1966	(Rabat)	Mike Tagg (Eng)	England
1967	(Barry)	Eddie Knox (Sco)	England
1968	(Tunis)	John Bednarski (Eng)	England
1969	(Clydebank)	Dave Bedford (Eng)	England

1970	(Vichy)	John Hartnett (Ire)	England
1971	(San Sebastian)	Nick Rose (Eng)	England
1972	(Cambridge)	Aldo Tomasini (Ita)	Italy
1973	(Waregem)	Jim Brown (Sco)	Spain
1974	(Monza)	Rich Kimball (USA)	USA
1975	(Rabat)	Bobby Thomas (USA)	USA
1976	(Chepstow)	Eric Hulst (USA)	USA
1977	(Dusseldorf)	Thom Hunt (USA)	USA
1978	(Glasgow)	Mick Morton (Eng)	England
1979	(Limerick)	Eddy de Pauw (Bel)	Spain
1980	(Paris)	Jorge Garcia (Spa)	USSR
1981	(Madrid)	Mohamed Chouri (Tun)	USA
1982	(Rome)	Zurubachew Gelaw (Eth)	Ethiopia
1983	(Gateshead)	Fesseha Abebe (Eth)	Ethiopia
1984	(New York)	Pedro Casacuberta (Spa)	Ethiopia
1985	(Lisbon)	Kimeli Kipkemboi (Ken)	Ethiopia
1986	(Neuchatel)	Melese Feysia (Eth)	Ethiopia
1987	(Warsaw)	Danda Kirochi (Ken)	Ethiopia
1988	(Auckland)		
1989	(Stavanger)		

WOMEN

1967	(Barry)	Doris Brown (USA)	England
1968	(Blackburn)	Doris Brown (USA)	USA
1969	(Clydebank)	Doris Brown (USA)	USA
1970	(Vichy)*	Paola Pigni (Ita)	Holland
	(Frederick, Md)*	Doris Brown (USA)	England
1971	(San Sebastian)	Doris Brown (USA)	England
1972	(Cambridge)	Joyce Smith (Eng)	England
1973	(Waregem)	Paola Cacchi (Ita)	England
1974	(Monza)	Paola Cacchi (Ita)	England
1975	(Rabat)	Julie Brown (USA)	USA
1976	(Chepstow)	Carmen Valero (Spa)	USSR
1977	(Dusseldorf)	Carmen Valero (Spa)	USSR
1978	(Glasgow)	Grete Waitz (Nor)	Rumania
1979	(Limerick)	Grete Waitz (Nor)	USA
1980	(Paris)	Grete Waitz (Nor)	USSR
1981	(Madrid)	Grete Waitz (Nor)	USSR
1982	(Rome)	Maricica Puica (Rum)	USSR
1983	(Gateshead)	Grete Waitz (Nor)	USA
1984	(New York)	Maricica Puica (Rum)	USA
1985	(Lisbon)	Zola Budd (Eng)	USA
1986	(Neuchatel)	Zola Budd (Eng)	England
1987	(Warsaw)	Annette Sergent (Fra)	USA
1988	(Auckland)		
1989	(Stavanger)		

(* In 1970, before the event came under IAAF patronage, two separate races were held, both of which have claims to be considered as the 'International' of that year).

English Men's Senior National Cross Country Champions

Year	Venue	Winner and club	Starters	Team winners
1876	(Epping)	Race declared void	32	
1877	(Roehampton)	Percy Stenning (Thames H and H)	33	Thames H and H
1878	(Roehampton)	Percy Stenning (Thames H and H)	33	Spartan H
1879	(Roehampton)	Percy Stenning (Thames H and H)	41	Thames H and H
1880	(Roehampton)	Percy Stenning (Thames H and H)	88	Birchfield H
1881	(Roehampton)	George Dunning (Clapton B)	105	Moseley H
1882	(Roehampton)	Walter George (Moseley H)	107	Moseley H
1883	(Roehampton)	George Dunning (Clapton B)	91	Moseley H
1884	(Four Oaks, Sutton Coldfield)	Walter George (Moseley H)	56	Moseley H
1885	(Manchester)	William Snook (Birchfield H)	66	Liverpool H
1886	(Croydon)	J 'Flyer' Hickman (Coventry Godiva H)	58	Birchfield H
1887	(Four Oaks, Sutton Coldfield)	J 'Flyer' Hickman (Coventry Godiva H)	54	Birchfield H
1888	(Manchester)	Edward Parry (Salford H)	88	Birchfield H
1889	(Kempton)	Edward Parry (Salford H)	82	Salford H
1890	(Sutton Coldfield)	Edward Parry (Salford H)	80	Salford H
1891	(Rock Ferry)	James Kibblewhite (Spartan H)	88	Birchfield H
1892	(Ockham)	Herbert Heath (South London H)	91	Birchfield H and Essex B (tie)
1893	(Redditch)	Herbert Heath (South London H)	81	Essex B
1894	(Blackpool)	George Crossland (Salford H)	83	Salford H
1895	(Wembley)	Steve Cottrill (Thames Valley H)	149	Birchfield H
1896	(Water Orton)	George Crossland (Manchester H)	104	Salford H
1897	(Trafford Park)	Syd Robinson (Northampton and CAC)	98	Salford H and Manchester H (tie)
1898	(Horton, Northants)	Syd Robinson (Northampton and CAC)	80	Salford H
1899	(Wembley)	Charles Bennett (Finchley H)	116	Highgate H
1900	(Rotherham)	Charles Bennett (Finchley H)	93	Finchley H
1901	(Leicester)	Alfred Shrubb (South London H)	113	Essex B
1902	(Lingfield)	Alfred Shrubb (South London H)	159	Highgate H
1903	(Haydock)	Alfred Shrubb (South London H)	146	Birchfield H
1904	(Wolverhampton)	Alfred Shrubb (South London H)	114	Highgate H
1905	(Lingfield)	Albert Aldridge (Highgate H)	125	Highgate H
1906	(Haydock)	Charles Straw (Sutton H and AC)	162	Sutton H
1907	(Colwall Park)	George Pearce (Highgate H)	186	Birchfield H
1908	(Newbury)	Arthur Robertson (Birchfield H)	252	Hallamshire H
1909	(Haydock)	James Murphy (Hallamshire H)	163	Birchfield H
1910	(Derby)	Fred Neaves (Surrey AC)	247	Hallamshire H
1911	(Taplow)	Fred Hibbins (Thrapston H and AC)	240	Hallamshire H
1912	(Haydock)	Fred Hibbins (Thrapston H and AC)	173	Hallamshire H
1913	(Wolverhampton)	Ernest Glover (Hallamshire H)	211	Birchfield H

Cross-country running

Year (Venue)	Winner	Time	Team
1914 (Chesham)	Charlie Ruffell (Highgate H)	273	Surrey AC
1915–1919 Not held			
1920 (Windsor Great Pk)	Joseph Guillemot (France)*		Birchfield H
	Charles Clibbon (Birchfield H)	271	
1921 (Doncaster)	Walter Freeman (Birchfield H)	205	Birchfield H
1922 (Hereford)	Joseph Guillemot (France)*		
	Harold Eckersley (Warrington AC)	236	Birchfield H
1923 (Beaconsfield)	Charles Blewitt (Birchfield H)	327	Birchfield H
1924 (Doncaster)	Cpl William Cotterell (R C Signals)	219	Birchfield H
1925 (Hereford)	Cpl William Cotterell (R C Signals)	245	Birchfield H
1926 (Wolverton)	Jack Webster (Birchfield H)	321	Birchfield H
1927 (Crewe)	Ernest Harper (Hallamshire H)	429	Hallamshire H
1928 (Leamington)	Jack Webster (Birchfield H)	375	Birchfield H
1929 (Beaconsfield)	Ernest Harper (Hallamshire H)	247	Birchfield H
1930 (Sheffield)	Wally Howard (Kettering Town H)	334	Birchfield H
1931 (Kettering)	Jack Potts (Saltwell H)	348	Birchfield H
1932 (Wolverton)	Alec Burns (Elswick H)	289	Birchfield H
1933 (Alderley Edge)	Tom Evenson (Salford H)	344	Birchfield H
1934 (Himley Park)	Sammy Dodd (Wirral AC)	297	Birchfield H
1935 (Beaconsfield)	Frank Close (Reading AC)	295	Belgrave H
1936 (Alderley Edge)	Jack Potts (Saltwell H)	285	Birchfield H
1937 (Stratford-upon-Avon)	Herbert Clark (York H)	315	Birchfield H
1938 (Reading)	Jack Holden (Tipton H)	288	Mitcham AC
1939 (Worsley)	Jack Holden (Tipton H)	392	Belgrave H
1940–45 Not held			
1946 (Leamington Spa)	Jack Holden (Tipton H)	239	Belgrave H
1947 (Apsley)	Archie Robertson (Reading AC)	274	Sutton H
1948 (Sheffield)	Sydney Wooderson (Blackheath H)	402	Belgrave H
1949 (Bromford Bridge, Birmingham)	Frank Aaron (Leeds St Mark's H)	449	Sutton H
1950 (Aylesbury)	Frank Aaron (Leeds St Mark's H)	493	Sutton H
1951 (Richmond, Yorks)	Frank Aaron (Leeds St Mark's H)	350	Sutton H
1952 (Great Barr, Birmingham)	Walter Hesketh (Manchester A & CC)	418	Victoria Park AAC
1953 (Caversham Park, Reading)	Gordon Pirie (South London H)	473	Birchfield H
1954 (Arrowe Park, Birkenhead)	Gordon Pirie (South London H)	419	Bolton United H
1955 (RAF Cardington, Beds)	Gordon Pirie (South London H)	544	South London H
1956 (Warwick)	Ken Norris (Thames Valley H)	509	Sheffield United H
1957 (Parliament Hill, London)	Frank Sando (Aylesford PMAC)	717	South London H
1958 (Arrowe Park, Birkenhead)	Alan Perkins (Ilford AC)	574	South London H
1959 (Fletton, Peterborough)	Fred Norris (Bolton United H)	617	Sheffield United H
1960 (Dartmouth Park, West Bromwich)	Basil Heatley (Coventry Godiva H)	662	Derby and CAC
1961 (Parliament Hill, London)	Basil Heatley (Coventry Godiva H)	796	Derby and CAC
1962 (Stanley Park, Blackpool)	Gerry North (Blackpool and Fylde AC)	696	Derby and CAC
1963 (Coldhams Common, Cambridge)	Basil Heatley (Coventry Godiva H)	857	Coventry GH

Year	Venue	Winner	Points	Team
1964	(Western Park, Leicester)	Mel Batty (Thurrock H)	853	Portsmouth AC
1965	(Parliament Hill, London)	Mel Batty (Thurrock H)	908	Portsmouth AC
1966	(Graves Park, Sheffield)	Ron Hill (Bolton United H)	919	North Staffs and SHAC
1967	(Agricultural Showground, Norwich)	Dick Taylor (Coventry Godiva H)	856	Portsmouth AC
1968	(Sutton Park, Sutton Coldfield)	Ron Hill (Bolton United H)	944	Coventry Godiva H
1969	(Parliament Hill, London)	Mike Tagg (Norfolk Gazelles)	1046	Tipton H
1970	(Agricultural Showground, Blackpool)	Trevor Wright (Hallamshire H)	1023	City of Stoke AC
1971	(Agricultural Showground, Norwich)	Dave Bedford (Shaftesbury H)	914	Shettleston H
1972	(Sutton Park, Sutton Coldfield)	Malcolm Thomas (Thames Valley H)	1021	Tipton H
1973	(Parliament Hill, London)	Rod Dixon (New Zealand)*		
		Dave Bedford (Shaftesbury H)	1195	Gateshead H
1974	(Graves Park, Sheffield)	David Black (Small Heath H)	984	Derby and CAC
1975	(Stopsley Park, Luton)	Tony Simmons (Luton United H)	1156	Gateshead H
1976	(Western Park, Leicester)	Bernie Ford (Aldershot, Farnham and DAC)	1314	Gateshead H
1977	(Parliament Hill, London)	Brendan Foster (Gateshead H)	1458	Gateshead H
1978	(Roundhay Park, Leeds)	Bernie Ford (Aldershot, Farnham and DAC)	1536	Tipton H
1979	(Stopsley Park, Luton)	Mike McLeod (Elswick H)	1672	Gateshead H
1980	(Western Park, Leicester)	Nick Rose (Bristol AC)	1710	Tipton H
1981	(Parliament Hill, London)	Julian Goater (Shaftesbury H)	1685	Tipton H
1982	(Roundhay Park, Leeds)	Dave Clarke (Hercules-Wimbledon AC)	1737	Tipton H
1983	(Stopsley Park, Luton)	Tim Hutchings (Crawley AC)	1762	Aldershot, F and DAC
1984	(Newark Showground)	Eamonn Martin (Basildon AAC)	1862	Aldershot, F and DAC
1985	(Campbell Park, Milton Keynes)	Dave Lewis (Rossendale H and AC)	1907	Aldershot, F and DAC
1986	(Town Moor, Newcastle)	Tim Hutchings (Crawley AC)	1819	Tipton H
1987	(Stopsley Park, Luton)	Dave Clarke (Hercules-Wimbledon AC)	2000+	Gateshead H

(* denotes actual race winner was a guest, ineligible for title)

English Women's Senior National Cross Country Champions

Year	Venue	Winner and club	Finishers (where known)	Team winners
1927	(Luton)	Anne Williams (Littlehampton AC)	108†	Middlesex LAC
1928	(Chigwell Row)	Lilian Styles (Littlehampton AC)	90	Middlesex LAC and LOAC tie
1929	( )	Lilian Styles (Littlehampton AC)	—	Middlesex LAC
1930	( )	Lilian Styles (Littlehampton AC)	—	Westbury H
1931	(Epsom)	Gladys Lunn (Birchfield HLS)	—	London Olympiades AC
1932	(Coventry)	Gladys Lunn (Birchfield HLS)	—	Birchfield HLS
1933	(Warwick)	Lilian Styles (Haywards Heath LAC)	—	Airedale H
1934	(Kettering)	Lilian Styles (London Olympiades AC)	—	London Olympiades
1935	(Birmingham)	Nellie Halstead (Bury & RAC)	—	London Olympiades AC
1936	(Ilford)	Nellie Halstead (Bury & RAC)	—	Small Heath H
1937	(Perry Barr, Birmingham)	Lilian Styles (London Olympiades AC)	—	Birchfield HLS
1938	(Luton)	Evelyne Forster (Civil Service LAC)	—	Birchfield HLS
1939	(Rugby)	Evelyne Forster (Civil Service LAC)	—	Birchfield HLS
1940–45	Not held			
1946	(Cheltenham)	P. Sandall (Birchfield HLS)	32†	Birchfield HLS
1947	(Oxford)	R. Wright (St Gregory's, Chelt)	—	Birchfield HLS
1948	(Sutton Coldfield)	Ivy Kibbler (Birchfield HLS)	—	Birchfield HLS
1949	(Worsley)	E. Johnson (Airedale H)	76	Birchfield HLS
1950	(Parliament Hill, London)	Avery Gibson (North Shields)	—	Birchfield HLS
1951	(Tadcaster)	Phyllis Green (Ilford AC)	—	Ilford AC
1952	(Birmingham)	Phyllis Green (Ilford AC)	—	Ilford AC
1953	(Woodgate)	Diane Leather (Birchfield HLS)	—	Birchfield HLS
1954	(Aylesbury)	Diane Leather (Birchfield HLS)	—	Birchfield HLS
1955	(Leeds)	Diane Leather (Birchfield HLS)	—	Ilford AC
1956	(Sutton Coldfield)	Diane Leather (Birchfield HLS)	—	Ilford AC
1957	(Enfield)	June Bridgland (Southampton AAC)	—	Ilford AC
1958	(Winton)	Roma Ashby (Coventry Godiva H)	—	Highgate H
1959	(Great Barr, Birmingham)	Joyce Byatt (Hampstead H)	—	London Olympiades AC
1960	(Morden)	Joyce Smith (Hampstead H)	—	Ilford AC

Year	Venue	Winner	Starters	Team
1961	(Sheffield)	Roma Ashby (Coventry Godiva H)	—	London Olympiades AC
1962	(Wolverhampton)	Roma Ashby (Coventry Godiva H)	—	London Olympiades AC
1963	(Richmond)	Madeleine Ibbotson (Longwood LAC)	—	Mitcham AC
1964	(Bury)	Madeleine Ibbotson (Longwood LAC)	—	Bury and Radcliffe AC
1965	(Birmingham)	Pam Davies (Selsonia LAC)	98	Maryhill LAC
1966	(Oxhey)	Pam Davies (Selsonia LAC)	105	Maryhill LAC
1967	(Blackburn)	Pam Davies (Selsonia LAC)	—	Barnet & DAC
1968	(Coventry)	Pam Davies (Selsonia LAC)	—	Cambridge H
1969	(Aldershot)	Rita Lincoln (Essex LAC)	—	Barnet & DAC
1970	(Blackburn)	Rita Lincoln (Essex LAC)	—	Cambridge H
1971	(Wolverhampton)	Rita Lincoln (Essex LAC)	—	Coventry Godiva H
1972	(Keep Hill, High Wycombe)	Rita Lincoln (Essex LAC)	179	Cambridge H
1973	(Rawtenstall)	Joyce Smith (Barnet & DAC)	—	Cambridge H
1974	(Leicester)	Rita Ridley (Essex LAC)	—	Barnet and DAC
1975	(Parliament Hill, London)	Deirdre Nagel (Eire)* Christine Tranter (Stretford AC)	167	Cambridge H
1976	(Blackburn)	Ann Ford (Feltham AC)	—	London Olympiades AC
1977	(Stoke on Trent)	Glynis Penny (Cambridge H)	162	Sale H
1978	(Hughenden Park, High Wycombe)	Mary Stewart (Birchfield H)	193	Sale H
1979	(New Town Park, Runcorn)	Kath Binns (Sale H)	239	Aldershot, F and DAC
1980	(Hagley Park School, Rugeley)	Ruth Smeeth (Aldershot, F and DAC)	279	Birchfield HLS
1981	(University of Essex, Colchester)	Wendy Smith (Boro of Hounslow AC)	255	Sale H
1982	(Carlisle Racecourse)	Paula Fudge (Boro of Hounslow AC)	235	Sale H
1983	(Lammas Field, Warwick Racecourse)	Christine Benning (Southampton and EAC)	344	Sale H
1984	(Knebworth Park, Herts)	Jane Furniss (Sheffield AC)	407	Aldershot, F and DAC
1985	(Arrowe Park, Birkenhead)	Angela Tooby (Cardiff AAC)	446	Crawley AC
1986	(Western Park, Leicester)	Carole Bradford (Clevedon AC)	566	Sale H
1987	(Footscray Meadows, Bexley)	Jane Shields (Sheffield AC)	514	Sale H

(* denotes actual race winner was a guest, ineligible for title)
(Benning nee Tranter; Ridley nee Lincoln; Smith nee Byatt; Shields nee Furniss)
(† number of starters)

Decker-Slaney, Mary

Her unfortunate collision with Zola Budd during the 1984 Olympic 3000m final in Los Angeles and the less than tactful outburst against Zola afterwards meant that Mary Decker first came to the attention of a large section of the British public through the surrounding controversy and its aftermath. As such, it rather overshadowed her rise to a position of world class after a long series of frustrating setbacks in her own colourful and often unsettled life.

Mary Theresa Decker was born in Flemington, New Jersey, on 4 August 1958, and began running at the age of 11 after her family had moved to California. She entered her first race, a cross-country event she had seen advertised, simply out of boredom, and ran with a friend. Her friend dropped out; but Mary won the race easily. So she joined the Long Beach Comets Track Club, where her training under coach Don DeNoon seems excessively hard. She set a 'world 12-year-old best' of 2:12.7 for 880 yards, but her training included such sessions as 40×440 yards in 80 seconds, or 25×50 yards at top speed. Far too much for a growing adolescent, although she apparently lapped up all the training and had even run a marathon in 3:09.43, by the time she was 13 she had developed ankle and heel injuries requiring plaster casts on both feet.

Yet in between injuries she progressed rapidly, and became a national figure in the USA in 1973 when, at the age of 14, she outsprinted Soviet Olympic silver medallist Niele Sabaite over 800m in a televised USSR v. USA match in Minsk. The following winter she set an indoor world best for 880 yards of 2:04.4, but there was a sign of her fiery temperament

Mary Decker-Slaney (here leading Chris Cahill) has long been one of the world's outstanding middle-distance runners

when, during a medley relay in an indoor international match in Moscow, a Soviet runner jostled her and Mary in retaliation threw her baton at the Russian not once, but twice! The Soviets were disqualified for the foul, and the Americans for unsportsmanlike behaviour.

It was the start of an unhappy period for Mary. Her parents divorced in 1974, and her mother had to work night and day as a barmaid to support young Mary and her brother and sister. Don DeNoon also bowed out after increasing criticism of the severity of his training programme and what he claimed was interference from outside.

Between 1975 and 1977 Mary's running career was constantly interrupted by chronic shin pain, which was eventually diagnosed as compartment syndrome, and successfully operated on in July 1977. But achilles tendinitis and further shin pain continued to restrict her progress. Coached now by the 1976 Olympic 5000m silver medallist Dick Quax, she finally began to show her best form in time for the 1980 Moscow Olympics, which the USA then boycotted due to the Soviet invasion of Afghanistan. Twice before those Games, and twice afterwards, she broke the US 1500m record, taking it below four minutes with 3:59.43.

Having split with coach Quax that summer, she was briefly coached by the almost legendary Bill Bowerman in Eugene, Oregon, where she now lived. It was a short-lived partnership, however, as Bowerman decided he did not have the time needed, and her training was then taken over by physiologist Dick Brown. Her private life was subject to similar instability. On 12 September 1981 she married 2:11 marathon runner Ron Tabb, but it was another relatively brief liaison, and they divorced in 1983.

That year Mary was in her finest form on the track. After setting US records of 1:57.60 for 800m and 3:57.12 for 1500m on the eve of the inaugural IAAF World Championships in Helsinki, she took on the might of the Soviet Union, whose athletes had been so awesome in the women's middle-distance events at the 1982 European Championships. But Mary showed no sign of being intimidated by their reputation, and won both the 1500 and 3000m gold medals from the front.

They were extraordinary performances from a girl who so often had to run way ahead of her rivals in the US, yet was equally able to repel her fast-finishing opponents in Helsinki. It was already clear that, while acclaiming her 1983 world titles, the American public would expect nothing less than victory from Mary in the Los Angeles Olympics, although she insisted that the only pressure she felt came from within herself 'because I want to win so much'.

In 1984 Mary did not give quite the same aura of invincibility as she had the previous year. Even in the US Olympic trials she unexpectedly lost to Ruth Wysocki in the 1500m, although she still won the 3000m comfortably, and decided to concentrate on the longer event in the Games.

The withdrawal of most of the Eastern Europeans from the Games, in retaliation for the 1980 boycott by the USA, made her task appear easier, although many people still favoured the blonde Rumanian, Maricica Puica. And while much publicity surrounded South African-born Zola Budd, who was controversially running for Britain, no real chance of victory was given to her. But it was Budd who proved, literally, to be Decker's downfall. On the fifth lap, with Budd leading, Decker somehow caught her foot on Budd's bare heels and fell on to the infield, tearing a groin muscle. Her race, and her gold medal hopes, ended in that moment.

Later Decker openly blamed Budd for causing the fall, but the damage had been done. Puica swept on to the gold medal as Mary was carried out of the arena by her new fiancé, British discus thrower Richard Slaney. Zola, meanwhile, faded to seventh place, insensitively booed by the crowd.

The anger which poured out of Decker after the race was undoubtedly heartfelt. Yet it lost her some friends and, later, some lucrative contracts as her public popularity dipped, even in the US. But what Decker was more concerned about was getting back into peak fitness for 1985, especially as the rest of 1984 had been

Track progress (i = indoors)

Born 4 August 1958

	800m	1500m	Mile	3000m	5000m	10,000m
1971	2:15.2		5:04.8			
1972	2:11.4	4:35.9				
1973	2:02.43	4:25.7				
1974	2:01.8i		5:00.8			
1975	2:08.3					
1976	2:12.6					
1977	2:15.2i					
1978	2:01.8	4:08.9	4:40.0			
1979	2:03.5	4:05.0	4:23.5			
1980	1:58.9i	3:59.43	4:17.55i	8:38.73		
1981	Injured					
1982	1:58.33	4:01.91	4:18.08	8:29.71	15:08.26	31:35.3
1983	1:57.60	3:57.12	4:21.65	8:34.62		
1984	2:05.1	3:59.19	4:22.92	8:34.91		
1985	1:56.90	3:57.24	4:16.71	8:25.83	15:06.53	
1986	(Maternity)					

wiped out through her injury. Once again she changed coaches, this time teaming up with the Brazilian Luis Oliveira, who is based in Eugene, Oregon, and coached Olympic 800m champion Joaquim Cruz.

After marrying Richard Slaney on 1 January 1985, Mary put together a fine summer season, which included victory in an over-dramatized 're-match' 3000m against Zola Budd (but not Puica) at Crystal Palace in July. And to culminate ten consecutive track wins (including a world mile record of 4:16.71 in Zurich in August, beating Puica and Budd), she won the 3000m in the IAAF Mobil Grand Prix Final in Rome in September in a US record of 8:25.83, again beating Puica and Budd, who were both dragged to national records. Mary was also the overall Mobil Grand Prix winner, earning $35,000.

She had at least confirmed her 1985 brilliance and superiority over Puica, even though some people remain unconvinced that Mary would have won the Los Angeles Olympic final. In any case, there was little more that Mary could do competitively in 1985, and later that year she revealed that she and Richard were expecting their first child.

Their daughter, Ashley, was born on 30 May 1986. Within a week Mary was jogging a mile, and within a month she was almost back to normal training (although she later admitted that was insufficient recovery). On 13 September 1986 she returned to competition, placing sixth in the Mercedes Mile, a road race along New York's Fifth Avenue, in 4:32.01, but a subsequent injury to her right Achilles tendon prevented her competing in the 1987 indoor season. Her goal remains the 3000m at the Seoul Olympics in 1988, by which time she will still only be 30.

Diary

Maintaining a daily training diary is the ideal method of recording running progress, and from its pages detecting any pattern which might emerge from the long succession of runs which may, eventually, stretch into many years.

Relying purely on memory to record where you ran, and how fast, is hazardous. There are probably runners still desperately trying to repeat racing and training times which they recall erroneously anyway.

Some runners like to keep very detailed accounts of every run, including the weather conditions, their personal state, the time of day, time elapsed, the route, their weight on completion of the run, and so on. For others, just a stark daily figure denoting the number of miles covered, or the number of minutes spent running, suffices. But from both methods it is possible to notice any trends which preceded a series of particularly good (or disastrously bad!) racing performances.

By studying the pattern over recent weeks and months, the self-coached runner can quickly assess whether he has been missing too many days training, undertaking too many long, slow runs, or too much track work, or perhaps going too long without a rest day. Without the record the training diary provides that may be difficult to detect.

Certainly for runners seeking advice from others, such as a coach, it is indispensable, for a generalized verbal account rarely pinpoints the potential problems; but a look at a runner's training diary can tell the experienced eye a great deal.

There are a number of specifically designed running diaries available, but any simple diary, or loose-leaf book, is quite adequate. The loose-leaf book in particular enables you to insert commemorative certificates, results sheets, relevant correspondence, or even newspaper cuttings related to your running career to complete the record.

E

Endorphins

Endorphins are chemicals produced by the pituitary gland at the base of the brain, which are increased during a training run and have the morphine-like ability to dull pain. In recent years they have been credited by some scientists as the physiological cause of 'runner's high', the feeling of euphoria experienced by some runners in training.

In females, the endorphin levels also increase considerably during pregnancy, probably as a way of making childbirth more comfortable. This link is being investigated by some researchers as possibly pointing to a cause of amenorrhoea in hard-training female runners where the increase in endorphins might somehow be fooling the brain into believing the woman is already pregnant.

See also *Runner's High*.

F

Fantasy

In the same way that schoolboy footballers playing in the local park imagine they are scoring the winning goal in the FA Cup Final, so runners of all levels admit that they often fantasize while training. The heavily sweating jogger coming down the road may be the only person on Earth to know that he is actually leading the Olympic marathon! But fantazising, even among successful international runners, is a harmless method of overcoming the boredom which sometimes sets in on long runs. It may even make the runner faster, as he can mentally stack up the odds and still be sure of an eventual historic victory. The danger is that if taken to extremes too often it can make the runner train too hard, and cause an inferior performance in an actual race, or even tempt the runner to miss real races for the safety of fantasy.

Some runners, however, do benefit from 'visualization', in which they repeatedly go through a race in their mind (not necessarily while running) and try to rehearse what they want to happen. The theory is that if executed effectively, the race itself should become like a pre-scripted play. The drawback, of course, is that the other runners may not have read the same script.

Fartlek

Originally a Swedish method of training (the word itself is Swedish for speed-play), its application to a wide range of circumstances has made it an integral part of most ambitious distance runners' training programmes.

It is now generally understood as meaning a session of pre-determined duration or distance in which the runner changes pace as often as he feels ready. It has no detailed structure, in contrast to Interval Training, and the runner could choose to run 800 metres hard, then jog 200 metres, sprint to the next tree, walk for one minute, run hard for five minutes, and so on, until the intended distance has been completed, or the time elapsed.

As such, it has the potential to become the hardest session – or the easiest – of the week. Apart from the relatively short, hard efforts, its value is in allowing runners to prod themselves into efforts which, on contemplation, might seem impossible. But with the loose structure of fartlek the athlete can run hard to, say, a lamp-post and then decide at the last moment not to stop there at all but to try to continue at the same pace for another forty metres to the pillar-box, and then again another thirty metres to the next lamp-post. The end result may be the discovery that he has not been pushing himself as hard as he previously thought possible.

For this reason, it is best executed alone, where the runner is in sole control of when to stop and start, without being influenced by anyone else's ambitions or weaknesses. Because it can be physically and mentally taxing, it is best kept to one session a week, or at most two sessions. But it provides variety, stimulation, and the chance to work into the weekly training programme any particular type of effort which would otherwise be lacking.

Its original architect was Gösta Holmér, the Swedish national athletics coach for thirty-three years up to 1958, and he designed it as a means of trying to give the Swedish distance runners of the thirties, who had been rather overshadowed by the Finns, a means of 'self creating'. In explaining the theory behind it, he rejected the alternatively popular method of Interval Training: 'Most orthodox interval training, and any methods which bind the athlete to fast running of shorter distances than his actual event, undoubtedly trim the human motor to high speeds, but they do not necessarily promote endurance. Training for endurance means learning to go on in spite of fatigue, to defy the pains of running.

'Fartlek promotes speed *and* endurance – but requires sound discernment from its practiser. A typical session during the building-up period would be to run at an easy speed for two minutes, increase it for half a minute, then run at an easy speed for two minutes, increase it again for half a minute, and go on repeating this for 20–40 minutes. Then, ignoring fatigue, the athlete would run at a higher speed for five minutes.

'The next day's outing might entail running for two minutes at a good speed, walking until the pulse rate is down to 80–90 beats a minute, then repeating the two-minute run until fatigue arises, when he should run at an even and good speed for five minutes.

'Another day, you would run in woods at an easy speed, maintaining it, despite the irregularities of the ground, for about fifteen minutes. Run the same way back, but after seven minutes increase the speed. After a week, the speed increase on the return journey is made after six minutes, the next week after five minutes, and so on until the whole homeward run is at an increased speed.'

Although Holmér himself saw fartlek as a daily training approach, most coaches these days incorporate it as simply one component among many in a more structured programme. But some runners may actually prefer the sheer freedom it offers. 'Fartlek brings us back to the games of our childhood,' wrote Holmér, 'where nature decided that we should expose our inner organs to much effort, so that our bodies will develop. A child plays while sitting, walks some steps, runs to its mother, walks or runs back to the playground, makes a longer excursion to get a toy, etc. To keep its balance, a child prefers running to walking. The swift, but short runs dominate and develop the inner organs.'

The fartlek method of training was particularly brought into focus through the successes of Swedish athletes like Gunder Haegg and Arne Andersson during the early forties. While much of the world was at war, the rivalry between these two in neutral Sweden brought the world mile record down from 4:6.4 to 4:1.3 between 1942 and 1945. Haegg himself set fifteen world records at different distances, and his unbeaten tour of the USA in 1943 had the Americans asking whether their own interval-type training sessions were still valid.

'Fartlek might open the eyes of the American runners,' observed Gösta Holmér in an article in the US magazine *Track and Field News* at that time, 'and teach them that the road to success is called *work*, hard work! And sleep and rest; that is, to give the body back what it has given out during the training. Lots of sleep and rest is just as important as the training itself.'

See also *Gösta Holmér*.

Fibula

The smaller of the two long bones in the lower leg is the fibula, which extends down the outer side of the leg from just below the knee to the ankle. Although it has to bear little weight (most of it being borne instead by its more robust partner in the lower leg, the tibia) the fibula is a common site of a stress fracture in the distance runner.

For although the fibula is mainly functional as a lever for muscle attachment, it does bend slightly at its 'waist', the narrowest point, to help dissipate some of the shock sent through the legs during running. It is this waist, some 5–8 centimetres above the lateral malleolus (that bony protrusion on the outside of the ankle) which is most likely to be the point of any stress fracture, caused mainly by the repetitive pulling of the muscles on the fibula.

See also *Stress Fracture*.

Fixx, James

The man who set hundreds of thousands of people running, American author James Fixx, became a role model for them because of the way in which he had reversed his own lifestyle through running. His father, a New York magazine editor, had suffered his first heart attack at the age of just 35 and died at 43, after years of inactivity, heavy smoking and stress.

Yet it seemed that his son was headed along the same road, also working long hours for New York magazines, smoking two packets of cigarettes a day, and allowing his weight to rise to nearly 16 stones (100kg). He was married with four children, and lived a stressful life.

But in 1964, at the age of 32, he decided to do something about it by increasing his physical activity, particularly through tennis. But a tennis injury started him running in 1967, and he became so enthusiastic about it that he began entering races. In his first, the Memorial Day 5-mile road race in Greenwich, Connecticut, he finished last.

His enthusiasm increased to the point where he ran 60–80 miles a week, and that enthusiasm for his new way of life was put on paper in his classic *The Complete Book of Running* (Random House, 1977). It sold around 1 million copies, and had sixteen foreign editions. It was published just as the running boom was reaching its peak, and Fixx's own story of a heavily overweight smoker becoming a fit marathon runner, although not having started running until the age of 35, was inspirational.

Jim Fixx, signing copies of his bestselling book, helped set the world running

He became a national celebrity, and other books followed. But the stress of promoting them and of meeting deadlines probably did not allow him the real benefit of his running. With tragic irony he collapsed and died while on a ten-mile run in Northern Vermont, where he had planned to spend a month working on his latest book, on 20 July 1984. He was 52.

The high-risk factors of heart disease in his family, and his own early neglect of his physical health, almost certainly contributed strongly to his apparently premature death. The anti-running lobby naturally claimed that Fixx's fate really did prove that exercise was a killer, but in fact without running he might have died much younger, as his father had done.

An autopsy by the state medical examiner showed that Fixx had died from a heart attack, and that his three main arteries were 95 per cent, 85 per cent and 50 per cent blocked. Traces of earlier minor attacks were also found, probably 2–4 weeks old. Curiously, given his background, Fixx apparently took little notice of warning signs, rarely underwent physical check-ups and felt that if he ran he must be virtually immune to heart disease.

In his running career, he completed eight Boston Marathons, with a best time of 3 hours 12 minutes in 1975. At 10km he did not break 40 minutes. In the same way that his life proved inspirational to so many, his death should also provide a note of caution to every runner. Running, in itself, is not dangerous. But it has to be complemented with due attention to the signs coming back from the body. This, apparently, is what Jim Fixx did not do. His legacy is a much fitter world, and even the shock of his death may indirectly help to save other lives.

Foot

The foot is very much in the front line, as it is the runner's only point of contact with the ground during many thousands of strides in an average training week. It is the foot which makes the first attempt to absorb the shock created on each stride, and although the quality and suitability of the training shoes worn can go a long way in reducing this, there is still a complicated and versatile piece of human machinery functioning inside each shoe.

The foot consists of twenty-six bones of greatly varying sizes and shapes, supported by ligaments and muscles, which allow both a considerable range of rotation and a strong leverage, as well as absorbing shock.

From the group of chunky bones at the rear of the foot, the skeletal mechanism divides into five separate 'strands' at the midfoot area, through the metatarsals and the phalanges (toe bones) to form the toes.

Overall, the bones of the foot also form two longitudinal arches to assist in transmitting forces during movement. The more pronounced of these arches, on the inside of the foot, is known as the medial arch, and it is this which may be said to have 'dropped' if it is low down or flat on the ground when standing. As a simple home test, stepping out of the bath on to a dry floor, with its resulting foot mark, may give the runner an idea as to whether he has dropped arches or not. So will his bare footprints across damp, firm sand on the beach.

If the arch has a degree of abnormality, an orthotic support may be needed to correct its mechanical function in running, for what might pass unnoticed in many people could lead to possible injuries to the leg or lower back in the serious runner.

The other, less prominent, longitudinal arch of the foot is on the outside, from the heel to the little toe, and is known as the lateral arch.

Along the length of the underside of the foot, just below the skin surface, lies the plantar

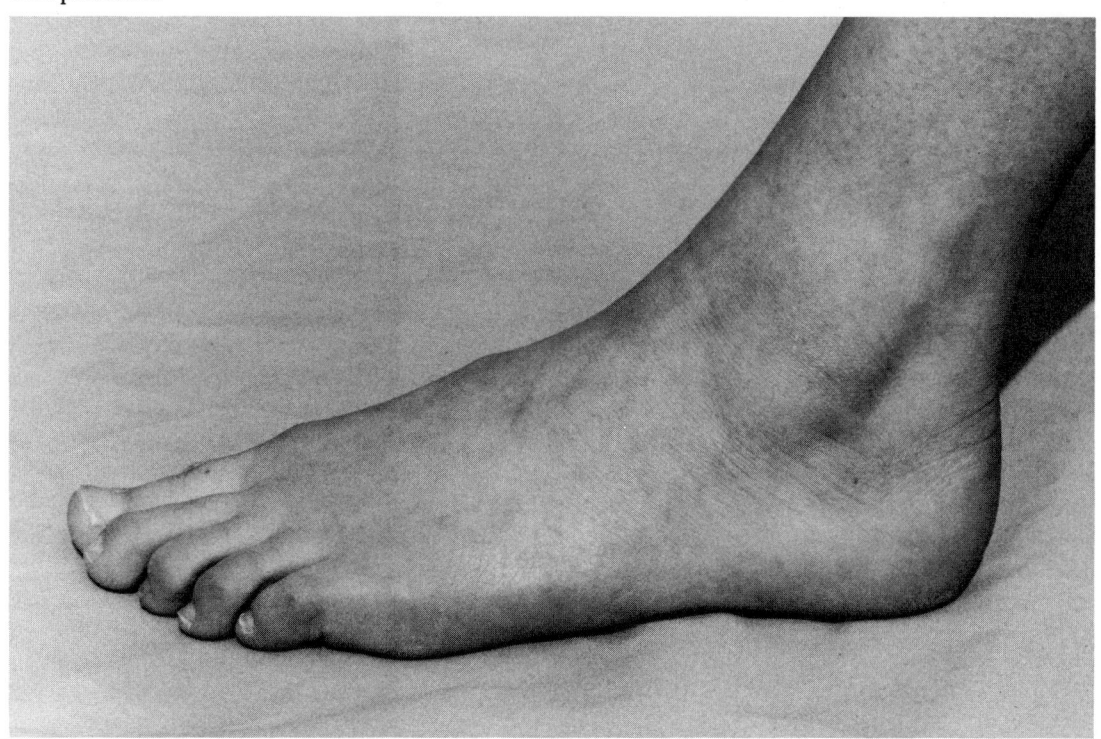

The foot is a complex mechanism of muscles and ligaments surrounding twenty-six bones, and needs the best protection

fascia, which is a firm band of connective tissue linking the heel to the base of the toes. Pain in this band, often beginning near the underside of the heel, is a potential problem for the runner and may be caused by plantar fasciitis.

See also *Ankle, Barefoot Running, Black Toenails, Blisters, Shoes, Socks.*

Four-minute mile

It is hard to adequately convey just how much fascination the very idea of a sub-four-minute mile held thirty-five years ago. Although it is a relatively common occurrence now in top-class athletics, with the world record standing around the three and three-quarter minute mark, it was for a long time held to be humanly impossible.

The challenge of trying to cross the symmetrical line of running four consecutive 440-yard laps at an average pace of one minute each was, at the time, considered the sporting equivalent of climbing the world's highest peak, Mount Everest. In the end, even Everest was conquered first.

By the time the world record stood to the diminutive, bespectacled Blackheath Harrier Sydney Wooderson at 4:6.4 in 1937, the sub-four-minute mile had become a distinct possibility. Between 1942 and 1945, while the rest of the world was engaged in other less sporting activities, two rival Swedes, Gunder Haegg and Arne Andersson, between them reduced Wooderson's world mile record in a series of great races to the 4:1.3 set by Haegg in neutral Sweden in 1945. But both men were declared professional for accepting illegal appearance money for their duels, which packed stadiums in Sweden, and their progress ended there. Although the rest of the world's athletes managed to pick themselves up fairly quickly in the post-war years, there was something of a vacuum in miling after Haegg and Andersson had to leave the scene.

Between 1946 and 1951 no one in the world ran faster than 4:5.4, and it was only at the end of 1952 that the race to be first under four minutes really began to develop in earnest. An Australian, John Landy, who had not qualified for the Olympic 1500m final in Helsinki that summer, suddenly produced a run of 4:2.1 in Melbourne in December. The 22-year-old agricultural student at Melbourne University used the advantage of the Australian summer to try to be first to four minutes 'because the Europeans are almost certain to better four minutes in 1953, and I'd like to get in before them'. In early January 1953 he ran 4:2.8 in Melbourne, then 4:4.2 on a grass track in Perth three weeks later.

Two other principal challengers for the honour of cracking the barrier were becoming clear. Britain's Roger Bannister, the 24-year-old medical student, who had decided to continue competition after a disappointing fourth place in the 1952 Olympic 1500m final, knocked over four seconds off his own best time with a British record of 4:3.6 at Oxford in May 1953. And in the USA, 21-year-old Wes Santee from Kansas joined the fray with runs of 4:2.4 (easily an American record) in California in early June, and 4:3.7 in Nebraska in late June 1953.

A week later Bannister, who had tried to avoid the Press as much as possible while public interest in the four-minute mile became intense, suddenly appeared in an invitation mile race during the Surrey Schools Championships at Motspur Park. His friend and training partner Chris Brasher was also in the field, but merely jogged the first two laps until the leaders caught him as they approached the three-quarter-mile point. Then, still fresh, he helped Bannister round the difficult final circuit in just over sixty seconds, so that Bannister's final time of 4:2, the third-fastest mile ever, was inside his own British record.

But the BAAB rejected the performance for ratification, stating that they did not consider it to have been achieved in a bona-fide competition, and that they did 'not regard individual record attempts as in the best interests of athletics as a whole'. Bannister accepted this philosophically and did not attempt to crack the barrier again that summer; Santee was meanwhile still failing in his attempts in the USA.

As a new season dawned in Australia late in 1953, John Landy opened a barrage of attempts with a personal best of 4:2 in Melbourne in mid-December, while Santee was still trying in the USA, with 4:4.2 (including a fifty-five second last lap) on the very last day of the year. But Landy could not get any closer, running between 4:2 and 4:3 on no less than six occasions before April, while Bannister, at home in England, awaited each race with increasing tension.

At times even Landy himself lost heart. 'It's a brick wall,' he said. 'I shall not attempt it again.' But he did, and when the Australian summer was over, he planned a further series of races in Europe from June 1954. And in the USA the new season had brought more attempts by Santee: 4:5.5 and 4:3.1 in April. So Bannister knew that he must use every suitable occasion if he was to be the first to four minutes.

On Thursday 6 May 1954 the long-standing match between Oxford University and the AAA was due to take place at Iffley Road track, Oxford, a venue familiar to Bannister from his own student days there. Although only a very few people knew of his intentions, the Press were there in force as Bannister was due to run the mile with his former Oxford University teammates and current training partners Chris Brasher and Chris Chataway. There was a rumour that they might try that evening, but the wind had been blowing hard all day, and even an hour before the race Bannister had been against attempting the four-minute barrier in such difficult conditions.

Shortly before the race began at 6 p.m., however, the wind dropped, and the key trio finally decided it was 'on'. After one false start, Brasher took the lead and, followed by Bannister and Chataway, went through 440 yards in 57.4 seconds and 880 yards in 1:58. The 1200 spectators present that historic night kept up a continual roar as Brasher faded on the back straight of the third lap, and Chataway moved into the lead to keep the pace going. With Bannister a stride behind him, he passed the three-quarter-mile point in 3:00.4, and with less than 250 yards remaining, Bannister hit the front. Covering the final furlong in twenty-nine seconds, he broke the tape in 3:59.4.

As he collapsed into the arms of waiting officials, Bannister had broken the world record by nearly two seconds and earned himself a place in history. But, more significantly, he had finally proved that the four-minute mile was humanly possible. Of course, we know that now; we didn't then.

See also *Sir Roger Bannister, Chris Brasher*.

Roger Bannister ensured his place in athletics history in 1954 by becoming the first man to run a sub-four-minute mile (below) at Oxford

World Mile Record Evolution since 1868

4:29.6	Walter Chinnery (UK)	Cambridge	10 Mar 1868
4:28.8	Walter Gibbs (UK)		3 Apr 1868
4:26.0	Walter Slade (UK)		30 May 1874
4:24.5	Walter Slade (UK)	Lillie Bridge	19 Jun 1875
4:23.2	Walter George (UK)		16 Aug 1880
4:19.4	Walter George (UK)	Stamford Bridge	3 Jun 1882
4:18.4	Walter George (UK)	Birmingham	21 Jun 1882
*(4:12.75	Walter George (UK)	Lillie Bridge	23 Aug 1885)
4:17.8	Thomas Conneff (Ire/USA)	Cambridge, Mass.	26 Aug 1893
4:17.0	Fred Bacon (UK)	Stamford Bridge	6 Jul 1895
4:15.6	Thomas Conneff (Ire/USA)	New York	28 Aug 1895
4:15.4	John Paul Jones (USA)	Cambridge, Mass.	27 May 1911
4:14.4	John Paul Jones (USA)	Cambridge, Mass.	31 May 1913
4:12.6	Norman Taber (USA)	Cambridge, Mass.	16 Jul 1915
4:10.4	Paavo Nurmi (Fin)	Stockholm	23 Aug 1923
4:09.2	Jules Ladoumegue (Fra)	Paris	4 Oct 1931
4:07.6	Jack Lovelock (NZ)	Princeton, NJ.	15 Jul 1933
4:06.7	Glenn Cunningham (USA)	Princeton, NJ.	16 Jun 1934
4:06.4	Sydney Wooderson (UK)	Motspur Park	28 Aug 1937
4:06.1	Gunder Haegg (Swe)	Gothenburg	1 Jul 1942
4:04.6	Gunder Haegg (Swe)	Stockholm	4 Sep 1942
4:02.6	Arne Andersson (Swe)	Gothenburg	1 Jul 1943
4:01.6	Arne Andersson (Swe)	Malmo	18 Jul 1944
4:01.3	Gunder Haegg (Swe)	Malmo	17 Jul 1945
3:59.4	Roger Bannister (UK)	Oxford	6 May 1954
3:57.9	John Landy (Aus)	Turku	21 Jun 1954
3:57.2	Derek Ibbotson (UK)	White City	19 Jul 1957
3:54.5	Herb Elliott (UK)	Dublin	6 Aug 1958
3:54.4	Peter Snell (NZ)	Wanganui	27 Jan 1962
3:54.1	Peter Snell (NZ)	Auckland	17 Nov 1964
3:53.6	Michel Jazy (Fra)	Rennes	9 Jun 1965
3:51.3	Jim Ryun (USA)	Berkeley, Ca.	17 Jul 1966
3:51.1	Jim Ryun (USA)	Bakersfield, Ca.	23 Jun 1967
3:51.0	Filbert Bayi (Tan)	Kingston, Jam.	17 May 1975
3:49.4	John Walker (NZ)	Gothenburg	12 Aug 1975
3:49.0	Sebastian Coe (UK)	Oslo	17 Jul 1979
3:48.8	Steve Ovett (UK)	Oslo	1 Jul 1980
3:48.53	Sebastian Coe (UK)	Zurich	19 Aug 1981
3:48.40	Steve Ovett (UK)	Koblenz	26 Aug 1981
3:47.33	Sebastian Coe (UK)	Brussels	30 Aug 1981
3:46.32	Steve Cram (UK)	Oslo	27 Jul 1985

(*This performance was achieved after George had turned professional.)

G

Gasparilla Distance Classic

This 15km road race is held each February in Tampa, Florida, during a city festival which commemorates an eighteenth-century pirate. Jose Gaspar (also known as Gasparilla), who sailed the seas off Florida for forty years, attacked and plundered ships from all nations before his eventual capture in 1821. The race, on an out and back course along Tampa Bay, was first organized in 1978 (when its 1600 runners false-started), and now attracts fields of around 6000, led by some of the world's best.

It remains one of the most prestigious events in the packed calendar of American road racing.

Recent winners

MEN

Year	Winner	Time
1980	Greg Meyer (USA)	43:40
1981	Ric Rojas (USA)	43:12
1982	Mike Musyoki (Ken)	43:09
1983	Rob de Castella (Aus)	42:47
1984	Mike McLeod (UK)	42:55
1985	Mike McLeod (UK)	43:02
1986	John Treacy (Ire)	42:59
1987	Marcos Barreto (Mex)	43:17

WOMEN

Year	Winner	Time
1980	Grete Waitz (Nor)	48:01
1981	Grete Waitz (Nor)	48:13
1982	Grete Waitz (Nor)	48:25
1983	Wendy Sly (UK)	48:18
1984	Grete Waitz (Nor)	47:52
1985	Grete Waitz (Nor)	48:10
1986	Ingrid Kristiansen (Nor)	48:00
1987	Grete Waitz (Nor)	48:50

Gateshead

A town synonymous now with world-class athletics, Gateshead for many years was known primarily as 'the dirty back lane leading to Newcastle'. But the deep-rooted love of running in the northeast of England, the successes of local athletes (and specifically Brendan Foster) in major competitions, and the wholehearted backing of the Gateshead Metropolitan Borough Council from the early seventies has helped turn the previously unfashionable town situated south of the River Tyne, facing Newcastle, into a centre renowned for athletic excellence and innovation.

Although the town's athletics club, Gateshead Harriers, was founded in 1904 by a local barber, Jack Nowell, and always enjoyed a degree of success, it was Brendan Foster in the seventies who really put it on the map. His consistent successes in major international championship events, including winning the 1974 European 5000m title, helped inspire the rest of his club which, in 1973, had become the first from the northeast to win the National senior team cross-country title, and went on to other team successes, including winning the AAA twelve-stage National Road Relay from 1975–77 and in 1979.

When the Gateshead Council agreed to install an all-weather running track at the town's stadium, Foster not only assembled a top-class international meeting to open the track on 3 August 1974, but with the new surface just ten days old, and the ground packed, set a world 3000m record of 7:35.2, as if to order.

Newly appointed as the town's sports and recreation officer, he also helped mastermind innovations like lunchtime jogging sessions and mass fun runs for the community, and assisted in attracting major events to the town. Although Foster is no longer employed by the town where he still lives, his legacy remains through an enthusiastic and no less ambitious recreation department. Apart from the regular international track and field meetings which continue to pack the stadium, and the annual international cross-country meeting, Gates-

Gateshead's most famous son, Brendan Foster, setting a world 3000m record at the opening of the town's track in 1974

head staged the IAAF World Cross-country Championships in 1983 and the IAAF Women's World 15km Road Race Championship in 1985.

The annual Great North Run half-marathon is another innovation, and passes the stadium, while the successes of Steve Cram (who was born in Gateshead, although he competes for the rival Jarrow and Hebburn AC), Charlie Spedding of Gateshead Harriers, and Mike McLeod, who runs for nearby Elswick Harriers, have made them the new heroes of the northeast.

See also *Great North Run*.

Gerschler, Woldemar

The German coach and physiologist who is credited with developing interval training, Gerschler achieved his greatest fame in the fifties through his work with Josy Barthel of Luxembourg, the surprise winner of the 1952 Olympic 1500m title, and Britain's Gordon Pirie. But before the war Gerschler, a graduate of Leipzig University, had coached the German Rudolf Harbig to a world 800m record of 1:46.6 in 1939, a mark which survived until 1955 (although Harbig was killed in the war).

Gerschler's tough demands on the athletes he helped made him a controversial figure, but he insisted that the physiological research he carried out after the war while in charge of the Freiburg University Institute of Education, in conjunction with Professor Hans Reindell, proved that athletes could withstand a great deal more training if it was correctly monitored and if much of the guesswork was subsequently taken out of their training schedules.

An all-round sportsman, Gerschler had qualified as a schoolteacher when offered the job of chief coach to Dresdner SC, one of Germany's top sports clubs before the war. Gerschler's wife, Hilde, was one of Germany's top high jumpers, although surprisingly for such a visionary he was against the idea of women racing further than 200m, and contested the introduction of the women's 800m in Germany. But this was more on grounds of femininity than physiology, because he also predicted that if he had the right material he could coach a woman to run under two minutes for the distance, at a time, in 1953, when the women's world record stood at 2:8.2. Born in 1904, he died on 14 June 1982.

See also *Interval Training*.

Glycogen

The principal source of energy for the working muscles during exercise is carbohydrate, which is stored mainly in the cells of the muscles and in the liver as an insoluble form of glucose known as glycogen. To release its energy, the glycogen is broken down in a process known as glycolysis. But the limitations of storage are such that if it had to use glycogen alone, the body would only be able to continue to exercise for 70–90 minutes.

But by calling upon its fat stores, in the form of free fatty acids, it is able to simultaneously burn a mixture of both, and thus make its glycogen stores last longer. Marathon runners have also successfully used dietary manipulation to artificially increase their glycogen stores, and thus delay the point at which they hit 'the wall', when those glycogen stores are finally depleted.

For the distance runner in hard training adequate refuelling between sessions in the form of a high carbohydrate diet, to top up the glycogen stores, is essential as otherwise there is likely to be a downward spiral in training performance.

See also *Carbohydrate Loading, Hitting the Wall*.

Gravity inversion

Many runners who suffer from lower back ache and sciatica-type problems induced by running many miles on road, with its subsequent shock-absorption in the lower back, have found relief through various forms of gravity inversion, in which the body is suspended upside down.

Whereas backache and sciatica can be caused by compression of the lumbar vertebrae in the lower back, gravity inversion reverses the process and helps to stretch out and decompress not only the back but also the sacroiliac and knee joints.

The techniques of gravity inversion range from special manacle-like boots with a hooking device by which the runner hangs, bat-like, from a horizontal bar set in a doorway, to a more sophisticated type of pivoting table on which he lies horizontally and which is then swung into a vertical position with his feet upwards, secured by ankle locks. The bodyweight in both cases helps the necessary stretching to take place, and hanging sessions can last from just a couple of minutes to 15-20 minutes at a time once the subject becomes used to the sensation.

The benefits are by no means confined to runners, of course, but anyone with high blood pressure or related circulatory problems is not advised to use the system. Additionally, it has to be remembered that while gravity inversion can reverse some of the causes of back pain it cannot repair actual damage, in which case conventional medical treatment will be necessary.

See also *Sciatica*.

The 1983 London Marathon winner Mike Gratton undergoing gravity inversion treatment in the author's garage

Great North Run

Inaugurated in the same year as the London Marathon, 1981, and with consistently larger fields, the Great North Run has earned its own niche in road running circles. It is an accurately measured half-marathon, starting in Newcastle-upon-Tyne, alongside Town Moor, and running out towards the coast, with the last mile along the seafront at South Shields.

It was the original idea of Brendan Foster,

Great North Run

Bigger even than the London Marathon, the Great North Run has become Tyneside's greatest annual running event

one of Tyneside's greatest running innovators and inspirations, and with 12,500 starters for the first event on 28 June 1981 it became Britain's biggest road race at that time. It could not have been launched at a more appropriate moment, with the running boom just taking off after the success of the London Marathon three months earlier, and the inspirational *Chariots of Fire* in the cinemas; indeed, passing through the tunnel leading to the Tyne Bridge after one mile in that first race thousands of runners joined in a spontaneous and echoing rendition of 'Jerusalem'.

Another local hero, Mike McLeod, won the first Great North Run, with a 20-year-old named Steve Cram making a daring mid-season step up in distance to place tenth in 1hr 7min 28sec. Foster himself was twentieth in 1hr 9min 34sec, and England soccer star Kevin Keegan 491st in 1hr 26min 25sec!

In succeeding years the fields quickly grew, with a 25,000 limit placed by the organizers, who could easily have doubled that total from the prospective entries. Big names like Carlos Lopes, Grete Waitz and Rosa Mota were added to the list of winners, and in 1986 a tremendous duel between Kenyan Mike Musyoki and Britain's Steve Jones resulted in a win for Musyoki in a world best time of 1 hr 00min 43sec, just sixteen seconds ahead of Jones, on a course which was double checked for accuracy and proved to be fifteen and a half yards over distance.

The Great North Run may be only half the length of the London Marathon, but the Tyneside crowds, estimated at between a quarter and half a million people lining the course to South Shields, at least match the enthusiasm of London, and make the event into an occasion for runners fast and slow.

Great North Run

Year	Starters	Finishers	Men's Winner	Women's Winner
1981	12,500+	10,681	Mike McLeod (UK) 1:03.23	Karen Goldhawk (UK) 1:17.36
1982	20,400+	19,000+	Mike McLeod (UK) 1:02.44	Margaret Lockley (UK) 1:19.24
1983	21,000+	20,700+	Carlos Lopes (Por) 1:02.46	Julie Barleycorn (UK) 1:16.39
1984	25,000+	24,247	Oyvind Dahl (Nor) 1.04.36	Grete Waitz (Nor) 1:10.27
1985	25,000+	23,848	Steve Kenyon (UK) 1:02.44	Rosa Mota (Por) 1:09.54
1986	25,000+	25,023	Mike Musyoki (Ken) 1:00.43	Lisa Martin (Aus) 1:09.45
1987	25,000+		Rob de Castella (Ans) 1:02.04	Lisa Martin (Aus) 1:10.00

H

Hamstring

The hamstring is actually a group of three distinct muscles at the back of the thigh and which flex the knee. These muscles (the semitendinosus, the semimembranosus and the biceps femoris) are powerful, but relatively inelastic and prone to damage at high speed if not kept fully stretched through regular mobility exercises.

All three muscles have their upper anchoring at the ischial tuberosity, situated in the lower rear of the pelvis and sometimes called the seat bone. But they then divide like an inverted 'V' to attach either side of the knee. The biceps femoris attaches at the outside of the knee to the head of the fibula, while the other two muscles attach at the inner side, to the upper end of the tibia.

The hamstrings complement the quadriceps muscles of the thigh, and it is important that a strength balance between the two groups is maintained if injury is to be avoided.

Hamstring strains tend to happen more frequently to sprinters, or to distance runners who use sprint training sporadically, than to distance runners who never sprint. But in all runners, pain at the rear of the thigh which is originally diagnosed as a hamstring strain but then fails to respond to treatment sometimes turns out instead to be inflammation of the sciatic nerve which also runs down the back of the upper leg.

See also *Gravity Inversion, Sciatica*.

The hamstring muscles are particularly prone to injury at high speed, frequently suffered by sprinters

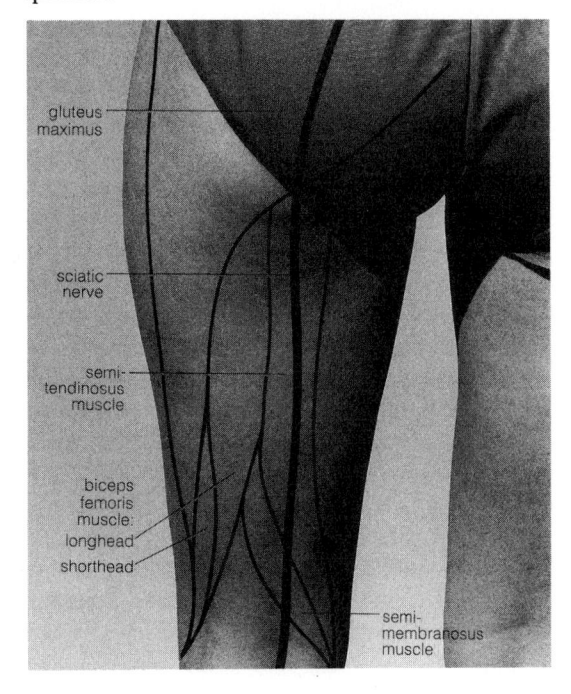

Heart

It may only be the size of a grapefruit, but the heart is the central pump of the body which keeps the blood circulating and sustaining life. During a twenty-four-hour period it will pump 9000 litres (2000 gallons) of blood along the 96,500km (nearly 60,000 miles) of veins, arteries and capillaries which, with the heart, make up the cardiovascular system.

Really the heart should be considered as two separate pumps, situated at the centre of a circulatory figure-of-eight. One of the pumps, on the right-hand side, is responsible for pumping the blood to the lungs to receive oxygen. The other pump, on the left-hand side, receives the newly oxygenated blood from the lungs and then pumps it out to the body's tissues.

After the de-oxygenated blood has been picked up from the tissues it is returned to the first pump and is then dispatched off to the lungs to collect more oxygen. And so the process continues, from birth until death, with the blood making the complete tour of the circulatory system more than 1000 times in every twenty-four hours.

Each of the heart's two pumps has a large chamber, known as its ventricle, and a smaller ante-chamber where the blood accumulates before being forced into the ventricle, and then pumped out again on its next journey.

When the blood enters the right ventricle, it is dark red and de-oxygenated before being pumped through the pulmonary artery to the lungs.

By the time it returns to the left ventricle it is bright red with its newly acquired oxygen, and ready to be pumped through the aorta, the largest and most important artery in the body, to the body's tissues. Then it will return, dark red, to the right ventricle again.

In middle- and long-distance running, a quick and plentiful supply of oxygen to the muscles is essential, and through training it is possible to enlarge the heart and improve its efficiency. In the average adult the pumping cycle is completed about seventy-two times a minute at rest. But the fitter you are, the stronger and larger the heart, and the fewer times it needs to beat to pump the same volume of blood. In top-class international endurance athletes, resting heart rates as low as thirty-two beats per minute have been recorded. Taking your pulse, in which you can feel each wave of blood as it is pumped by the heart through the arteries, can give you an indication of your heart rate.

Training for an endurance event like distance running can keep the arteries and veins clear and efficient, and may cause the creation of more capillaries to help keep the blood speeding around the body in hard exercise. But in the non-exercising body, the arteries of even quite young people can become narrowed and less efficient, particularly if the diet is too high in fats, or they are a smoker. This condition is known as arteriosclerosis, which reduces the amount of blood able to reach the heart. Brisk exercise, such as jogging, even for the non-competitor, is known to play a considerable part in helping to prevent the scourge of modern society, heart disease, whch claims so many victims prematurely and apparently unnecessarily every year.

In the rare cases of sudden death while running, it is usually found afterwards that there was a genetic or other pre-existing problem which had remained undetected. And despite suggestions from the anti-exercise lobby, there is no evidence that running itself will ever harm a normal, healthy heart. Instead, there appears to be ample evidence that it will improve its condition.

See also *Blood, Blood Pressure, Breathing, James Fixx, Lungs, Pulse*.

Heat

An activity like distance running generates a great deal of heat, and when it takes place in conditions which are also hot, the joint effects of the exercise and the weather are on a collision course. So unless the situation is given due respect, the runner could end up with heat stroke, or worse.

The body temperature is normally regulated

by cells in the brain, which maintain the level of 37°C (98.4°F). But sustained running, where nearly three quarters of the total energy generated is released simply as heat rather than powering the muscles, could lead to the temperature rising dangerously out of control without the assistance of three mechanisms through which the runner can lose heat: convection, heat radiation and sweating.

Convection is the simple cooling of the skin by the air, where a light breeze on a reasonable amount of exposed skin surface can reduce the amount of heat stored in the body. Heat radiation involves the transport of heat by the blood from the muscles to the skin surface, although it also means that blood will be diverted away from the working muscles to perform this task, in turn reducing the amount of oxygen available to the muscles.

The third mechanism, sweating, where water and salt are secreted by the sweat glands in the skin, can be the most efficient form of heat loss, but only as long as the sweat is able to evaporate in the atmosphere. The sweat is released on to the skin, absorbs heat from the skin, and in evaporating takes heat away. But in a particularly humid atmosphere, where the air is already practically saturated with water, this evaporation becomes very difficult.

Runners can lose two litres of sweat per hour, and much of it must be replaced quickly through taking drinks, as a fluid loss of more than 3 per cent of the body weight can bring on the first stages of dehydration, itself a major threat in hot weather. Pure water should be taken during exercise because it is most rapidly absorbed; adding sugars or minerals will actually slow down the process, and offer no significant assistance during the event.

Taking extra drinks before an event like a marathon on a warm day can ensure that the runner starts fully hydrated. But he should also take advantage of the drinks offered early in the race, before he even begins to feel thirsty. To ignore the body's need for liquid could lead to heat exhaustion, with the athlete feeling dizzy, nauseous, uncoordinated and even becoming delirious. Dehydration would raise the body temperature still further, creating a vicious circle as it has already caused a reduction in sweat rate, which will become more acute as the body temperature continues to rise.

From its normal level of 37°C (98.4°F), the temperature of a runner taking part in even a 10km race on a mild day may rise to 39.4°C (103°F). If allowed to reach 41.1°C (106°F), the functioning of vital organs, particularly the liver and kidneys, begins to be impaired, with possible complications, which could even lead to death.

In the 1912 Olympic marathon at Stockholm, a 21-year-old Portuguese, Francisco Lazaro, who was an experienced runner and pronounced medically fit, collapsed after nineteen miles and died next day from sunstroke and heart failure. At the 1978 Falmouth Seven-mile Road Race in the USA, held in 75 per cent humidity, American runner Alberto Salazar collapsed after the finish and was actually given the last rites by a Roman Catholic

The effects of heat exhaustion clearly seen in Switzerland's Gabrielle Andersen-Schiess near the finish of the 1984 Olympic women's marathon

priest. Salazar's temperature was found to be 42.2°C (108°F), but hospital treatment in an ice bath helped him make a fairly rapid recovery.

Salazar was a particularly dogged and determined runner, almost too much so for his own good. So was Jim Peters, whose collapse at the finish of the 1954 Empire Games marathon in Vancouver is regularly cited as a graphic example of the draining effects of the marathon. In fact, Peters was perfectly able to cope with the distance, as he had repeatedly proved in the past. However, on that August day, with the temperature over 26.7°C (80°F), he would not compromise his style of flat-out racing and literally ran himself into the ground, even though he was leading the race by some two miles.

These days most marathons are held in spring or autumn, and when a major championships is staged at the height of summer, the marathons are usually given a starting time which will keep the competitors out of the strongest heat.

Training runs, of course, can usually be adapted to the coolest parts of the day, in early morning or evening, when necessary. But if a runner is taking part in a race in hot weather, then it is important to adapt as well as possible to the conditions. Kit should be light coloured, which helps to reflect the sun's rays, rather than the dark colours which absorb them, and loose fitting where possible to enable maximum circulation of air. Mesh, or mesh-panelled, vests also contribute to ventilation, while underwear for both sexes should be kept to the minimum required for comfort, support and decency.

Some runners like to wear a sun hat, but others feel that as a third of the body heat is normally lost through the head, then wearing a hat of any type may interfere with this process. One compromise solution is a mesh sun hat, or one with holes cut in it to allow heat to escape.

Drinks should be taken before the race, and the hotter or more humid it is, the more frequently drinks should be taken during the event. Sponges should also be accepted whenever offered, and used to wipe down the thighs, face and neck in particular to aid body temperature regulation. A water-soaked handkerchief worn round the neck will help keep the body cool, although it will need to be re-soaked whenever possible during the race as it will quickly dry out. Some runners have placed ice lumps inside such handkerchiefs, so that as they slowly melt, the supply of cooling water is at least available for longer.

Because the demands of the body to keep cool divert some of the blood away from its normal role of oxygen transportation during distance running, performance levels tend to suffer on hot days, unlike the sprints and field events, where overheating is not a problem, and hot weather will actually enhance performance by allowing the muscles to be looser. Therefore ambition in terms of times achieved in distance races should be moderated on hot days; the conditions may not give the runner an accurate reflection of his current best form. For this reason, a high priority should be given to assessing the factors which will enable him to perform at his best in the prevailing weather, which may include setting a more restrained pace than on cooler days. Finishing in a slower time is at least preferable to not finishing at all.

See also *Humidity, Sweating*.

Hill training

Training on hills is often characterized solely as runners punching their way up a steep gradient, sometimes in loose sand, and is considered to be a relatively short, explosive exercise. But there are two distinct ways of hill training (and that does not mean up and down!).

Firstly, there is indeed the series of fast repetitions on a short, steep hill, with the runner jogging or walking back down after each effort as a form of recovery. This type of training is primarily for track runners who want to improve their sprinting ability, which can be enhanced by maximum exertion of the lifting muscles of the thighs and the driving muscles of the arms when running hard uphill. The resistance of the slope brings about muscle fatigue much more quickly than flat running, and therefore for the fit runner this can be a particularly time-efficient method of improvement.

The second method of hill running affects the road runner more significantly. It is to run a series of hills, which would ideally be spaced around a repeatable road circuit, in as relaxed a style as possible. For while the track runner is aiming for a dynamic driving action up the hill, the longer distance runner should be seeking economy of effort in tackling any hill which presents itself in competition. And while the first method of hill training will certainly provide physiological improvement, to indulge mainly or exclusively in this form of hill training could cause a reflex action at the sight of any hill in a race. The danger then is that the runner could find himself subconsciously speeding up and putting in unnecessarily extravagant effort, which in a long race would be detrimental.

So by running a continuous circuit, and consciously relaxing on the hills, while working the arms a little harder where necessary but resisting the onset of tension in the upper body, the distance runner can develop both the stamina and relaxation necessary for his event. The aim must be to allow the challenge of the hill to make as little difference to the natural running style and effort during the race as possible, so it is essential to run smoothly up and over the top of the hill without dramatically increasing the breathing rate or rhythm.

In trying to evaluate the more suitable style of hill training for himself, the runner has to consider whether he is training for a relatively short race which he wants to complete as fast as possible, or a longer race which he wants to complete as economically and efficiently as possible.

See also *Resistance Training*.

Hip

Unlike the ankle, which moves only forward and back, the hip is a far more mobile joint, with the rounded head of the femur (thigh

Sebastian Coe demonstrates the higher knee lift and arm drive used by track runners when hill training

bone) fitting into a hollow surface, known as the acetabulum, near the base of the pelvis. This forms a ball-and-socket joint, allowing a wide range of movement and firmly protected by strong ligaments. The joint also aids stability and absorbs shock.

The hip abductor muscles, which pull the thigh outwards, are the gluteus medius and the gluteus minimus. They both extend from the outer side of the hip bone to the top of the thigh bone at its outer extremity, the knobble known as the greater trochanter. If you stand with your fingers on your hips, slightly to the rear, and then move your leg outwards you can feel them working.

The main hip flexor muscles are psoas major and iliacus, which move the thigh upwards at the hip. The psoas major extends from the lumbar vertebrae at the lower end of the spine, across the hip joint itself, to attach at the inner top of the thigh bone. Iliacus is spread across the front of the whole hip bone, but also narrows down to attach inside the thigh bone, and these two main flexors are known as 'iliopsoas' as they work so closely together. Any activity which involves exaggerated leg-lifting action, such as running uphill, or performing sprint drills, puts a high work load on these flexors; so does the sheer repetition of a long run. Gradually increasing pain in these muscles, or in the abductors, may well be from overuse, and if it is felt more acutely on one side than the other it could be due to an imbalance caused by a lack of flexibility in the joint on that side.

Rest, and gradually improving the flexibility through exercises, is the best treatment in such cases, as it can also help to prevent a recurrence once healed. Swimming, at any stroke which does not cause discomfort, is also a good form of rehabilitation from an overuse hip strain.

Pain in the hip joint itself should always be referred to a doctor for investigation, as conditions such as osteoarthritis can follow often-undetected degeneration inside the joint. In extreme cases the whole joint can actually be replaced artificially in a comparatively simple surgical operation which has already allowed some older runners a whole new lease of life.

Hitting the wall

During a prolonged running event, such as a marathon, the body's natural energy source of glycogen which is stored in the muscles and liver will usually be completely used after several hours of hard exercise. When this happens, the runner's pace is almost immediately reduced while the body switches to burning fats for its energy supply, and the runner realizes he is getting slower for more effort. This point in a marathon, experienced by the faster runners at around 18–22 miles, is known as 'hitting the wall'.

A form of dietary manipulation, called carbohydrate loading, has helped some runners postpone this point in the race, but the system also has its drawbacks. Women seem to experience the phenomenon of 'hitting the wall' far less

The draining effects of the marathon can reduce even fit runners to a walk when they 'hit the wall'

frequently than men, possibly due to their greater stores of body fat and more efficient method of using it to supplement their existing glycogen stores.

See also *Carbohydrate Loading, Glycogen.*

Holmér, Gösta

The Swedish Olympic coach for thirty-three years, until his retirement in 1958, Gösta Holmér (born 23 September 1891) was the man generally credited with the development of Fartlek as a popular training form. He was an Olympic bronze medallist in the decathlon in 1912, and fourth in 1920, with ten Swedish titles in the decathlon, pentathlon and 110m hurdles, and also played first-division soccer. He coached athletes in all events, including world record breakers in the hurdles, javelin and discus, but claimed his greatest satisfaction was the development of Fartlek.

Humidity

The level of humidity, or moisture in the atmosphere, is significant to the distance runner because if it is too high it will interfere with the efficiency of the sweating process by which he disposes of excess body heat. Sweat is secreted by the sweat glands on to the skin, where it absorbs heat produced during exercise, and then takes it away from the skin by evaporating.

But if there is a high degree of humidity, with a lot of water already in the air, the evaporation becomes much more difficult. Heat regulation by this method in those circumstances is poor, so the body temperature rises further, sweating increases, and could eventually lead to dehydration.

See also *Heat, Sweating.*

Hypothermia

Although hypothermia is normally associated with elderly people whose bodies have lost much of their ability to retain heat in cold weather, even fit, experienced long-distance runners have been known to fall victim to this chilling of the body, which can in extreme cases lead to death.

In March 1972 hundreds of competitors in the English National Cross-country Championships at Sutton Coldfield suffered mild hypothermia when a sudden bitter storm of snow and sleet descended during the senior nine-mile event. And in October 1981 three fit young New Zealand runners died from exposure during a club run in an isolated, hilly part of Wellington after an unexpectedly heavy shower of sleet and snow, together with plummeting temperatures, caught the lightly clad runners unaware.

In distance running, even on cold days, the body normally generates sufficient heat to maintain a safe core temperature. So much so, in fact, that runners tend to train or race in minimum amounts of clothing and, as long as their pace remains largely constant, there is no problem.

But if, through circumstances, they have to slow drastically or stop, because of chronic fatigue, injury, illness, blisters, or losing their way, their body temperature will start to fall. The problem will be aggravated by strong, cold winds, especially if they are wearing clothing made wet by rain or sleet.

As it gets colder, the body tries to retain some of its heat by forming goose pimples on the skin, and starting to shiver. But if these early symptoms of hypothermia are ignored, the body temperature will continue to fall, and the runner may become drowsy and disorientated. If isolated, the runner may no longer be in a position to take self-help measures, which would include urgently seeking warmth and shelter. If accompanied, the companion should endeavour to warm up the victim by covering him with all dry clothing available, and if he can still walk or run, encouraging him to move as fast as possible to the nearest form of shelter. A warm bath, with the legs and arms raised out of the water, is an effective way of restoring the body to normal temperature. Warm drinks can also help, but alcohol should be avoided because this will actually provoke further heat loss by sending more blood

As they finish, these marathon runners are given foil 'space blankets' to prevent hypothermia before their tracksuits are retrieved

towards the skin, rather than to the brain, where it is urgently needed.

Runners in the closing miles of a marathon are particularly vulnerable to hypothermia in poor weather conditions, and should be aware of the rule which empowers the officially appointed medical staff to order them to retire from the race if it is considered necessary on health grounds. Usually the medical officer will be in a much better position to make such a decision, as a runner suffering from hypothermia may be irrational. Trying to continue in a fatigued state, where hypothermia is developing and warm shelter is being offered, would be foolish. The drop in body temperature usually continues downwards in a spiral, and once below the 35°C (95°F) point, technically considered the border line of hypothermia, could reach 28°C (82.4°F) relatively quickly. This would probably lead to unconsciousness and, without urgent help, a further drop in temperature to 25°C (77°F) which could be fatal.

But the race competitor is probably less at risk than the lone runner who ventures into isolated territory on a long training run in poor weather. In such circumstances, the runner should always ensure that someone knows exactly where he is going, and when he is due back.

See also *Cold*.

I

IAAF

The world governing body for all aspects of track and field athletics, road and cross-country running and race walking is the International Amateur Athletic Federation (IAAF), which was formed in Stockholm on 17 July 1912, two days after the last athletics event of the Olympic

Games. Seventeen countries attended that inaugural meeting, and by the end of 1986 no less than 179 countries were affiliated to the IAAF.

The Federation holds a biennial congress, but much of its work in such matters as rule changes, world record approval, technical developments and so forth is carried out throughout the year by its twenty-one-member council, its permanent bureau in London, and by its six special committees: Technical, Women's, Walking, Cross Country and Road Running, Veterans and Medical.

An annual handbook, containing its rules, committee composition and international addresses is published in English and French, together with a monthly colour magazine and a wide range of its own statistical and coaching booklets, wall charts, and video-cassettes of its own major events.

The IAAF now promotes its own World Championships in track and field every four years (the 1991 Championships being staged in Tokyo), with annual World Cross-country Championships for men and women every March. Additionally, the World Cup, the World Marathon Cup, World Indoor Championships, World Junior Championships and World Race Walking Trophies are staged under its control, and it is also responsible for the track and field programme at the Olympic Games.

The IAAF headquarters are at 3 Hans Crescent, Knightsbridge, London SW1 0LN. Tel. 01–581 8771.

Ice

As a method of treatment for relieving pain, reducing swelling and internal bleeding, and assisting recovery, the careful application of ice to a soft tissue injury can be extremely effective.

The cold temperature causes superficial vasoconstriction, the constriction of a vein close to the body surface, which in turn reduces the blood flow to the injured tissue, and can limit swelling. Research in Canada has also indicated that ice can relieve pain by stimulating the body's production of endorphins and stopping pain messages from reaching the brain.

Treatment by ice (known as cryotherapy) can be performed in a number of ways. An ice cube held on the affected area is quite effective, although some form of barrier between the skin and the ice should be employed: olive oil smeared on the skin first, or wrapping the ice in a wet towel, will not interfere with the transmission of cold but can save the skin from an ice burn, blister or even frostbite if the ice is kept in place too long. Usually 5–10 minutes at a time, repeated at intervals of 45–60 minutes can suffice. The essential sign is a deep pinkening of the skin (or darkening if you are dark-skinned), which shows the treatment is working.

Other methods of applying ice include putting a number of ice cubes in a plastic bag, which allows the home-made ice pack to be wrapped or shaped around the injured area, or using a strip of commercially produced ice-

Dr Primo Nebiolo, the Italian President of the IAAF, has instigated many of the sport's recent innovations

cube moulds in polythene form which can also be wrapped around the injured area. In emergencies, soft packets of frozen peas have been used, although caution should be exercised if the food inside becomes de-frosted in use; it should not be re-frozen.

If water is frozen in a polystyrene cup, the bottom of the cup can be cut off and the ice block applied to the injury in a massaging movement, in the style of a solid deodorant stick, with the ice pushed further through the cup as and when it melts.

There are re-usable cold packs containing a special gel which remains pliable even when below freezing point, but they need to be kept in a refrigerator in the first place. For injuries which occur during training, the sooner ice is applied the better, and some coaches equip themselves with specially manufactured chemical packs which have two compartments. When crushed together, the chemicals inside make an ice-like substitute. The packs are expensive and cannot be re-used, but they are easy to carry and can save a lot of time if there is no other source of ice quickly available. In emergencies, cafés, restaurants, pubs and fishmongers are among the first places to visit!

Injury

The vast majority of injuries experienced by distance runners are those termed 'over-use' injuries; they have simply been caused through constant repetition of an exercise (running) thousands and thousands and thousands of times. Other types of sports injury include 'direct' injury, involving physical contact, such as in a crushing soccer tackle, or the 'indirect' injury, where the damage is caused by a violent force not involving physical contact, such as twisting an ankle by stepping in a hole. Direct injuries are extremely rare and always accidental in running; indirect injuries are more common, but still overwhelmed in number by over-use injuries.

For a runner covering just 20–30 miles a week will still take around 2,000,000 strides a year, while a runner covering 100 miles a week will take about 9,000,000. And every single one of those strides, which involve some thirty muscles working closely in harmony, will create a force some 3–4 times greater than the runner's bodyweight every time the foot lands. That could be around 500lb in a ten-stone runner, which has to be absorbed in the legs and lower back.

The human body is designed to work in symmetry, but if one small aspect of the machine goes wrong, the whole works is thrown out of synchronization. If the exercise is continued while disregarding the original problem, a whole new group of problems can occur. The runner who tries to keep running on an injured knee, for example, may soon find that the ankle on his opposite leg starts to hurt, where he has been 'favouring' the leg. So if an injury occurs, he should wait until that is healed before continuing normal training. It is frustrating, but often the lesser of two evils.

Most distance runners' injuries occur at the knee and below, with any occurrence of a sharp on-the-bone pain as warning of a possible stress fracture particularly to be noted. Invariably, distance running training causes some fatigue and stiffness, plus relatively minor ailments like blisters and cramp. But any ailment which causes prolonged pain over and above normal stiffness may need medical attention.

Apart from the wear and tear of an excessive volume of repetitive training, other prime causes for injury include:

* Sudden and overenthusiastic addition of hill training (particularly a cause of Achilles tendon strains).
* Favouring an injury on the other leg, and running 'awkwardly'.
* Running in shoes which are worn down, or excessively distorted through pronation.
* Trying to run flat out with insufficient (or absence of) warm-up.
* Too much running on the side of a cambered road.
* Irregular training (three times a week, every week, is better than seven days a week for one week, then nothing for a fortnight).

A number of hospitals hold regular NHS

Injury is the greatest problem of the distance runner, who has to push his body hard in training

sports injury clinics, where it is possible to make an appointment to be seen by a doctor or physiotherapist who specializes in such ailments. But normally an introductory letter from your own GP will be necessary first. There is also an increasing number of private sports injury clinics and hospital departments.

Insomnia

Several variations of insomnia, or difficulty in sleeping, can apply to the runner, quite apart from the type of insomnia found among non-runners who are tense, anxious or sensitive to minor discomfort or disturbance.

Generally, distance running training is an excellent way of relieving tensions and creating a deeper, more relaxing sleep. The physical toll may even dictate the need for more sleep.

But to step up the training load to a point where you are eventually over-training can actually bring about a form of insomnia where you almost feel too tired to sleep. Coupled with other stress signs, such as loss of appetite, over-anxiety and a rising pulse rate at rest, it should be taken as the need for easing down the training load. Greater recovery after training is required, as to reach this level of fatigue is counterproductive.

The second, much more temporary, type of insomnia may afflict the runner on the night before or after an important race, where the mind has become overactive in contemplation or reflection of the race and the body has almost become physically ready to run it at that moment. Restricted sleep on the night before a race is unlikely to adversely affect performance, although if it has become a regular experience for some days it is more likely to do so.

Re-running a race in the mind afterwards, whether it was successful or not, is a habit into which runners of every standard find themselves drawn. After winning the 1986 European 5000m title, Jack Buckner found he could not sleep for three nights.

Avoiding stimulating drinks like coffee or tea

at night, taking a warm milky drink before going to bed instead, and maintaining regular getting-up and going to bed times, can help you avoid long-term insomnia.

See also *Over-training*.

Interval training

Interval training is a physically demanding but frequently effective method of improving oxygen debt tolerance, and is now used in one form or another by the vast majority of middle- and long-distance runners.

The innovators in this field were the German coach Woldemar Gerschler (1904–82) and his colleague, physiologist Dr Hans Reindell. Their principles were based on the fact that physical exercise increases the heart rate, and rest slows it down. Eventually, the training effects of repeated physical exercise will slow down the resting heart rate, which indicates that the heart has increased the volume of blood it can pump on a single stroke. A normal, healthy, untrained adult may have a pulse rate of around 70–74 beats per minute, for instance, but a highly trained international athlete's larger, more efficient heart may need only 32–34 beats per minute to pump the equivalent amount of blood at rest.

Gerschler and Reindell assessed the results of their experiments with some 3000 subjects and concluded that by asking the athlete to run a specific distance at a fast pace, then allowing a set recovery 'interval' before the athlete repeated the run, an efficient and controlled system of performance improvement could be devised. The optimum speed/distance of the run was that which pushed the runner's pulse rate up to 180 beats a minute, and the optimum recovery period was that which allowed the pulse to drop to 120 beats a minute before the run was repeated.

For example, a run of 400m in 59 seconds might achieve the 180 pulse rate in Athlete A, and a recovery jog of 200m might allow his pulse to drop to 120, by which time he would be ready to repeat the hard run. But in Athlete B a run of 400m in only 65 seconds might achieve the same 180 pulse rate, and he might need a longer recovery to drop to 120 beats a minute. But Gerschler and Reindell maintained that if the heart took longer than 1min 30sec to drop to 120 beats a minute in recovery, then the preceding run had either been too fast or too long, and should be adjusted accordingly.

In practice, relatively few athletes probably observe the exact rise and fall of their pulse rate in training, although it is becoming much easier now with the development of a number of digital pulse counters. An alternative is to count the number of beats in ten seconds and multiply by six, or to time thirty beats with a stopwatch. But a great many runners simply use the interval method of running hard, recovering, and running hard again, even if some of them are not quite sure why.

Some runners believe, erroneously, that interval running sessions have to be performed on a track. The advantages of doing so are that distances can be measured accurately and that the same session can be comparably performed in different venues, or on opposite sides of the world if necessary. But the disadvantage is that it can become too monotonous or mechanical, and some runners, of course, do not have access to a track.

In that case, the distance between lamp-posts, trees in the park, or any other objects which are unlikely to move or disappear in the foreseeable future, can be utilized. As long as the distance used is constant from comparable session to session, it really does not matter what length is actually covered.

In order to monitor progress over weeks or months, it is important that certain sessions are correctly recorded. For example, if the runner chooses to run ten times between the big oak tree in the park and the tennis court fence, allowing himself a two-minute jog recovery in between, and timing each run, the session will only be truly comparable if the jog is exactly two minutes each time. To allow it to drag on in a moment of weakness renders comparison with another occasion useless.

Similarly, an *average* time for the runs is more significant as a sign of improving fitness than the fastest time of the series. In a session of 10 × 400m on the track, an average of 58.6 seconds would be much more meaningful, for instance, in terms of demonstrating fitness than running the first one in 51 seconds and the rest in 65!

The variations in an interval session are endless, with the main variables being a) the number of runs undertaken; b) the distance to be run; c) the length of recovery interval; d) the type of recovery – static? walking? jogging?; and e) the intensity of each run.

A typical interval session for a middle-distance runner might be:

12 × 400m in 63 seconds, with 200m jog recovery;

or

6 × 600m in 96 seconds with 200m walk/200m jog recovery;

or, a mixture –

4 × 300m in 42 seconds, with 300m walk recovery. Then, 2 × 600m in 95 seconds, with 3 minutes static recovery. Then, 6 × 150m fast strides, untimed, walking back after each;

or, using sets of intervals –

four sets of 2 × 300m flat out, with 100m jog between runs, and 5 minutes walk/static rest between sets.

The number of variations is infinite, with the middle-distance runner generally aiming for a high number of repetitions at a relatively gentle pace during the winter build-up, and gradually switching to an emphasis on fewer, faster runs with a longer recovery at the height of the track season. The principle is always the same: run hard, recover, and then run hard again.

Iron

A deficiency of iron through a poorly balanced diet, or heavy menstrual loss, could lead to a downturn in racing and training form for the runner. For the lack of iron reduces the ability of the red blood cells to transport sufficient oxygen around the body to keep pace with demand, while continual excessive fatigue or shortness of breath may be symptoms of iron-deficiency anaemia.

Iron-rich foods like liver, molasses, kidney, dried apricots, sardines and beef can help regain correct levels, although supplementary iron tablets may be needed in more severe cases.

Women are more prone to iron deficiency, and should ensure adequate intake of the mineral during menstruation, pregnancy and lactation.

See also *Anaemia*.

J

Jacuzzi

The relaxing benefits of hydromassage derived from the whirlpool bath now known colloquially as the 'jacuzzi' and enjoyed by many sportsmen and women of all standards, were first noticed by its pioneer, Candido Jacuzzi, in 1942. An Italian by birth, Jacuzzi had moved to the USA with his family during the First World War, and after some considerable success with a family business specializing in aircraft propeller design, Jacuzzi spotted the beneficial effect which sea bubbles and waves had on his 15-month-old son who was almost paralysed with rheumatoid arthritis.

So Jacuzzi developed a pump which could be used in the home bath, and from it evolved and patented the whirlpool bath, later known as the jacuzzi, in the fifties. It became an enormous success, developing into a multi-million dollar industry as the fashionable device in many middle-class American homes and later spreading to Europe. Jacuzzi died in Sun City, Arizona, at the age of 83, on 7 October 1986.

Jogger's nipple

A painful chafing of the nipples, caused by repetitive rubbing of the runner's vest across the chest, during a long training run or race. Precautions such as smearing a petroleum jelly like Vaseline across the vulnerable areas, or the use of protective plasters, like Elastoplast or Band-Aid, can prevent or reduce its occurrence.

See also *Chafing*.

Jones counter

A device which attaches to the front axle of a bicycle being used to accurately measure road race courses. It was invented by a New York runner, Clain Jones, and measures by counting the number of wheel revolutions of the bicycle when ridden over the shortest possible line the runners could take. It has helped to simplify the art of course measurement and thus lead to more accurate courses, bringing a uniformity to road events approaching that in track races.

See also *Course Measurement*.

K

Knee

The knee is one of the three great stabilizers for the runner, along with the ankle and hip. But it inevitably absorbs a tremendous amount of shock in the course of even a single run. Knee pain can be a frustrating form of injury, because of the inaccessibility of its complex workings, the wide range of possible causes of pain, and the usually unavoidable need for a break in training while it is healing.

The knee is the joint where the lower end of the thigh bone (femur) meets the upper end of the shinbone (tibia) to form what is basically a

The Jones Counter (pictured next to a 20p piece), with which accurate course measurement on a bicycle can be made

damaged by, say, a bad tackle or sharp turn in soccer, where the bones may produce a grinding effect.

For runners, though, the most common type of knee pain is the condition known as chondromalacia patellae, or runner's knee. This affects the area around the knee-cap (patella), which is the third bone involved in the joint. It is small, rounded and flat, and is enclosed within the tendon which stretches down the front of the knee, joining the quadriceps muscles at the front of the thigh to the upper end of the shin bone. The function of the patella is to provide increased leverage at the joint.

The growing use of arthroscopy in knee surgery has meant that the joint is not quite the stubborn challenge to the medical world it used to be, but it is still the area in which specific expertise is most needed for diagnosis of injury.

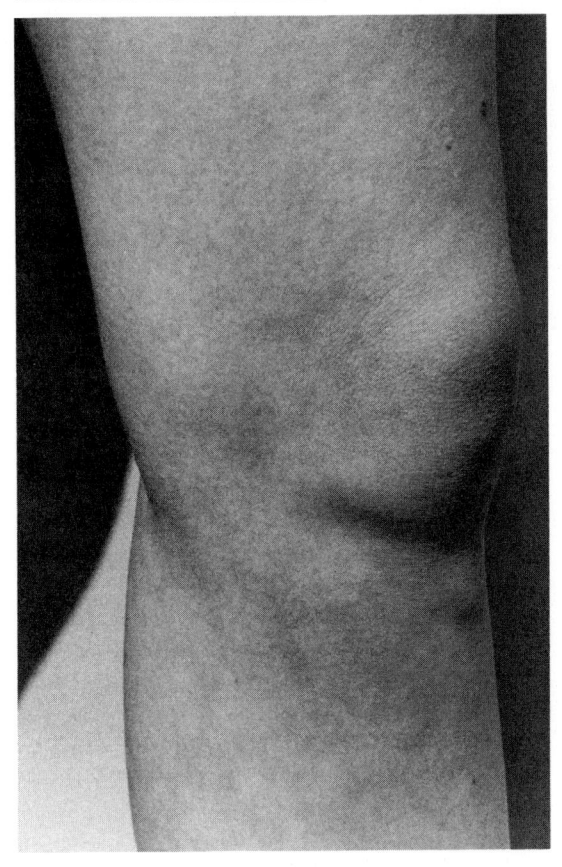

The most complicated joint in the body, the knee, is also the site of a number of painful and frustrating running injuries

hinge, but with some limited rotational movement.

In what is the largest and most complicated joint in the human body, there are two pairs of ligaments to provide stability and prevent abnormal movement of the joint; the cruciate and the collateral ligaments.

The strong cruciate ligaments, situated deep in the centre of the joint, serve to limit extension and rotation, while the collateral ligaments are the two 'side struts', linking the upper and lower leg, and preventing too much movement sideways.

Within the knee are two semilunar-shaped cartilages, or menisci, which act as cushioning. It is this type of cartilage, rather than the normal connective tissue on joint surfaces, which may have to be surgically removed if

Kristiansen, Ingrid

For some female athletes, motherhood means a scaling down, or even an end, to top-class competition. But for Norway's Ingrid Kristiansen, the ascent to the highest level of world-class distance running occurred only after she had given birth to a son in 1983. All of her major achievements, including two world records at 5000m, two world records at 10,000m and the world marathon record, followed motherhood.

But before that, she had already packed a lot into her varied sporting career. At just 15, in 1971, she ran 1500m for Norway in the European Championships, but fell. Soon afterwards, she abandoned athletics for cross-country skiing, and ranked among the best in Norway, three times placing second in the national championships. Her two careers even merged briefly, as she returned to running and finished tenth out of twenty-five in the 1978 European 3000m Championship in Prague.

When the women's marathon was first introduced as a major championship event, at the 1982 European Championships in Athens, Ingrid realized that the excellent cardiovascular

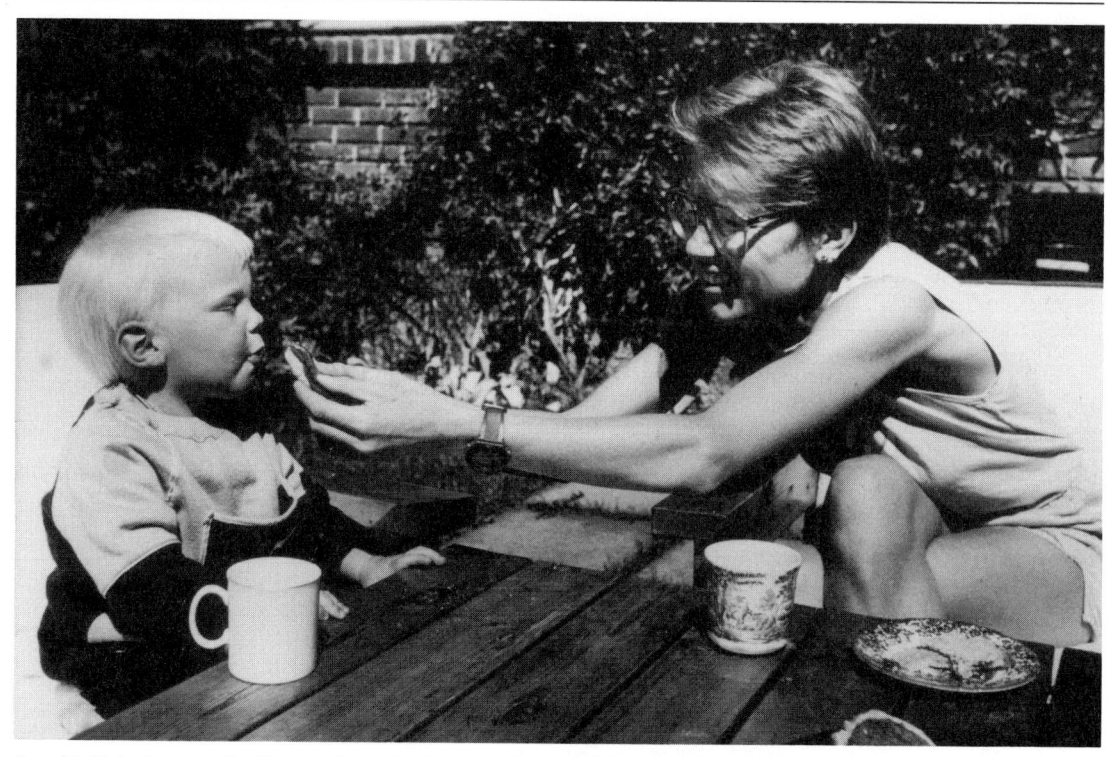

Ingrid Kristiansen, the Norwegian who has revolutionized women's distance running records, with her young son Gaute

fitness she had developed from cross-country ski-ing would provide a good background for the event. So she finally left competitive ski-ing to concentrate on running instead, and the unpredicted bronze medal she earned in the European Championship marathon was her first international success.

A disappointing thirty-fifth place in the 1983 World Cross-country Championships was explained when it turned out she was four months pregnant, but after the birth of her son, Gaute, she was training again within nine days.

'Gaute added something new to Ingrid's life,' said her husband, Arve Kristiansen, himself a 2hr 34min marathon runner. 'I'm sure that helped her become a great runner.'

Whether that development was physical, as some scientists suspect, or simply psychological, the effect was still significant. Despite the problems of living in Oslo, which is snowbound during the winter months, (and which she overcame by training on an electric treadmill in the basement to supplement the cross-country ski-ing which still forms part of her training), she reached new levels in 1984. In April she won the London Marathon in a European record of 2hr 24min 26sec, and then became the first woman to beat fifteen minutes for 5000m with 14:58.89 in Oslo in July.

So her fourth place in the Los Angeles Olympic marathon two months later was a major disappointment to her, especially as the race provided a chance to come out of the shadow of her better-known countrywoman Grete Waitz; as it was, Grete finished second. They remain friendly rivals, both living in Oslo, but approach their competitions quite differently. Like Grete, Ingrid is very ambitious, but outwardly she is more carefree and extrovert.

In 1985, determined to make up for the disappointment of LA, Ingrid took Joan Benoit-Samuelson's world marathon record with 2hr 21min 6sec in winning the London

Track and road progress

Born 21 March 1956.

	800m	1500m	3000m	5000m	10,000m	Marathon
1971	2:18.7	4:22.6				
1972	2:16.9	4:26.4	9:43.2			
1973		4:39.3	9:32.2			
1974		4:39.1	9:47.0			
1975						
1976		4:44.6	9:26.0			
1977	2:17.0	4:23.9	9:09.7			2h45:15
1978	2:14.6	4:19.3	9:01.3			
1979		4:26.3	9:07.92			
1980		4:18.5	8:58.8			2h34:25
1981	2:09.7	4:16.34	8:57.5	15:28.43		2h30:09
1982	2:12.18	4:13.5	8:51.79	15:21.81		2h33:36
1983	(Maternity)					2h33:27
1984		4:13.27	8:39.56	14:58.89		2h24:26
1985		4:10.17	8:40.34	14:57.43	30:59.42	2h21:06
1986		4:05.97	8:34.10	14:37.33	30:13.74	2h24:55.

Marathon again. She also set a world 10,000m track record of 30:59.42 in front of her adoring Oslo fans in July, but although she also bettered her own 5000m world best in London in August with 14:57.43, she was beaten in that race by Zola Budd, who ran 14:48.07.

When Ingrid raced Olympic champion Joan Benoit-Samuelson in the 1985 Chicago Marathon in October, the American again came out the winner, only just missing Ingrid's world best by fifteen seconds with 2hr 21min 21sec. But against the clock in 1986 Kristiansen was in a class of her own and quite unstoppable, setting new targets for female runners. In July, she improved on her own world 10,000m record by nearly forty-six seconds, again in Oslo, with 30:13.74. A month later she regained the 5000m world record in Stockholm with 14:37.33. She also finally won a gold medal when she took the inaugural European women's 10,000m track title held in Stuttgart in just over half a minute with 30:23.25.

Ingrid has shown that Norway has more than one great woman athlete capable of overcoming the difficult climate and lack of tradition, and she has convinced many women (particularly mothers) that there is still room for hope and ambition in the sporting field after starting a family.

Ingrid's maiden name was Christensen, and she was born in Trondheim, on the northwest coast of Norway, on 21 March 1956.

L

Lactic acid

Lactic acid is produced by the muscles when you are trying to run too fast for too long, and is the cause of the severe muscular pain and fatigue felt particularly in races lasting 1–2 minutes. When the body is demanding energy at a more intense rate than it can convert sufficient oxygen, notably in events like the 400 and 800 metres, the lactic acid system (known as anaerobic glycolysis) comes into action.

The whole process takes place within the muscle, where glycogen is converted into pyruvic acid. When, in the absence of oxygen, this is joined with hydrogen, energy is produced through the breakdown of the glycogen, in the process known as glycolysis. But a significant by-product of this is lactic acid, which accumulates in the muscles and inhibits their normal contraction.

Eventually, however hard the runner is trying, he has to slow down, as in the final straight of a 400-metre race, where the runner is often said to be 'treading water' or even 'drowning in a sea of lactic acid!'. Certainly, there is a lot of accuracy in the saying that the winner of the 400 metres is not the runner who finishes fastest, but rather the one who slows down the least.

For the body can only continue this form of energy production without oxygen (that is, anaerobically) for a limited period, enduring what is known as 'oxygen debt', before the lactic acid levels rise to a point where the muscles can no longer work properly. When the 400-metre runner has finished, he has to stop and gasp in vast amounts of oxygen to repay that debt, and allow the lactic acid to be washed from his muscles by freshly oxygenated blood.

Afterwards, the removal of the remaining lactic acid can be accelerated by light aerobic exercise, such as a warm-down jog. But to take no further exercise after a hard racing effort extends the time needed for lactic acid removal, and if it is not properly cleared away muscle stiffness may result.

The longer the event, the less that lactic acid is likely to play a part in performance, although even in a 10,000m track race an athlete who starts his final sprint too soon may also suffer from its effects and possibly lose a race he might otherwise have won.

For 400- and 800-metre runners, regular training at speeds and distances which create lactic acid will help to improve the body's tolerance of the pain and ability to break down the lactic acid more efficiently. Because of its physical discomfort, it is an area of training from which athletes tend to shy away; but it is an essential part of preparation for competitive improvement.

Lebow, Fred

Fred Lebowitz helped build the New York City Marathon from its modest start in 1970 to a position as the world's largest and most innovative within a decade. As its race director, and as president since 1972 of the promoting body, the New York Road Runners Club, he has been a particularly visible figurehead.

Lebow was born in Arad, Western Rumania, on 6 March 1932, into an orthodox Jewish family. After the war, when life under the Russian liberators began to get hard, he escaped from the country with his brother in 1947 and worked his way round post-war Europe. In 1951 he decided to move to the USA, where a scholarship to a Talmudic academy in Brooklyn earned him entry as a student. He changed his name to Lebow to obtain a work permit, and some years later that name change became legalized when he was granted US citizenship.

After working in the textile industry in New York, he started jogging in 1968, at the age of 36, simply to get fit for his only other sporting interest, tennis. But the attraction of running soon developed into a compulsion, and he joined the New York branch of the Road Runners Club of America (which later became the New York Road Runners Club).

Although displaying no great talent as a runner, and finishing next to last in his first race, his long-term experience as a salesman, entrepreneur (and, some would say, wheeler-dealer) helped him in later promoting the New York Marathon, obtaining world-class runners, enlarging the field, and producing a sporting spectacle which lent itself to worldwide television coverage. He was also instrumental in obtaining the 1984 World Cross-country Championships for New York, and developing the Fifth Avenue Mile, which brought some of the top middle-distance runners in the world to race a straight mile down elegant Fifth Avenue.

Fred Lebow, the much-travelled President of the New York Road Runners Club and founder of the New York City Marathon

Not without his critics and enemies, Lebow has nevertheless been one of the small band of promoters who at one point sailed dangerously close to the wind in their interpretation of the rules regarding legitimate payments to athletes. But in doing so he helped nudge the IAAF out of its lethargy and thus helped to bring about changes more in keeping with the current sporting climate. He has run sixty-six marathons himself, with a best of 3:29.18.

See also *New York City Marathon*.

Ligaments

Ligaments are strong bands of white fibrous tissue which hold together the two bones in a joint, preventing them from dislocating, but which may themselves be strained by a sudden unaccustomed movement. The ligaments in the foot, ankle or knee, for example, may be damaged by stepping in a hidden rut while on a training run. Rest is the best self-treatment, with the application of ice in the first twenty-four hours to help restrict the damage. Ligaments can also be strained in over-use injuries, where again rest, together with a change of activity (and possibly footwear) can help recovery. Physiotherapy and, in extreme cases, injections may also be needed to promote healing.

London Marathon

Without doubt the London Marathon has been a major contributory factor to the British running boom of the eighties. From its first year in 1981 it caught the public imagination, particularly after the graphic BBC Television coverage which caught both the dramatic and the humorous as well as conveying the unique atmosphere. Soon many thousands of non-runners were getting into training in the hope of participating in the following year's race, and it spawned a marathon mania which, at its peak in 1983, saw 130 marathons staged in the UK.

Subsequently there was a levelling off, as the newly converted runners realized that shorter events, like 10km and the half-marathon, could offer their own satisfaction and were less demanding. But demand for a place in the London Marathon itself did not subside, and there were still some 86,000 applications for the record 27,500 places on offer for the 1987 race.

The London Marathon was the brainchild of Chris Brasher, the 1956 Olympic steeplechase gold medallist and later the athletics correspondent of the *Observer*. In October 1979 he had made his own marathon debut in the New York City Marathon, and was overwhelmed by the way in which such an event could unite a notoriously volatile city and its population for at least one day of the year, and he suggested a similar event should be held in London.

At that time a marathon was already planned for central London in August 1980, the Avon Women's International Marathon, which began in Battersea Park and finished at the Guildhall. It was aimed at highlighting the lack of a marathon for women in the Olympic

Games, which would finish the day before in Moscow. The Avon race was successful in its own way, but no follow-up was planned for London.

So Brasher, and his business partner and former Olympic teammate John Disley (1952 Olympic steeplechase bronze medallist), began to set the wheels in motion. A board of governors for a projected London Marathon was established, and a sponsor, Gillette, came forward with £50,000. In October 1980 a 'shadowing party' of eight officials travelled to the New York Marathon to watch in detail how the event was organized behind the scenes, and the inaugural London Marathon was set for Sunday 29 March 1981.

For a proposed limit of 8000 runners, no less than 20,000 applications were received, and the numbers had to be judiciously pruned down, as they have been every year since.

The race route, developed and measured by John Disley, has remained largely unchanged. From its start on Blackheath, it passes the famous clipper Cutty Sark at Greenwich ($6\frac{1}{2}$ miles), crosses Tower Bridge northwards ($12\frac{1}{2}$ miles), then loops the Isle of Dogs to pass under Tower Bridge (22 miles) and on towards the Victoria Embankment. The runners then head up the Mall towards Buckingham Palace, and in 1981 the history-making deliberate dead-heat finish between American Dick Beardsley and Norwegian Inge Simonsen actually took place on Constitution Hill, alongside Buckingham Palace. But from 1982 onwards the runners turned left instead at Buckingham Palace, to finish on Westminster Bridge, with Big Ben in the background.

The course is flat and fast, as the women's world bests set by Grete Waitz in 1983 and Ingrid Kristiansen in 1985 indicate, and it has been painstakingly measured as accurate. Only the relatively short stretch of cobblestones alongside the Tower of London in the last four miles could be described as a less than ideal running surface, but it does add to the tradition of the race for the thousands and thousands of runners for whom a couple of seconds lost there is of minor importance.

Competitors in the London Marathon seen from the top of Tower Bridge as they approach the halfway point in the race

London Marathon

The race was sponsored by Gillette from 1981–83, and by Mars since 1984. Its growth and quality are indicated by the following statistics related to the total entry accepted by the organizers (the actual applications are much higher), and the winning times.

Year	Entry	Starters	Finishers	Men's winner	Women's winner
1981	7747	7055	6418	Dick Beardsley (US) tied with Inge Simonsen (Nor) 2:11.48	Joyce Smith (UK) 2:29.57
1982	18,059	16,350	15,758	Hugh Jones (UK) 2:09.24	Joyce Smith (UK) 2:29.43
1983	19,735	16,500	15,776	Mike Gratton (UK) 2:09.43	Grete Waitz (Nor) 2:25.29
1984	21,142	16,992	15,649	Charlie Spedding (UK) 2:09.57	Ingrid Kristiansen (Nor) 2:24.26
1985	22,274	17,500	15,840	Steve Jones (UK) 2:08.16	Ingrid Kristiansen (Nor) 2:21.06
1986	25,300	19,261	18,175	Toshihiko Seko (Jap) 2:10.02	Grete Waitz (Nor) 2:24.54
1987	28,364	21,485	19,545	Hiromi Taniguchi (Jap) 2:09.50	Ingrid Kristiansen (Nor) 2:22.48

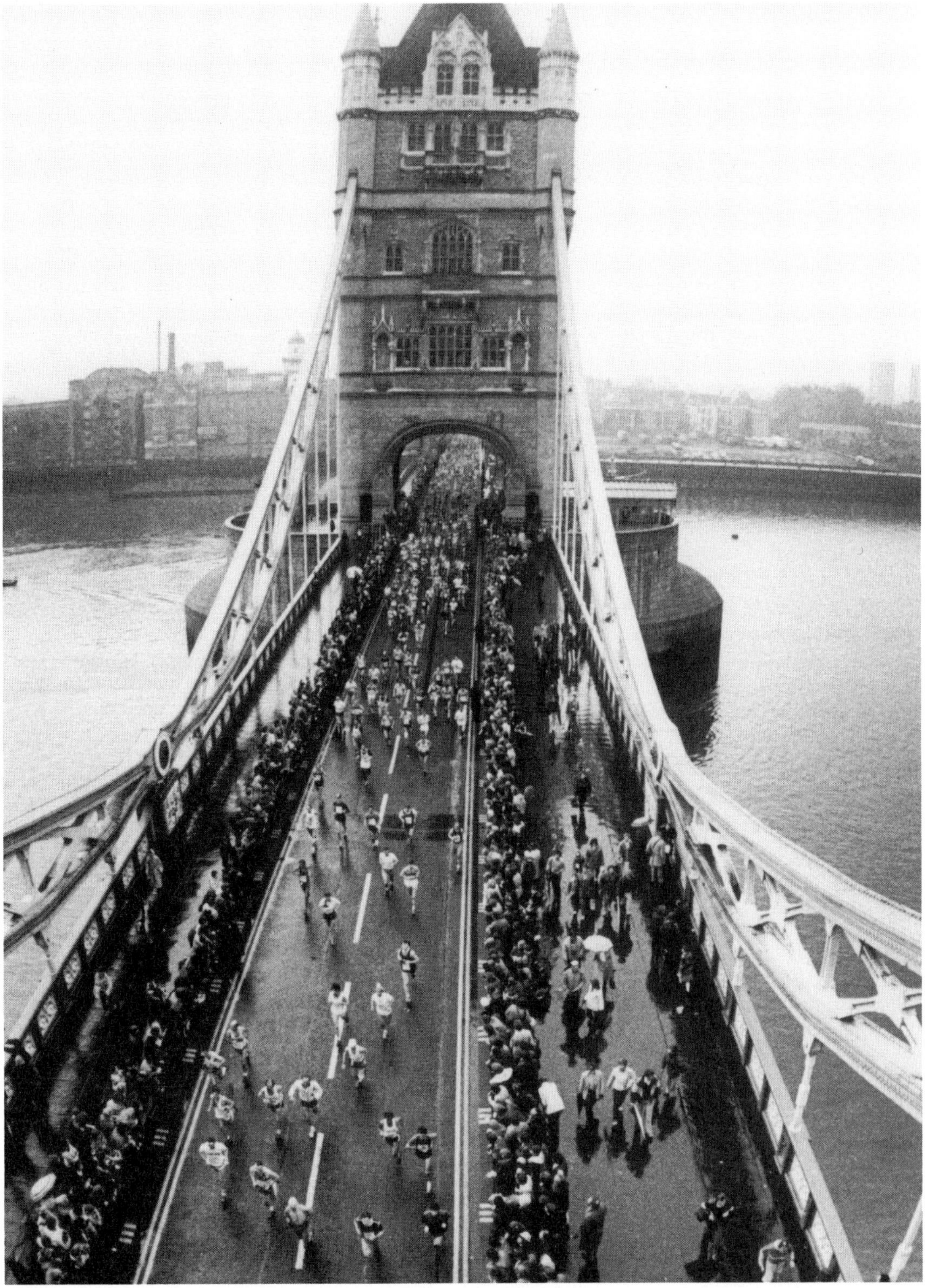

LSD (Long Slow Distance)

The term LSD has become, in the past decade or so, the popular name for the most comfortable form of running which, despite its simplicity, has a particular importance for all runners however seriously they view the sport.

The initials stand for Long Slow Distance, and were first used in this context by the American runner and author Joe Henderson, who published a book entitled *Long Slow Distance – The Humane Way to Train* in 1969. In the book, Henderson, a long-time competitor of self-admitted modest ability, turned runners back to an aerobic way of training at a time when a surfeit of emphasis on interval training and phrases like 'no gain without pain' were burying the more enjoyable side of running.

He later admitted that with hindsight he would have left the word 'train' out of the original title because it was misconstrued by some people who assumed he was recommending LSD as the best way to train for racing. He admitted it was not, and that speed-work was still essential for racing improvement, but that LSD in itself could be enjoyed.

LSD means running at an aerobic pace; that is at a speed which only raises the pulse to around 130 beats per minute and does not leave the runner gasping for breath. By continuing the run for a substantial time, it is possible to build up a considerable base of stamina and improve the cardiovascular system to the point where the pace of the comfortable running actually becomes faster over weeks and months without any conscious effort or noticeable raising of the steady pulse rate.

For some runners, a continuous pursuit of this type of running makes them fit enough to be able to participate in long-distance races, including marathons, without the use of any other sort of training. The mental relaxation and the physical exertion of being pleasantly tired but not in discomfort are sufficient in themselves.

At a more modest level than Henderson was originally preaching, jogging picked up enormous popularity in the seventies, using the same principles. And there is really no dividing line between jogging and running; running is simply jogging faster!

For the more ambitious runner, other forms of training, such as interval training and fartlek, are needed to supplement LSD and to push the pulse rate up beyond 180 beats a minute. But before such exercises can be undertaken, even the greatest Olympic champion has to undergo a substantial period of LSD-type running, and all year round it is likely to remain a significant part of their weekly training. For the champion needs an input of steady running to offset the mental and physical toll of hard, fast running. The body needs to be used gently in between spells of the type of temporary discomfort necessary to improve racing performance.

Trying to find the correct formula is what keeps coaches and runners forever experimenting, but there is no single universal answer. Each runner has their own, if they can but find it. A move towards high volumes of LSD for track runners in the early seventies (with some athletes covering as much as 200 miles in a week) has fortunately been reversed following the inevitably high proportion of over-use injuries. Now even the hardest-training track runners rarely cover more than 100–120 miles at the peak of their winter build-up, preferring instead to try to find a more even balance between quantity and quality. And, as a way of reducing still further the over-use injuries (which are caused by sheer repetition of the running action), many runners are now substituting several sessions a week of steady-state cycling or swimming for running. By raising their pulse rate to a similar level to LSD, around 130 beats per minute, on a stationary bike or by swimming lengths of the pool, they can retain cardiovascular fitness without subjecting their bodies to quite as much shock-absorption as in running.

The most important aspect of LSD running is the discovery (or rediscovery) for many people that running need not be a flat-out, gut-busting effort, despite what their PE teachers may have tried to make them believe at school.

Lungs

The lungs are the organs which provide the facility for fresh oxygen to be absorbed into the blood and the unwanted carbon dioxide, created by energy production, to be sent back out of the body through expiration.

They are situated in the chest area, light and spongy in texture, and are worked by the bellows-like action of the chest and the diaphragm muscles together. When breathing in (inspiration), the lungs expand to their maximum volume as air is taken in through the nose and mouth, and down the windpipe (the trachea). This divides at the breastbone into the left and right lungs, and then sub-divides again within the lungs themselves into branches known as bronchioles.

The bronchioles again divide, terminating in numerous air sacs, known as alveoli, which form in clusters and resemble tiny bunches of grapes. There are some 300 million alveoli in an adult pair of lungs, and each is covered with a network of blood capillaries which come from the pulmonary artery (bringing with them used blood cells high in carbon dioxide for expulsion from the body) and then return to the pulmonary vein, taking back blood cells which have been replenished with fresh oxygen.

This 'exchange' of old for new takes place in the capillary bed, through the very thin membrane which lines the alveoli, after which the oxygen-rich red cells are whisked off to the muscles to help in the creation of more energy.

When breathing out (expiration), the lungs are squeezed by the action of the lowering chest and the raising of the diaphragm muscles, and so the carbon dioxide is forcibly exhaled.

In normal, quiet breathing, this process occurs around 12–15 times a minute, and each such gentle subconscious breath draws in approximately half a litre of air. But the maximum volume of the lungs, known as the vital capacity, can be measured on a special device known as a spirometer, into which the subject exhales as completely as possible after taking one very deep breath.

Although age, sex and pulmonary condition naturally have to be taken into account when evaluating the readings, the volume is generally in the range of 3.5 to 6 litres for an adult male, with distance runners tending towards the higher level. Females may record nearer to 4–4.5 litres.

When running, the breathing rate increases quite considerably, usually up to fifty times a minute, as the need for oxygen in the muscles becomes much greater. Training helps this process to improve by increasing lung efficiency, particularly in the area of exchange of carbon dioxide and oxygen at the alveolar wall of the lungs. A single red cell may be in contact with the wall for as little as 0.3 sec., yet still be almost completely saturated with oxygen. Particularly in middle-distance events this efficiency can be crucial, as the muscles cry out for more oxygen, and the value of training sessions which simulate this situation and thus help the body adapt to it in preparation for a race can be realized.

See also *Blood, Breathing, Heart, Oxygen*.

Lydiard, Arthur

Although a great many coaches can be said to have influenced distance running training in the past 25 years, few have had as wide an influence as the New Zealand coach Arthur Lydiard. A former national marathon champion (and 13th in the 1950 British Empire Games marathon), Lydiard first came to world prominence as a coach in 1960 when three of his athletes won medals in the Rome Olympics: Peter Snell, a surprise winner of the 800m; Murray Halberg, the 5000m champion; and Barry Magee, the marathon bronze medallist. Snell in particular went on to even greater things, setting world records at the 800m, 880 yards, 1000m and mile, and won the Olympic 800 and 1500m titles in 1964.

Lydiard, born in Auckland on 6 July 1917, became associated with a training regime of 100 miles a week, which was in fact only one part of his schedule. He believed that this amount of steady running was necessary as a stamina base, even for 800m runners, to enable them to

Peter Snell (466), whom Arthur Lydiard coached to three Olympic titles

reproduce their full natural speed in races. But whereas the subsequent sections of his training routines, outlined initially in his 1962 book *Run to the Top*, went on to advocate hill training and interval training in the usual way, some runners mistakenly tried to run fast 800m races on nothing but 100 miles a week of steady running and then wondered why it did not work for them.

Later in professional demand by countries like Finland, where he first went in 1966, Mexico and Denmark, he has had a lasting influence on the training ideas of most of today's leading coaches. He was also one of the earliest advocates of jogging for the sake of health, and his influence on the American coach Bill Bowerman, who visited New Zealand in 1963, helped to transport the jogging phenomenon to the USA.

See also *Bill Bowerman*.

M

Marathon

The longest running race on the standard international programme, the marathon of 26 miles 385 yards (42.195km) has evolved over almost a century from an event with an almost frightening aura into one which, although still extremely arduous, is within the eventual reach

---

The 1908 Olympic Marathon from Windsor to White City gave the event its classic 26 miles 385 yards distance

From an event for elite runners only to a mass participation run the marathon has, in many senses, come a long way

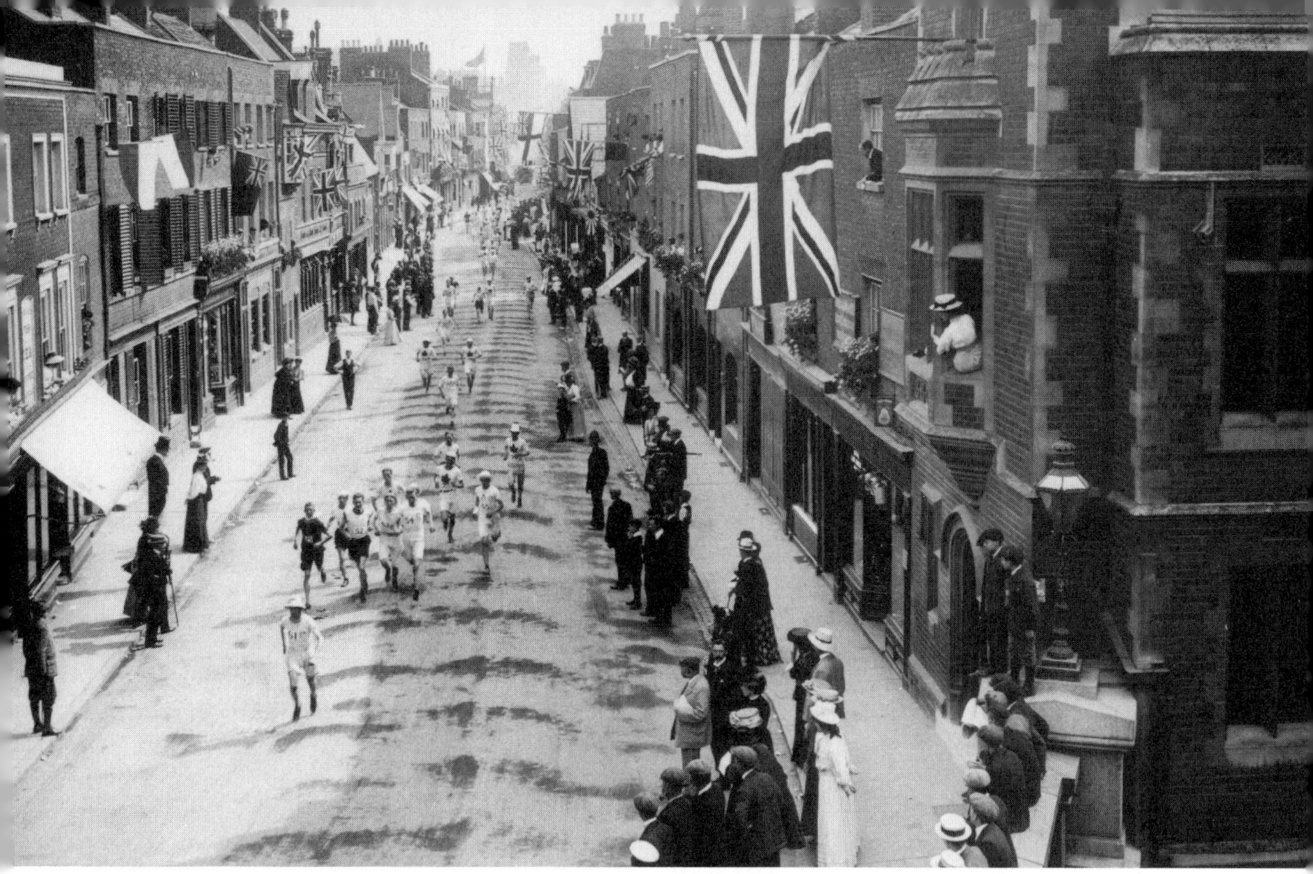

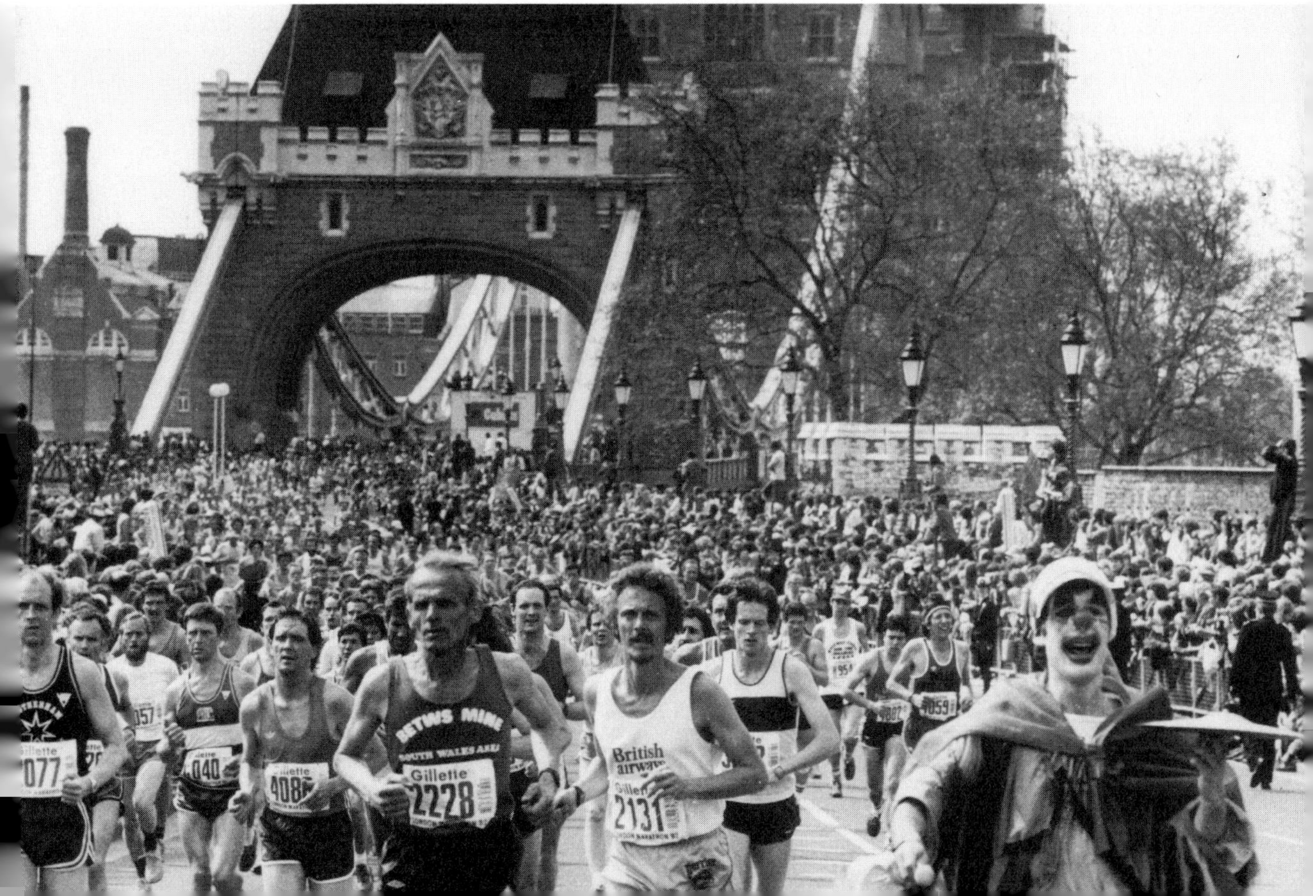
BETWS MINE
SOUTH WALES AAU
Gillette
2228
British
2131

of most dedicated, even if not necessarily talented, runners. The huge fields at mass races like the London and New York marathons are packed with first-timers who simply want to get round the course, even if it takes them four or five hours, around twice the time of the fastest runners.

Marathons like New York and London and their many imitators allowed the opportunity for the slower runner to tackle the distance for, until the mid-seventies, there were very few chances for runners expecting a time outside three and a half hours to take part in a marathon. It was still such an 'elite' area that the officials would previously not have expected any participants slower than that worthy level. But the marathon boom has helped re-define the event as simply a very long road run.

The origins actually only stretch back to the end of the nineteenth century, although its spirit goes much further. It commemorates a run reputed to have been made in 490BC by an Athenian messenger named Pheidippides from the village of Marathon (some twenty-three and a half miles northeast of Athens). The Athenians had defeated the Persians in a great battle there, and according to legend Pheidippides ran back to Athens with news of the victory. Gasping out 'Rejoice, we conquer!' he then reputedly fell dead before the city elders.

There is still a great deal of doubt over whether this incident ever took place, or whether it was just the use of dramatic licence by subsequent historians, like the Roman Plutarch nearly six hundred years later. But the Greeks certainly used the trained runner, or *hemerodromoi*, to convey urgent messages.

In 1894, when the Frenchman Baron Pierre de Coubertin was making preparations for the inaugural modern Olympic Games (staged in Athens two years later), he received a suggestion from a historian and linguist at the Sorbonne, Michel Breal, that the new Games should include some form of endurance race along the route allegedly taken by Pheidippides, as a way of further reflecting Greek history. The idea was taken up, and provided the highlight of those first Games when, on 10 April 1896, a Greek shepherd, Spiridon Louis, gave the host nation its only victory, covering a course of just under twenty-five miles in 2hr 58min 50sec.

The event rapidly caught the public imagination, and later in 1896 marathon races were staged from Paris to Conflans in France, and from Stamford to New York in the USA. Most of the US competitors in the Athens Olympics had been members of the Boston Athletic Association, and in 1897 they persuaded the Association to stage a marathon in the city. So the first Boston Marathon was held on 19 April 1897, and it remains the world's oldest annual marathon.

The curious distance, now universally recognized at 26 miles 385 yards, dates back to the 1908 Olympics held in London. The marathon course began at Windsor Castle and finished at White City Stadium, West London. To allow the children of the Royal Family to watch the start, it was staged in the private grounds of the Castle and the distance from there to the finish opposite Queen Alexandra's royal box in the Stadium was measured at 26 miles 385 yards. There was still no standard distance for the event, and the 1912 and 1920 Olympic marathons were held on courses of slightly different length. But in 1921 the International Amateur Athletic Federation decided to standardize the marathon distance for Olympic Games at 26 miles 385 yards, as from the 1924 Games. Eventually all other marathons came into line.

It took a lot longer for the event to be considered suitable for women, even though the first recorded instances of unofficial female participation go back as far as the race itself, when two Greek women are recorded as having covered the tough Marathon to Athens route in 1896. In March of that year, Stamatia Rovithi, a 35-year-old mother of seven children, did so in five and a half hours, while a girl named Melpomene is said to have joined in the inaugural Olympic race, covering it in four and a half hours.

There are further isolated instances, but in the sixties more women runners began gatecrashing men's marathons to show that they, too, could run that far. In 1972 women were officially allowed to compete in the Boston Marathon, and in 1974 an international all-women's marathon was staged in Waldniel, West Germany. Medical reports indicated that there was no specific risk in women racing that far (indeed, some experts contended that with their greater fat reserves, women were actually more suitably equipped for endurance events than men). By 1980, the Norwegian runner Grete Waitz had lowered the women's world best to 2hr 25min 41sec, and there could be no further argument. From 1982, and the European Championships (in, appropriately, Athens), the women's marathon was added to the programme of all major international games including, from 1984, the Olympics.

Massage

Although massage seemed to go out of fashion for some time, its value has been rediscovered in recent years by most of the world's leading distance runners as a means of speeding up recovery between training sessions and reducing their chances of overuse injury.

Properly applied, massage restores the state of the muscle tissues, improves the blood supply and helps relieve the type of muscular tightness which, if trained on, can lead to injury. It can be particularly helpful following a physically exhausting session, such as a very long run, a hard interval session or a race, where the muscles have been worked to the limit.

Injury treatment by massage is best left to experienced and qualified masseurs, who are finding a growing call for such attention among runners, dancers and exponents of other demanding physical activities. But as a therapeutic aid to training it is possible for a friend

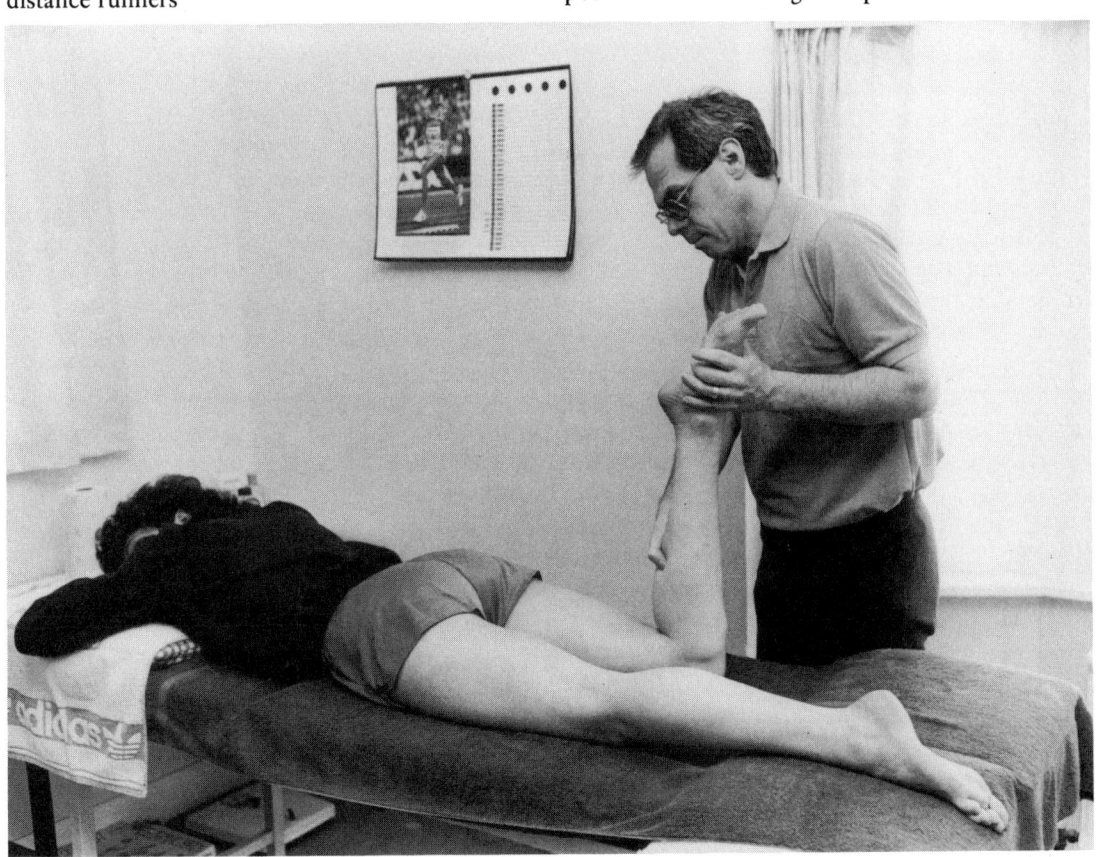

As a form of assisting recovery and preventing injury, massage is increasingly employed to help distance runners

or relative to provide a simple, relaxing massage. The basic essential is always to massage towards the heart, using fairly slow, deep pressure. To make it easier a lubricant, such as baby oil, massage cream or even talcum powder, should be lightly spread on the masseur's hands first while the runner should lay on a firm surface which has been covered with a towel.

Fortunately, some of the less agreeable associations which had become attached to the very word *massage* have faded, and it has been restored to its rightful place as a highly beneficial accessory to the rigours of modern running training.

Advice on obtaining professional treatment from a masseur experienced in treating sportsmen can be obtained from The British College of Neuropathy and Osteopathy, 6 Netherall Gardens, London NW3 (01-435 7830) or the British School of Osteopathy, 1-4 Suffolk St, London SW1 (01-930 4640).

See also *Cramp, Rest, Restless Leg Syndrome*.

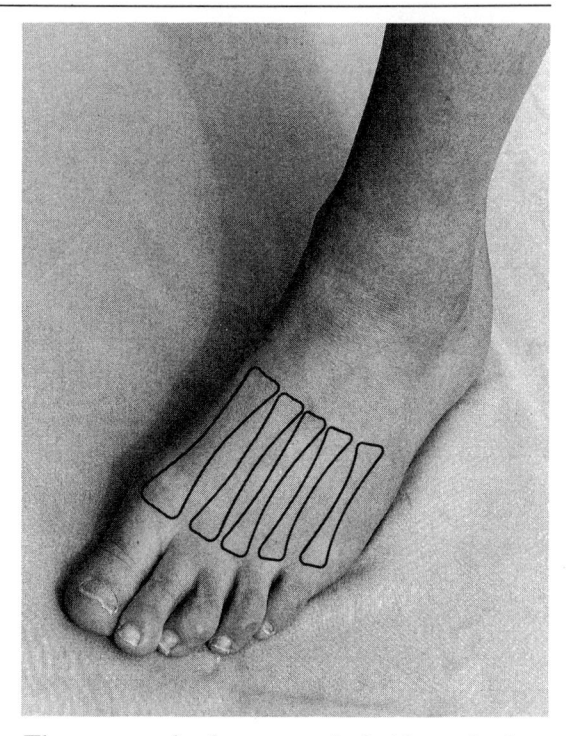

The metatarsals, the narrow-shafted bones in the forefoot, are particularly vulnerable to stress fracture from overuse

Metatarsals

The five long, narrow-shafted bones in each foot, located between the midfoot and the phalanges (toe bones), are called the metatarsals. Because of their shape, they are particularly vulnerable to stress fracture in runners who increase their training load too quickly. Army recruits who suddenly find themselves on unaccustomed long marches in heavy boots are similarly prone to metatarsal stress fractures, which have consequently become known as 'march fractures'.

Individually, the metatarsals are numbered from first to fifth, working outwards from the big toe to the little toe, but the first metatarsal has a considerably greater diameter than the other four because of its weight-bearing functions, and is thus less liable to a stress fracture. The middle three are more usually affected, with a sharp pain midway along the shaft of the metatarsal, often accompanied by some localized swelling, a warning sign.

General pain in this area may also be due to metatarsalgia, causing pain under the ball of the foot, where the ligaments supporting the metatarsal heads may have become strained, possibly through running in shoes with insufficiently thick soles.

A more specific, but sporadic, pain may be caused by two of the metatarsal heads rubbing together and squeezing the nerve which lies between them and which may occasionally become slightly swollen. A pad under the metatarsals involved may relieve the condition.

See also *Foot, Stress Fracture*.

New York City Marathon

Although it was to become the world's biggest marathon, and blueprint for many other city-centre races (including the London Marathon), the New York Marathon had a modest start. It was created by Fred Lebow, a Rumanian refugee working in New York. He put up the idea of a New York Marathon in 1970 and the first race, on 13 September of that year, attracted just 127 entrants, who ran a five-lap course around the city's Central Park. New York fireman Gary Muhrcke won that first race in 2hr 31min 39sec, with Lebow finishing forty-fifth of the fifty-five finishers in 4hr 12min 9sec. Lebow himself was to play a crucial role in the race's development.

It became an annual event, and although the entries increased each year until they were over five hundred in 1975, it was only when the present course, which passes through each of the city's five boroughs, was used for the first time in the bi-centennial year of 1976 that the race really took off. The entry that year topped 2000, and within four years it was over 11,500. Soon it was surpassing 14,000, with many thousands more disappointed as the entry limit precluded them.

The dramatic start of the New York City Marathon on the Verrazano Bridge, completely taken over by the runners

Its distinctive route, with the spectacular start on the Verrazano Bridge, and its tour through the city's varied and cosmopolitan districts, from Harlem to Fifth Avenue, gave the race a character of its own. With its halfway point on the slope of the Pulaski Bridge, and its final three miles run inside Central Park, the New York Marathon demonstrated how a marathon could show off a city to the world, be a great sporting spectacle in itself, and at the same time unite, at least temporarily, so many different communities.

New York City Marathon

The race was held within Central Park from 1970–75, but from 1976 it has used the current course from the Verrazano Bridge, which links Staten Island with Brooklyn, to the finish at the Tavern on the Green, the smart restaurant in Central Park.

Year	Entry	Starters	Finishers	Men's winner	Women's winner
1970	127	127	55	Gary Muhrcke (US) 2:31.39	
1971	246	246	168	Norm Higgins (US) 2:22.55	Beth Bonner (US) 2:55.22
1972	284	284	187	Sheldon Karlin (US) 2:27.53	Nina Kuscsik (US) 3:08.42
1973	406	406	282	Tom Fleming (US) 2:21.55	Nina Kuscsik (US) 2:57.08
1974	527	527	278	Norbert Sander (US) 2:26.31	Kathy Switzer (US) 3:07.29
1975	534	534	339	Tom Fleming (US) 2:19.27	Kim Merritt (US) 2:46.15
1976	2090	2090	1549	Bill Rodgers (US) 2:10.10	Miki Gorman (US) 2:39.11
1977	4823	4823	3885	Bill Rodgers (US) 2:11.29	Miki Gorman (US) 2:43.10
1978	11,142	9875	8588	Bill Rodgers (US) 2:12.12	Grete Waitz (Nor) 2:32.30
1979	13,210	11,533	10,477	Bill Rodgers (US) 2:11.42	Grete Waitz (Nor) 2:27.33
1980	16,005	14,012	12,512	Alberto Salazar (US) 2:09.41	Grete Waitz (Nor) 2:25.41
1981	15,816	14,496	13,233	Alberto Salazar (US) 2:08.13	Allison Roe (NZ) 2:25.29
1982	15,906	14,308	13,599	Alberto Salazar (US) 2:09.29	Grete Waitz (Nor) 2:27.14
1983	16,988	15,193	14,546	Rod Dixon (NZ) 2:08.59	Grete Waitz (Nor) 2:27.00
1984	18,376	16,315	14,590	Orlando Pizzolato (Ita) 2:14.53	Grete Waitz (Nor) 2:29.30
1985	19,230	16,705	15,881	Orlando Pizzolato (Ita) 2:11.34	Grete Waitz (Nor) 2:28.34
1986	23,898	20,502	19,689	Gianni Poli (Ita) 2:11.06	Grete Waitz (Nor) 2:28.06

The tremendous rapport between the runners and the spectators made it a particularly vivid experience for the participants, and when world records were broken on the far-from-ideal potholed course it gave the event yet another dimension. Grete Waitz was totally unknown in the USA when she set her first world mark of 2hr 32min 30sec in 1978, but in setting two more records in succeeding years she quickly became synonomous with the event. The race's greatest day may have been in October 1981 when first American Alberto Salazar (2hr 8min 13sec) and then New Zealander Allison Roe (2hr 25min 29sec) apparently set world bests in the same race. But subsequent checking of the course showed that it had been measured one metre from the kerb, instead of along the shortest line the runners could take. It was estimated that it would have been possible to have run 250 metres under the marathon distance by taking the shortest route on bends, and consequently the performances by Salazar and Roe were removed from the record books.

In more recent years the New York race has perhaps been somewhat overshadowed in terms of quality by its great rival, the Chicago Marathon. But there can be no doubting the place the Big Apple deserves in running history as the first event to popularize the mass participation marathon, where the 6hr 8min jogger was as welcome as the 2hr 8min star.

See also *Lebow, Fred*.

Night running

Most runners have to undertake at least part of their training at night, and in winter this can particularly pose some hazards. Even a runner on the pavement has to cross roads from time to time, and the suddenness of a figure running out from behind a car, even if the runner knows they have time to cross, can cause an accident.

A runner training around the roads will automatically expect to see traffic, and will adjust accordingly. But drivers will rarely be on the lookout for runners. Thus the runner has to advertise his presence as vividly as possible to catch the driver's attention.

Some training shoes now have reflective material on the heels, and tracksuits and rainsuits can be purchased with reflective strips which show up clearly when caught by car headlights, like the cat's eyes in the centre of the road. Reflective belts, of the type worn by motor cyclists and pedal cyclists for similar reasons, can be used without causing the runner any undue discomfort, and there are reflective mesh 'bibs' which can be worn over the runner's choice of training gear. Heavy orange or yellow jackets of the type worn by road or rail maintenance workers have excellent visibility, but in practical terms usually make the runner too hot while running.

In the absence of reflective patches, an outer layer of clothing which is as light coloured as possible, even if it means pulling a white T-shirt over a tracksuit top, aids safety.

The worst type of clothing to wear while training at night is a black, blue or navy blue tracksuit, which renders the runner virtually invisible to traffic. He should wherever possible run on the pavement, not the road, and always facing oncoming traffic.

Nurmi, Paavo

Of the many great Finnish runners this century, Paavo Johannes Nurmi, born in Turku on 13 June 1897, remains on a level of his own. Between 1920 and 1928 he won nine Olympic gold medals (six individual and three team), plus three silver medals, and between 1921 and 1931 he set no less than twenty world records at distances ranging from 1500m to 20km.

Nicknamed the Flying Finn, Nurmi won his first three Olympic golds at the 1920 Games in Antwerp. In the 10,000m he beat France's Joseph Guillemot (who three days earlier had beaten him for the 5000m title), then went on to win team and individual golds in the cross country event.

In the 1924 Olympics in Paris (the 'Chariots of Fire' Games), Nurmi had what could be described as his finest hour, winning the 1500m gold medal in 3:53.6, and just 60 minutes later

Track progress

Born 13 June 1897.

	1500m	3000m	5000m	10,000m
1914	—	10:06.9	—	—
1915	4:37.4	9:30.6	15:57.4	—
1916	—	—	15:52.8	34:35.0
1917	—	9:47.8	15:47.4	—
1918	4:29.2	10:10.2	15:50.7	—
1919	4:23.0	8:58.1	15:31.5	32:56.0
1920	4:05.5	8:36.2	15:00.0	31:45.8
1921	—	—	14:53.8	30:40.2
1922	3:59.8	8:28.6	14:35.3	—
1923	3:53.0	8:27.8	14:39.9	—
1924	3:52.6	8:32.0	14:28.2	30:06.1
1925	3:56.2i	8:26.8i	14:38.0i	30:40.2
1926	3:52.8	8:20.4	14:34.0	31:12.2
1927	3:59.5	8:31.4	14:54.4	—
1928	3:57.3	8:29.6	14:40.5	30:18.8
1929	—	8:38.5i	14:55.4	—
1930	4:03.0	8:35.0	14:40.7	31:04.6
1931	—	8:24.4	14:47.6	30:50.6
1932	—	—	—	30:40.9
1933	3:55.8	8:27.5	14:46.6	31:33.0
1934	—	8:55.4	15:12.0	31:39.2

also taking the 5000m title, after a desperately close race with his Finnish teammate Ville Ritola. Nurmi won by one-fifth of a second in 14:31.4, then several days later took further gold medals in the cross-country event and the 3000m team race (both events subsequently dropped from the Olympic programme).

In 1928, at the Amsterdam Olympics, Nurmi beat Ritola again, this time over 10,000m, but subsequently lost to him in the 5000m. But his domination of world distance running was otherwise immense. Between 1926 and 1931 he lost only three important races. He also became renowned for running while holding a stopwatch, which he constantly consulted.

Of his world records, his performances on 19 June 1924 in Helsinki were probably the most notable. In virtually a rehearsal of the Olympic timetable, Nurmi set a world 1500m record of 3:52.6, then just an hour later ran 5000m in 14:28.2, another world record.

His international career ended under a cloud, unfortunately, when on the eve of the 1932 Olympic Games in Los Angeles, where Nurmi was hoping to win the marathon in his final appearance, he was declared ineligible for the Games because of professionalism. However, he competed for another two years in Finland as a 'national amateur', even winning the 1933 Finnish 1500m title at the age of 36.

It was an emotional moment, then, when the mystery figure who ran into the Helsinki Olympic Stadium with the flaming torch at the Opening Ceremony of the 1952 Olympic Games, was seen to be none other than Finland's former hero, Nurmi himself, aged 55.

A statue of Nurmi stands now outside the Helsinki Olympic Stadium, honouring the greatest of their many national champions. He died on 2 October 1973, at the age of 76.

Orthotics

An orthotic is a specially shaped insert worn in the runner's shoe to correct an abnormality in foot motion which in turn may have been the root cause of an injury in the leg, knee, hip or lower back. The orthotic is usually made of a rigid material, like fibreglass or steel, which will firmly resist abnormal movement in the foot, restoring it to a mechanically correct action, with the intention of removing the cause of the injury elsewhere.

But because everyone's feet and their movements are intricately different, the most effective form of orthotic is one which has been custom-made for the runner from a specially taken plaster cast of the foot, in conjunction

Two examples of orthotics: on the left a ready-made, but adjustable, orthotic, and on the right a custom-made plastic orthotic

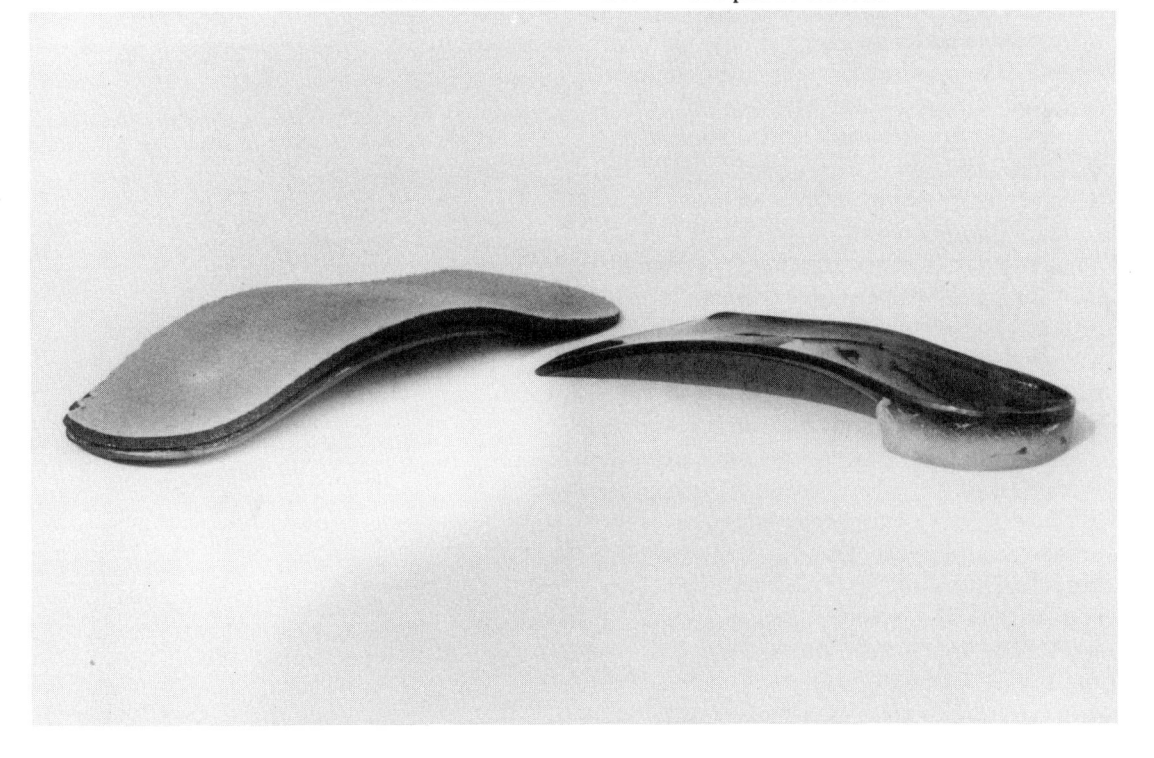

Paavo Nurmi's 20 World Records

Date	Event	Time	Location
22 Jun 1921	10,000m	30:40.2	Stockholm
27 Aug 1922	3000m	8:28.6	Turku
4 Sep 1922	2000m	5:26.3	Tampere
12 Sept 1922	5000m	14:35.4	Stockholm
23 Aug 1923	Mile	4:10.4	Stockholm
24 Aug 1923	3 miles*	14:11.2	Stockholm
19 Jun 1924	1500m	3:52.6	Helsinki
19 Jun 1924	5000m	14:28.2	Helsinki
31 Aug 1924	10,000m	30:06.2	Kuopio
1 Oct 1924	4 miles*	19:15.4	Viipuri
1 Oct 1924	5 miles*	24:06.2	Viipuri
24 May 1926	3000m	8:25.4	Berlin
13 Jul 1926	3000m	8:20.4	Stockholm
18 Jun 1927	2000m	5:24.6	Kuopio
7 Oct 1928	15,000m*	46:49.6	Berlin
7 Oct 1928	10 miles*	50:15.0	Berlin
7 Oct 1928	1 hour run	19,210m	Berlin
8 Jun 1930	6 miles*	29:36.4	London
3 Sept 1930	20,000m	64:38.4	Stockholm
24 Jul 1931	2 miles*	8:59.6	Helsinki

*Event no longer recognized for world records by IAAF.

with careful measurements of the foot and observation of the running action by a foot specialist, who is usually known as a podiatrist.

From this plaster cast, which is sent to a company specializing in the production of orthotics, the corrective insert can be made. It may take the subject some weeks to adapt to the wearing of the orthotics (which may be required in either or both shoes), but if the device has been correctly prescribed and manufactured, some improvement should be noted fairly quickly.

Ironically, the injuries resulting from foot-action abnormalities like over-pronation are rarely in the foot itself, which is why foot action should always be considered when assessing the cause of any other injury. Conversely, though, not all injuries can be corrected by orthotics, and their careless use, or the use of poorly made orthotics, can actually create worse problems. Seeking expert advice is therefore recommended, although such advice, and the orthotics themselves, may be expensive. An estimated cost should always be obtained before having orthotics specially made since, once produced, they will be of no relevance or value to anyone else's feet.

Some forms of ready-made orthotic devices made of pliable thermoplastic which can be adapted by heating can be bought in sports shops and are rated in shoe sizes. But while that may be a worthwhile interim measure (and certainly cheaper than custom-made orthotics), obtaining individual advice may eventually be inevitable for some chronic problems. Not all orthotics are rigid, as corrective devices may also be required to aid shock absorption, and so will be made of softer materials, like cork or leather. But their function is basically the same: to restore the foot to a state of mechanical soundness.

Corrective devices in shoes were first developed at the end of the nineteenth century, but it was not until the 1960s that a Californian podiatrist, Dr Merton Root, developed the assessment of bio-mechanical foot problems and the orthotic insert on which much of this area of specialist treatment is now based. The word orthotic itself derives from the Greek 'orthos', meaning straight or correct.

During the 1970s the relevance of orthotics to running was more deeply explored, since it was the most basic and simple form of sporting foot action to correct, but now, following more complex research, orthotic devices are available to treat abnormalities affecting a much wider range of sports. In running, they are most applicable to those who suffer frequent injury related to their foot action. For those whose injuries are unrelated to foot action, or for those who have foot abnormalities which nevertheless do not appear to cause injury, orthotics are best left alone.

See also *Pronation, Shoes, Supination*.

Osgood Schlatter's disease

In young athletes, excessive amounts of training may cause pain on the tibial tuberosity, the bony lump just below the knee. This is a growth point of the bone, and to place too much con-

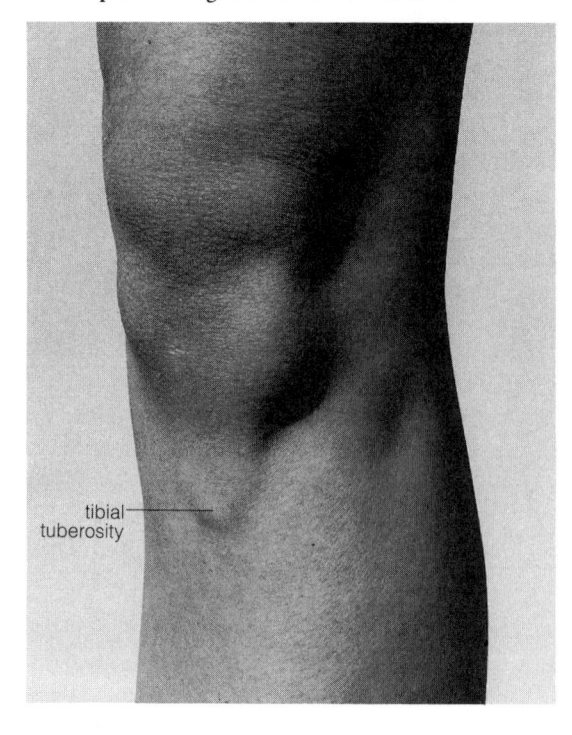

The tibial tuberosity, just below the knee, is the site of pain in Osgood-Schlatter's disease

tinuing stress on it is not only painful but can have adverse long-term effects. The condition is known as Osgood Schlatter's disease, although it is not in fact a disease. Substantial rest and patience while the bone growth is completed (usually by the age of 16–17) is necessary, and an alternative activity, such as swimming, can help to maintain a level of fitness, use up excess energy and ease frustration.

See also *Children*.

Over-training

Just as lack of training can prevent the runner making improvement, so can the negative effects of over-training, where the athlete piles session upon session without allowing his body the chance to recuperate in between.

The result is continual fatigue and a deterioration in performance, which all too often leads the runner to believe he is training insufficiently and adding still more work to his load. Physical signs like insomnia through over-fatigue, mouth ulcers and other infections, and susceptibility to over-use injuries, spell out the message that a period of rest, followed by a better-balanced training programme which mixes the hard training necessary for improvement with easier training and rest days, is required.

See also *Insomnia, Rest*.

Ovett, Steve

The colourful career of Steve Ovett, whose activity at the top level of international middle distance running has spanned fifteen years, has been widely but incompletely documented. His brilliance as a runner, his unconventional approach, and his reticence to reveal too much about himself in the media has led to him being misunderstood and, on occasions, misrepresented. For that, he must share at least a portion of the responsibility. But it is difficult to misrepresent his remarkably consistent and successful career, which is, he insists, far from over.

During the mid-seventies, when British athletics was in something of a lull, it was the sudden and seemingly unanswerable bursts of speed from the tall Brighton-based runner at the end of middle distance track races which set the British crowds alight. The sheer ease with which he could pull away from his straining rivals gave him a particular aura, and for years he was unchallenged at 1500m by anyone in the world.

Steven Michael James Ovett was born in Brighton on 9 October 1955. His father, Mick Ovett, a trader in Brighton's Open Market, and mother Gay were already keen sports fans and used to attend some of the major athletics meetings at London's now-demolished White City Stadium.

At the age of 15 Steve had already established himself as one of Britain's leading young runners at 400 and 800m (and had long jumped over 20 feet at the age of 14). He set a UK age-15 best of 1:55.3 for 800m in 1971 and won the AAA Youths 400m title. But unlike most of his young contemporaries then, his athletics career was destined to be long and successful.

Tall, muscular, and possessed of both speed and endurance, Ovett showed he could also rise to the big occasion by winning the 1973 European Junior 800m title in Duisburg, West Germany, edging out Willi Wulbeck in the last couple of strides. By 1974 he was competing in the senior European Championships and at the age of just 18 took the 800m silver medal there behind the Yugoslav Luciano Susanj. But he was deeply disappointed with it; even then, he wanted gold.

In July 1975 Ovett won the 800m in the European Cup semi-final at Crystal Palace, and an incident after that race sparked off a lengthy wrangle with the Press. At the post-race interview, he said that he would not be running for Britain in the final a month later as he would be hitch-hiking around Europe on holiday instead. One journalist told him he was being 'unpatriotic', and as a consequence of that remark Ovett decided that he did not require such instant judgements. He declined to attend any post-race interviews at Crystal Palace (and most other venues) for eight years. Ironically, he did run anyway in the Europa Cup final, held in Nice, and recorded one of his most emphatic victories, despite risking disqualification by physically clearing a path through the other runners in his break for the line.

After leaving Varndean Grammar School, he had begun to study art in Brighton, but was by then veering towards becoming a full-time athlete, supported by his parents. With coaching advice from Harry Wilson, plus a regular training partner and respected sounding board in local distance runner Matt Paterson, Ovett was in an excellent situation from which to aspire to fulfilling his enormous potential.

In the 1976 Olympic Trials he won the 800m comfortably and the following weekend lined up for the 1500m too. His inexperience showed, and with 50m left he was badly boxed as the runners fought for their Olympic places. Then suddenly a gap opened in front of him and he zipped through it to victory. But as he did so, still 30m from the line, in his surprise and delight at his redemption, he spontaneously turned and raised both arms to wave to his parents in the stands. This gesture, which delighted some people and infuriated others, was to develop into his trade-mark of the home straight victory wave in subsequent years.

But not at the Montreal Olympics in 1976. There, drawn in lane eight in the 800m final (and at a time when an experimental rule of running the first 300m in lanes meant the outside runner usually saw no-one until the first home straight), he finished a disappointed fifth, and also failed to qualify for the 1500m final.

But in 1977, having taken the 1500m more seriously, Ovett ran what many believe remains his best race ever. Competing for the Europe Select team in the inaugural World Cup in Düsseldorf, he devastated the 1500m field, which included the 1976 Olympic champion John Walker, with his speed over the final 200m. The first 100m of his sprint took only 11.9 seconds, and his time of 3:34.5 was a UK record. He made it look so ridiculously easy, relaxed and waving down the home straight, that it seemed he had found his real event and that he would be unbeatable.

In 1978 Ovett declined selection for the Commonwealth Games in Canada as he felt they would interrupt his build-up to the European Championships in Prague several weeks afterwards, and where he intended to race both 800m and 1500m. But the emergence of Sebastian Coe in 1977 as a world-class 800m runner in Britain always hinted at what would actually become the first act of the Ovett and Coe saga, and when they both lined up for the European 800m final in Prague it was impossible to predict which of the pair would win. In fact, neither did. Coe led through 400m in an overstretched 49.3 seconds, Ovett moved past him in the home straight, but both were unexpectedly beaten in the closing stages by the little known East German Olaf Beyer. Ovett took the silver (in a UK record of 1:44.09) and Coe the bronze. Later in the championships Ovett made sure of the gold in the 1500m, which proved to be the only British title of the championships, as he outsprinted Eamonn Coghlan of Ireland in a championship record of 3:35.6.

Ovett completed the season by setting a world 2 miles best of 8:13.5 at Crystal Palace, beating the prolific Kenyan Henry Rono, then set a UK mile record of 3:52.8 on a cold night in Oslo, and finally made the long journey to Tokyo to win the Dubai Golden Mile in 3:55.5.

The following summer, he declined an invitation to defend that Golden Mile title when the race was due to be held in Oslo. He said he thought it should be held in London, and that whoever won it would be gaining a hollow victory. But not everyone agreed when Sebastian Coe, who had twelve days earlier unexpectedly set a world 800m record of 1:42.33 in Oslo, not only won the Golden Mile from a classy field, but added the world mile record to his collection with 3:48.95.

Already there was animated speculation as to when and where the two Britons would race each other, with the first opportunity apparently coming in Zurich a month later. Coe was running the 1500m, but Ovett was turned down for the race by the meeting organizers, who

Steve Ovett's best race? He follows John Walker and Thomas Wessinghage before winning the 1977 World Cup 1500m in Düsseldorf

feared it would develop into a slow tactical event, whereas Coe was promising to attack the world record there. The snub felt by Ovett who was, after all, reigning European champion and World Cup winner, can be imagined. And while Coe did indeed set a world 1500m record in Zurich with 3:32.03, he was shortly afterwards obliged to end his own season because of injury.

Ovett, meanwhile, who had previously maintained that he was not interested in records, only in winning, decided that his own form was so good that he would indeed attack Coe's new marks. A little attempted revenge perhaps? But he failed narrowly. At Crystal Palace in late August he ran easily his fastest ever mile with 3:49.57, little more than half a second outside Coe's world best. Then at Brussels a few days later he came even closer to Coe's world 1500m record, clocking 3:32.11, just 0.08 seconds outside the mark (which would be ratified as 3:32.1).

Little wonder, then, that demand for the two runners to race each other grew to vast proportions. But with the 1980 Olympics looming, there was no chance they would do so beforehand. On the eve of the Games, in Oslo, they both competed in the Bislett Games, and both set world records in different events within an hour. Coe ran 2:13.4 for 1000m while Ovett finally broke Coe's world mile record with 3:48.8. Several weeks later Ovett actually equalled Coe's official 1500m record of 3:32.1, although his exact time of 3:32.09 was slightly inferior to Coe's 3:32.03.

Finally, in Moscow, their anxiously awaited clashes both turned out against the odds. In

Track progress

Born 9 October 1955.

Year	800m	1500m	Mile	3000m	2 miles	5000m
1970	2:00.0	4:10.7				
1971	1:55.3					
1972	1:52.5	4:02.0				
1973	1:47.3	3:44.8	4:00.0			
1974	1:45.8	3:46.2	3:59.4			
1975	1:46.1	3:39.5	3:57.0			
1976	1:45.4	3:37.9	—			
1977	1:48.3	3:34.5	3:54.7	7:41.3	—	13:25.0
1978	1:44.1	3:35.6	3:52.8	7:39.7	8:13.51	—
1979	1:45.0	3:32.2	3:49.6	—	—	—
1980	1:45.40	3:31.36	3:48.8	7:52.44	—	13:27.87
1981	1:46.40	3:31.57	3:48.40	7:50.9	—	—
1982	1:46.08	3:38.48	4:04.4	7:43.87	—	—
1983	1:45.25	3:30.77	3:50.49	—	—	—
1984	1:44.81	3:34.50	—	—	—	—
1985	—	3:37.74	3:55.01	7:49.83	—	—
1986	—	3:33.78	3:52.99	7:50.01	—	13:20.06

the 800m, Coe was slightly favoured but ran a very poor tactical race and left himself with far too much to do in the home straight, as Ovett ran home a comfortable and delighted winner in 1:45.4. But in the 1500m, for which Ovett's experience should have told, the hunger and determination of Coe (aided by some hard mid-race running by the East German Jurgen Straub), resulted in Coe winning in 3:38.4, with Straub second and Ovett only third.

Some slight consolation came for Ovett on 27 August 1980 when, in Koblenz, West Germany, he claimed the world 1500m record as his own with 3:31.36.

In 1981 speculation over Ovett and Coe's 'rivalry' was at its hottest. They continued to avoid each other in competition, but both showed brilliant form, and in one nine-day period in August they actually swapped the world mile record three times. Coe broke Ovett's mark with 3:48.53 in Zurich on 19 August; Ovett took it back with 3:48.40 in Koblenz on 26 August; and Coe regained it with 3:47.33 in Brussels on 28 August.

But 1981 was memorable for Ovett in other ways. On 18 September he married former athlete Rachel Waller, who had been a county level hurdler for Medway AC and whom he had met while training at Crystal Palace. And in December he accidentally ran into some church railings while on a training run, damaging his right knee so badly that an operation was required to repair it. He was not able to resume training until March 1982.

There was also a celebration at the award of the MBE in the New Year's Honours list, while in May 1982 at a press conference in London it was announced that Ovett and Coe would be taking part in a three-race series during that summer: a 3000m at Crystal Palace on 17 July, 800m in Nice on 14 August, and a mile in Eugene, Oregon, on 25 September.

But the series, aimed at satisfying public interest, was doomed. Coe withdrew from the first race with shin soreness, and Ovett, having been ill in France just before, could finish only tenth behind winner Dave Moorcroft.

The other races were wrecked when, in

August, Ovett pulled his left hamstring while training at Brighton's Withdean Stadium. He was not only out of the series with Coe (who was to have his own further medical problems anyway), but also out of that summer's European and Commonwealth Games. Instead, he showed a new talent by acting as in-studio comments man for BBC TV during their coverage of both championships.

There he watched the final emergence of Steve Cram as double 1500m gold medallist, and the following summer Ovett found himself also having to give best to the increasingly confident young Cram in the inaugural World Championships in Helsinki. Ovett, perhaps not fully back to his best anyway, ran an uncharacteristically poor tactical race, being badly boxed at the bell, and despite a despairing sprint down the home straight could finish no higher than fourth, as Cram won.

Several weeks later Ovett also lost his world 1500m record to the South African-born American Sydney Maree, who ran 3:31.24. A first attempt by Ovett to quickly regain it at his favourite Koblenz track was wrecked when the pacemaking went awry. But in Rieti, Italy, a few days afterwards Ovett successfully reclaimed the world mark with 3:30.77.

The season ended with a magnificent mile race between Cram and Ovett at the IAC Coca-Cola meeting at Crystal Palace. Cram won by a stride, in 3:52.56, but the capacity crowd appreciated seeing a great race between two of Britain's top stars, rather than the musical chairs-type avoidance of confrontation they had experienced for years.

Ovett's disappointment at the 1984 Los Angeles Olympic Games, where he bravely and perhaps foolishly disregarded medical advice against competing after being badly affected by a viral illness, was not the note on which he would want to leave the Olympic arena. Last in the 800m final, in which he started as defending champion, and having to drop out of the 1500m final at 1150m with pains in his chest and arm, is not how he would want to be remembered. But the preparatory period had been a trying time, as his new business interests had proved financially disastrous.

In 1985 injury wrecked Ovett's season again, while in 1986 things began to look up with a successful move to 5000m, including a gold medal at the distance in his first appearance in the Commonwealth Games at the age of 30. But in the European Championships, a few weeks later in Stuttgart, ill health struck again and he was forced to drop out midway through the 5000m final. He insists he is far from finished, however, and intends to further extend an international career which has already stretched over 14 seasons.

See also *Sebastian Coe* and *Steve Cram*.

World Records

1500m

3:32.09	Oslo	5 July 1981
	(ratified as 3:32.1)	
3:31.36	Koblenz	27 August 1980
3:30.77	Rieti	4 September 1983

Mile

3:48.8	Oslo	1 July 1980
3:48.40	Koblenz	26 August 1981

2 miles (unofficial distance)

8:13.5	Crystal Palace	15 September 1978

Oxygen

The utilization of oxygen from the air around us to combust energy fuels stored in the muscles is the basis of all middle- and long-distance running events. While sprinters can perform their events without oxygen (anaerobically), and make up the so-called 'oxygen debt' afterwards, endurance runners require a continual supply of oxygen. The volume they can obtain, and the efficiency with which they use it, governs the level of their performance.

Air, which contains 21 per cent oxygen, is breathed into the lungs, where some of that oxygen is then absorbed into the red blood cells by combining with the pigment haemoglobin. They then carry the oxygen to the muscles, where it is used to create energy, and afterwards the same red cells carry off the resulting waste product of carbon dioxide for expiration from the lungs and to obtain fresh oxygen supplies. By the time it leaves the lungs, the air has had its oxygen content reduced to 14.5 per cent, and 5.5 per cent carbon dioxide added.

The maximum oxygen uptake (VO_2), which is the maximum volume of oxygen (as opposed to the volume of inhaled air), which can actually be utilized by the individual in one minute, is a frequently used physiological measurement which can be obtained in clinical conditions. The subject performs some carefully monitored physical exercise at submaximal heartrate, usually on a running treadmill or stationary bicycle, which can be made more difficult by increasing the gradient or speed of the treadmill or the resistance of the bicycle.

Meanwhile, the subject's expired air is collected through a mouthpiece and tube and stored in large bags for later analysis of its oxygen content. The results are adjusted according to the subject's weight, since larger people have higher aerobic capacities, and are then expressed as a value of millilitres of oxygen used per kilogram of body weight per minute. A normal 20-year-old male would have a value in the region of 45ml per kg per minute, whereas most male endurance runners have values in the 70ml per kg per minute range, with one of the highest recorded being the late Steve Prefontaine, the American Olympic 5000m runner, who showed a value of 84ml per kg per minute.

Women tend to record values in the region of 70–75 per cent of the men's readings, with the great Norwegian runner Grete Waitz among the highest recorded with 73.8ml per kg per minute. But if the difference in body fat percentages between men and women is taken into account (since the female's extra fat content has to be oxygenated too), male and female values tend to be intrinsically similar.

See also *Altitude, Anaemia, Blood, Breathing, Lungs*.

P

Pacemaker

Although frowned upon by officialdom, the pacemaker is an integral part of the middle-distance track events at many international invitation meetings. The pacemaker is an athlete nominated (and usually well rewarded) by the meeting promoter to set off at a pace close to, or inside, record level as a way of enticing or assisting the best athletes in the race towards record times. Usually the pacemaker has little or no intention of completing the full distance himself, and often drops out once the rest of the field has caught and passed him.

The public hunger to see record attempts has created the demand for the pacemaker, whose front-running takes some of the psychological pressure off the main contenders until late in the race. For although it requires the same physical effort, mentally it is easier to follow someone else than to lead. Sometimes even two or three pacemakers are asked to lead specific portions of the race, before falling away like spent rocket boosters and leaving the 'star' on his own for the last lap.

It is not a recent phenomenon by any means, and the first four-minute mile, run by Roger Bannister in May 1954, was achieved with the assistance of two pacemakers, Chris Brasher and Chris Chataway, who between them led Bannister up to the last 300 yards.

Ironically, an attempt the previous year, in which Bannister had run in 4:2, was turned down for ratification as a British record because on that occasion Brasher had jogged the first two laps, allowing himself to be caught by the leaders, before speeding up and helping Bannister through the difficult stage of the race. To Bannister's later relief, it was not in this fashion that the four-minute mile was eventually achieved, and today the IAAF rules clearly state that 'Any competitor lapped or about to be lapped ... in a race shall not be allowed to act as a pacemaker'.

A familiar sight on European tracks as American 'rabbit' James Mays sets a record-schedule pace for Steve Cram

Earlier attempts to rule out pacemakers altogether have now been abandoned because of the difficulty in proving that a runner's fast start was pacemaking rather than a genuine tactical ploy (and perhaps also because of the public's appetite for records, and their readiness to accept pacemakers in what is, at the highest levels, a form of entertainment these days).

An alternative type of pacemaking which does constitute assistance for which an athlete could be disqualified, is when another person who is not in the race, such as a coach or fellow athlete, runs alongside them on a course open to the public (as in road or cross-country racing), and provides some encouragement.

But the rule-makers are having a hard task keeping up with developments in the sport.

Pacing 'by any kind of technical device' is actually banned under IAAF rules, yet many athletes wear digital watches capable of bleeping to a pre-set time pattern. And with men and women running together in marathons, there is no rule which at present stops a male athlete from running alongside, and theoretically pacing, a female athlete. Or the other way round, of course.

Peaking

The art of peaking is one which has eluded some of the greatest runners in the world. It involves producing your best form on the day which matters most, for there are many athletes who run their fastest times too early or too late in the season. In recent years the Finnish runner Lasse Viren was a fine example of peaking: he won the 5000 and 10,000m gold medals at the 1972 and 1976 Olympics, despite winning very little else in between.

Even for the club runner of whatever standard there is a satisfaction in knowing that in a race which was important to him, his performance was at least as good as it could have been. There is nothing more frustrating for the runner after a race than feeling that he has often run better in training.

Yet reaching a peak is simply a matter of careful planning, based on the knowledge that hard training is only of value if it is allowed time to be consolidated through recovery. To improve, the runner needs to train hard, but cannot also expect to race at his best at the same time as he is engaged in that hard training. The best races come later.

For a track runner, the peak may be required to last 3–4 weeks, to cover a number of important races at the height of the season, while for a long-distance runner, a specific marathon may be the aim, with everything being poured into that one effort.

But planning for a peak needs to be done over at least a three-month (and preferably a six-month) period, with the first two thirds of that time consisting of a large quantity of training. In the final third, there is a change of emphasis towards greater speed and less volume, with the last 2–3 weeks introducing a much lighter training routine, with several under-distance races as sharpeners (800m and 1500m races, for example, in preparation for a big 5000 or 10,000m, or a 10km road race in preparation for a marathon).

It is like bringing together the necessary ingredients for a cake, and the overriding desire to excel in the specific race some months hence should help to offset any disappointment over possibly sub-par racing performances during the early part of the heavy training build-up. It is impossible for the body to absorb the level of training which will assist in a notable improvement later on and yet still be sufficiently fresh to race well simultaneously. The runner may even wish to cut down his racing commitments in the early part of the build-up to concentrate on training.

Sufficient attention to diet, rest and injury-prevention should also be paid at this vulnerable time, which will occupy about two thirds of the total allocated to reaching the peak. Of the remaining one third, the first 50 per cent will involve reducing total mileage and trying to run shorter sessions faster. Then in the final phase, when training is reduced to a minimum, some local low-key under-distance races may be substituted where possible. There is a great tendency to over-train at this time, simply because after months and months of hard training, it feels unnatural not to be continually tired.

But this easing-off, or 'tapering-down', period is as important to the final result as the hard training. If the work was put in during the early part of the build-up, the rest will complement it, not undermine it, although having confidence to believe that there are such times, when *not* running will do more good than running, is not always that easy!

Ideally, the athlete should arrive at the day of his most important race of the season feeling stronger than ever, faster than ever, but above all well rested, and ready to produce a run worthy of all the training and planning. That is peaking.

Penile frostbite

A new hazard to male runners was identified in the *New England Journal of Medicine* in January 1977, which featured a report of a 53-year-old circumcised physician who undertook a customary thirty-minute jog in a local park at 7p.m. on a midwinter evening, with the temperature at −8°C (17°F) and a severe wind chill factor. Through insufficient protection to the more sensitive parts of his anatomy, he reported sustaining a rare form of frostbite, and urged other runners not to overlook the importance of maintaining adequate body heat. A Maryland company responded by marketing, apparently in all seriousness, a fleecy-lined supporter.

Pietri, Dorando

Like Jim Peters, the Italian marathon runner Dorando Pietri became more famous for a race he did not win than for his victories. But his collapse at the end of the 1908 Olympic Games marathon, from Windsor Castle to the White City Stadium, helped to create the dramatic aura which surrounded the event for many years afterwards.

Pietri, who was born in Mandrio, Italy, on 16 October 1885, was a late selection for the Italian team, only securing his place through a 40km track race just seventeen days before the Olympic event. In the marathon itself, the first over the classic 26 miles 385 yards distance, Pietri started steadily among the fifty-six entrants on a hot afternoon. After twenty miles he was still four minutes down on the leader, Charles Hefferon of South Africa, but caught and passed the fading Hefferon at twenty-five miles.

As Pietri entered the stadium he was close to collapse from the effort, and with just two thirds of a lap of the track to run, he at first turned right rather than left. During the final struggle to the tape he fell five times, before being helped across the line by sympathetic officials in a time of 2hr 54min 47sec. But the assistance he had received had ensured his subsequent disqualification, and the race was awarded instead to the American Johnny Hayes, who followed Pietri into the stadium and finished in 2hr 55min 19sec, with Hefferon of South Africa officially second in 2hr 56min 6sec.

The public had taken to Pietri, the diminutive pastrycook from Capri, and when the medals for the event were presented by Queen

Dorando Pietri is assisted across the line at the 1908 Olympic marathon, causing his inevitable disqualification

Alexandra (who had witnessed the event) three days later there was a special gold cup for Pietri, accompanied by a card headed Buckingham Palace, and in the Queen's own writing 'to Pietri Dorando in remembrance of the Marathon race, from Windsor to the Stadium, 24 July 1908, from Queen Alexandra'.

Pietri quickly recovered from his ordeal, and within three months had turned professional in the USA, where as a postscript to the dramatic Olympic marathon, a professional circuit thrived for several years. In the first race, which pitched Pietri against the official Olympic winner Johnny Hayes, the pair ran a tortuous 260-lap marathon on the indoor track at Madison Square Garden in New York, with thousands of spectators gambling vast fortunes on the outcome. The pair ran practically together, with Pietri leading most of the way, before the Italian pulled away in the final mile to win in 2hr 44min 21sec.

Less than three weeks later Pietri lined up again on the same track, this time to race the Canadian Indian runner Tom Longboat, winner of the 1907 Boston Marathon, but who had dropped out of the London Olympic race. Longboat turned the tables on Pietri, himself pulling away over the final mile to win in 2hr 45min 6sec, while Pietri himself collapsed just before the end. In all probability he had not recovered from the previous race. But both runners received 25 per cent of the race receipts, which at $3750 each was not a bad reward.

Pietri still won fifty of his sixty-nine races as a professional over a range of distances, and usually in simple head-to-head races, before his retirement in 1911. He died in San Remo on 7 February 1942, his name indelibly linked with the marathon.

Polytechnic Marathon

Although not one of the world's biggest marathons, rarely televised, and with a field measured in hundreds rather than thousands, the

An historic race in an historic setting: the Polytechnic Marathon competitors set off from Windsor Castle

Polytechnic Marathon, held annually in Windsor, remains a history-rich link with the earliest days of the marathon.

It was first held in 1909 and, although having faced extinction several times in recent years, it is still part of the fixture list nearly eighty years later. Its origins extend back to the poor British performances in the 1908 Olympic marathon in London, where the collapse of Dorando Pietri claimed the attention, but the first British runner home had placed no higher than twelfth of the twenty-seven finishers, to the disappointment of home supporters.

The daily newspaper the *Sporting Life* almost immediately offered a silver trophy worth £500 for a road race to be held annually over a distance of not less than twenty-five miles (the exact marathon distance was still not established at that time), with the intention of encouraging and improving British distance running.

The west London club Polytechnic Harriers duly arranged the first such event on 8 May 1909; they had already organized one of the pre-Olympic trial races as well as the actual 1908 Olympic marathon from Windsor to the White City Stadium.

For the inaugural 'Poly' Marathon, a route from Windsor Park to Stamford Bridge was chosen and the race was won, appropriately, by Polytechnic Harrier Harry Barrett in 2hr 42min 31sec. It was a world best for the distance of

Polytechnic Marathon winners

Windsor–Stamford Bridge (via Uxbridge and Hanwell)

1909	Fred Barrett (Polytechnic H)	2:42.31
1910	No race owing to death of the King	
1911	Henry Green (Herne Hill H)	2:46.39
1912	James Corkery (Can)	2:36.56*
1913	Alexis Ahlgren (Swe)	2:36.07
1914	Ahmed Djebelia (Fra)	2:46.31
1915–18	Not held	
1919	E. Woolston (Machine Gun Corps)	2:52.31
1920	Arthur Mills (Leicester H)	2:37.41
1921	Arthur Mills (Leicester H)	2:51.42
1922	Arthur Mills (Leicester H)	2:47.31
1923	Axel Jensen (Denmark)	2:40.47
1924	Dunky Wright (Scot)	2:53.18
1925	Sam Ferris (RAF)	2:35.59
1926	Sam Ferris (RAF)	2:42.25
1927	Sam Ferris (RAF)	2:40.33
1928	Sam Ferris (RAF)	2:41.03
1929	Sam Ferris (RAF)	2:40.48
1930	Stan Smith (Birchfield H)	2:42.24
1931	Sam Ferris (RAF)	2:41.55
1932	Sam Ferris (RAF)	2:35.31

Windsor–White City (via Datchet, Western Avenue)

1933	Sam Ferris (RAF)	2:36.33
1934	Dunky Wright (Scot)	2:56.30
1935	Bert Norris (Polytechnic H)	2:48.38
1936	Bert Norris (Polytechnic H)	2:35.20
1937	Bert Norris (Polytechnic H)	2:48.40

Windsor–Chiswick

1938	Henry Palme (Swe)	2:42.00
1939	Henry Palme (Swe)	2:36.56

Windsor Great Park

1940	Leslie Griffiths (Herne Hill H)	2:53.42

Chiswick

1941	Gerry Humphreys (Woodford Green)	3:12.36
1942	Leslie Griffiths (Herne Hill H)	2:53.57
1943	Leslie Griffiths (Herne Hill H)	2:53.14
1944	Tom Richards (Mitcham AC)	2:56.40
1945	Tom Richards (Mitcham AC)	2:48.45

Windsor–Chiswick

1946	Harry Oliver (Reading AC)	2:38.12
1947	Cecil Ballard (Surrey AC)	2:36.53
1948	Jack Holden (Tipton H)	2:36.45
1949	Jack Holden (Tipton H)	2:42.52
1950	Jack Holden (Tipton H)	2:33.07
1951	Jim Peters (Essex Beagles)	2:29.28
1952	Jim Peters (Essex Beagles)	2:20.43

(* 360 yards short)

Year	Winner	Time
1953	Jim Peters (Essex Beagles)	2:18.41
1954	Jim Peters (Essex Beagles)	2:17.40
1955	Bob McInnis (RAF)	2:36.23
1956	Ron Clark (Herne Hill H)	2:20.16
1957	Eddie Kirkup (Rotherham H)	2:27.05
1958	Colin Kemball (Wolverhampton)	2:22.28
1959	Dennis O'Gorman (St Albans City)	2:25.12
1960	Arthur Kelly (Derby & County)	2:19.06
1961	Peter Wilkinson (Derby & County)	2:20.25
1962	Ron Hill (Bolton United H)	2:20.59
1963	Buddy Edelen (Hadleigh Olympiads)	2:14.26
1964	Basil Heatley (Coventry Godiva H)	2:13.55
1965	Morio Shigematsu (Jap)	2:12.00
1966	Graham Taylor (Cambridge H)	2:19.04
1967	Fergus Murray (Oxford University)	2:19.06
1968	Kenji Kimihara (Jap)	2:15.15
1969	Phil Hampton (Royal Navy AC)	2:25.22
1970	Don Faircloth (Croydon H)	2:18.15
1971	Phil Hampton (Royal Navy AC)	2:18.31

Windsor–Chiswick, but 29 miles by error

Year	Winner	Time
1972	Don Faircloth (Croydon H)	2:31.52

Under-distance, Windsor

Year	Winner	Time
1973	Bob Sercombe (Newport H)	2:19.48

Windsor

Year	Winner	Time
1974	Akio Usami (Jap)	2:15.16
1975	Not held	
1976	Bernie Plain (Cardiff AAC)	2:15.43
1977	Ian Thompson (Luton United)	2:14.32
1978	Dave Francis (Westbury H)	2:19.05
1979	Mike Gratton (Invicta AC)	2:19.53
1980	Tony Byrne (Salford H)	2:22.28
1981	Bernie Plain (Cardiff AAC)	2:24.07
1982	Graham Ellis (Holmfirth H)	2:23.28
1983	Alan McGee (Southampton & E)	2:22.55
1984	David Catlow (Cheltenham)	2:26.02
1985	Terry Donaghy (London RRC)	2:33.02
1986	Hugh Jones (Ranelagh H)	2:26.11

WOMEN

Year	Winner	Time
1978	Gillian Adams (Aldershot)	2:54.11
1979	Jane Davies (Epsom/Ewell H)	3:21.23
1980	Gillian Adams (Aldershot)	2:45.11
1981	Caroline Rodgers (Highgate H)	2:51.03
1982	Kath Binns (Sale H)	2:36.12
1983	Val Howe (Bracknell AC)	2:05.40
1984	Sarah Foster (Woking AC)	2:54.06
1985	Pam Davies (Belgrave H)	3:22.28
1986	Frances Guy (Belgrave H)	2:51.15

26 miles 385 yards, matching the distance of the 1908 Olympic race.

In succeeding years the Polytechnic became one of the world's most prestigious marathons. Until 1932 it was held between Windsor and Stamford Bridge, and from 1933 to 1938 the finish was at White City Stadium, scene of the 1908 Olympics. Then from 1938 until 1972, perhaps its most illustrious era, it was held on a course between Windsor and the Polytechnic Stadium at Chiswick. It was on this course that Jim Peters set world best performances in three consecutive years, from 1952–54, with his 1954 time of 2hr 17min 40sec being still good enough to have won the race frequently in the seventies and eighties!

Further world bests were set on the course by the American Buddy Edelen (2hr 14min 28sec in 1963), Britain's Basil Heatley (2hr 13min 55sec in 1964) and the Japanese Morio Shigematsu (2hr 12min in 1965), but the gradual increase of other marathons in the UK and elsewhere undermined the importance the race had enjoyed for so long. In 1972, its final year on the classic Windsor to Chiswick route, the competitors took the wrong route and ran twenty-nine miles by error, and by 1973 the increasing traffic and marshalling problems had forced it on to a new route entirely within Windsor. Some of the magic of a race in which eight world bests had been set, and which had been started by three reigning monarchs, was lost.

In 1975, through lack of support, the race was not held at all, but was revived in 1976 following new sponsorship from Goldenlay

Eggs. In 1978 women competed for the first time (Gillian Adams winning in 2hr 54min 11sec), but the race did not benefit very much from the marathon boom in the early eighties as its strict qualifying standards for entry kept out many of the new-wave runners who, with better promotion and a warmer welcome, might have helped elevate the race, at least financially.

By 1986 this long and special link with history seemed destined to end when no new sponsor could be found to help absorb the rising costs of staging the event. But at the eleventh hour the investment company United Greenfield stepped in with an offer to help sustain the race at least through to its seventy-fifth staging in 1988. By then perhaps some of its former glory may have been restored.

Pregnancy

If the idea of a woman running for recreation would have shocked the Victorians, one hesitates to guess what their reaction to heavily pregnant women setting out for a thirty-minute jog would have been. But modern research has shown that continuing to exercise during a normal, healthy pregnancy is not only perfectly safe, but actually desirable.

Women have continued to run through all stages of pregnancy, right up to the day of birth, and where they have stopped running at an earlier stage it has usually been because of the awkwardness of carrying the extra 20–25lb lump, rather than any ominous side effects.

The pregnant woman should be guided by her own feelings, and if there is nausea, morning sickness or excessive fatigue, all common in the first fourteen-week trimester of pregnancy, she may not feel like running anyway. But on other days a steady run can help relieve the tensions and stimulate the circulation. The pace should be comfortable rather than a full effort, since a relatively under-researched area is the effect of maximum heart rate on the foetus, and whether the mother sustaining considerable oxygen debt by running flat out would also deprive the growing baby of oxygen. So a safe pulse rate ceiling of around 140 beats a minute is usually suggested, for these are difficult areas in which to perform human experiments.

General medical advice, therefore, is to keep all running at a sub-maximal effort. Thus, serious racing is not recommended while pregnant, although *participating* in races is not necessarily ruled out. In 1983 Ingrid Kristiansen even competed in the World Cross-country Championships without realizing that she was four months pregnant, but there were no complications.

Clare Temple, the author's wife, enjoying a steady run in the sixth month of pregnancy

As the pregnant woman becomes larger, training shoes with extra cushioning are recommended, as well as running on soft surfaces where possible, and as the baby develops inside the womb the mother will have to gradually adjust to her changing centre of gravity. But the baby is well protected inside its sac of amniotic fluid, and would be far more at risk from the mother smoking, drinking heavily or taking drugs during pregnancy than from being bounced up and down during a training run.

The pregnant runner will want to wear lightweight, airy clothes with the minimum of tight elastic, even around the ankles, although a more supportive bra may be needed during the later months of the pregnancy, and afterwards, when feeding the baby.

The final months may also find the mother feeling uncomfortable when running, and she may have to be content with just walking and jogging for short sections alternately. Mary Decker-Slaney, in her first pregnancy, ran daily for the first five months, but had to cut down to walking and jogging a mile every two or three days after that. But other runners have been able to run up to 5–6 miles practically up to the day of delivery.

Swimming can be a good substitute for running when it becomes uncomfortable, since the water supports much of the extra weight. Exercises which can be performed simply at home should also be maintained as long as possible since they can improve the mobility and strength needed during delivery.

Pregnancy is not an illness, but a perfectly healthy, normal condition, which has to be maintained by adequate nutrition and rest, and can be enhanced by the right amount of moderate exercise.

Following the birth, and assuming no complications, gentle jogging can be resumed, if comfort allows, after about three weeks (or six weeks after a Caesarean delivery). From a performance aspect, there are many examples of runners who produced their fastest times after motherhood, including Ingrid Kristiansen, who set world records at 5000m, 10,000m and the marathon. In the Soviet Union, research among the leading female distance runners caused a leading physiologist, the late Professor Vladimir Kuznetsov, to observe: 'The birth of a child seems to strengthen the organism physiologically and gives some form of reserve of energy, perhaps in preparation for a second birth. Psychologically, it seems that women are more prepared to train hard after giving birth.'

One of the best Soviet runners, Tatyana Kazankina, was a case in point. She won the 800 and 1500m at the 1976 Olympics, gave birth in 1978, then retained her Olympic 1500m title and broke the world 1500m record in 1980. Following a second birth, she set a world 3000m record in 1984. In the USA, sprinter Valerie Brisco-Hooks was the mother of a 2-year-old son when she won three gold medals in the 1984 Olympic Games, while Evelyn Ashford (who was already pregnant when she set a world 100m record in 1984) gave birth to a son in May 1985, and made a successful comeback in 1986.

In Britain, Joyce Smith, the mother of two daughters, has had one of the longest and most successful careers in distance running, including running in the 1984 Olympic Marathon at the age of nearly 47, while other international athletes who continued their success in distance running after motherhood include Christine Benning, Ann Ford, Paula Fudge and Glynis Penny.

While the changing routine and the additional demands of motherhood may reduce the opportunities for training, physiologically there seems no reason to suppose a female runner should not be every bit as good, if not better, in her standard of running following the birth of her children.

Pre-race preparation

The period leading up to a race is a time of apprehension for any runner, and the more important that race is to the runner, the greater their concern is likely to be. But there are certain ways to direct pre-race thoughts constructively. At the highest levels of track competition, for example, the mental approach to the race is almost as important as the training build-up. There are many athletes who have been brilliant on the training track, but disappointing in races; and vice versa.

Some people believe, incorrectly, that nervousness is a fault. In shorter, explosive events like sprints or the shorter middle-distance events (such as 800/1500m) nervousness is a sign that the body is gearing itself up ready for maximum effort. Indeed, an athlete in these events who does not feel nervous before such a race (and assuming he normally does) should gently attempt to deliberately raise his level of apprehension by mentally rehearsing what the last few minutes before the gun will be like.

A coach can achieve the same effect, if necessary, through talking the athlete into the right mental state. However, this process, known as 'psyching up', is best achieved by a coach who knows the athlete well, since it is all too easy to go over the top and almost scare the athlete into inhibition. Alternatively, the coach may sometimes have to calm an athlete down, if he is becoming too agitated. But in longer events, where careful pace judgement and conservative tactics are needed, the level of apprehension can be somewhat lower, since getting a poor start, or being caught in a tactical 'box', is less crucial to the result.

For the vast majority of runners, however, pre-race preparation is mainly a question of making sure you know where the race starts, at what time, and how to get there. Apart from a little nervous joking among colleagues on the start line, and several extra visits to the toilet, the apprehension usually remains largely submerged.

But the inner apprehension may start several days before the race, and gradually build, so that in the final few hours some runners appear alternately pre-occupied, or snappy and irritable, even to close family and friends. Other runners behave differently, becoming increasingly talkative and active as the race approaches. Some runners prefer to be on their own with their thoughts; others are desperate to be in the company of fellow runners for reassurance. There is no definitive 'norm', except that the competitive runner's usual behaviour often changes to some degree near race time.

In the days before a race, the normal training schedule is reduced, to allow full recovery beforehand. A low-key race may simply call for the weekly rest day to be taken the day before, but a more important race may mean easing down the workload for 2–3 days beforehand. And in the case of a marathon which has been long-awaited, the training may be eased over the final 10–14 days.

An early night before a race is not always a good idea if the runner merely tosses and turns restlessly. Often, going to bed a little later than usual instead may help achieve a more relaxed night's sleep. But even if insomnia intervenes, it is unlikely to adversely affect the next day's performance.

A light breakfast should be sufficient until after the race, even if it is an afternoon event, with simple, easily digested snacks being taken to bridge the gap. But an extra hour than normal should be allowed for digestion on race days, because the heightened nervousness tends to slow down the digestive process, and can result in stitch.

For a road race, the runner's bag (ideally packed the night before, using a check list) should contain: all running kit, including spare laces; safety pins; petroleum jelly; sticking plasters; towel; soap; toilet tissue; loose change for telephone/public toilet if necessary; notebook and pencil (for writing down results); several large black plastic sacks, including one for storing tracksuit at the start if necessary, and one, with head and arm holes, to wear in case of wet weather before the race begins! The storing bag should be labelled with your home address, in case you become separated from it. At some races it is relatively easy to find your gear afterwards; at others, much more difficult. And if you travel to the race in your running kit, ensure you take a complete change of clothes in case it pours down during the race.

If there is a long queue for the changing-room toilets before the race, it may be worth seeking out alternative public facilities in any nearby park, public building or railway station: in such circumstances, the cost of a platform ticket may be well invested!

See also *Peaking*.

Pronation

Every time a runner's foot lands, part of the inward movement which occurs in the foot before it pushes off again is termed pronation. It is not, in itself, an injury; every runner pronates. But problems occur when the runner *over*-pronates, causing a distortion in the action of the leg which in turn, repeated often and severely enough, can eventually cause injury. When a runner says 'I pronate', he means 'I over-pronate'.

Pronation is actually a necessary part of the foot action because it helps to spread the shock which is absorbed by the foot on every stride.

The effects of constant over-pronation on this right shoe are clearly visible from the distortion of the suede-covered plastic heel counter

If you can picture yourself running, imagine your foot approaching the ground in slow motion. The outer edge of the heel probably touches first, then the rest of the heel spreads on to the ground, followed by the midfoot and forefoot as your leg straightens up and passes over the heel. By the time you are pushing off with the forefoot and toes, the heel has lifted off the ground again.

Between the heel landing and lifting, a movement of the foot inwards occurs just below the ankle joint, in what is called the subtalar joint. This joint, unlike the ankle joint itself, allows movement to occur on three planes, but mainly from side to side. After allowing the inward movement of the foot on landing, the joint should then go into reverse, moving outwards in the opposite direction, in a motion called supination, which straightens the foot ready for the next stride.

Without this flexibility of the subtalar joint to reduce the shock, every stride would be a jarring experience, even though the body is designed to also spread the shock through the leg, knee, hip and back. But if the subtalar joint allows too much inward movement, and does not perform its opposite reaction to straighten the foot but remains over-pronated, then the carefully balanced process of absorbing the shock will be askew. Instead of being spread evenly, too great a dose may be directed at an angle into the knee, or hip, or back, where eventually some form of over-use injury may also become apparent as the muscles work to counteract the inefficiency resulting from the over-pronation.

To assess whether you over-pronate, the clearest sign is to look at the backs of a well-used pair of your training shoes. Stand them on a flat surface at eye level, and look at the reinforced sections which wrap around the heels of the shoes, known as the 'heel counters'. Their purpose is to control the side to side movement of the subtalar joint, but even the best-made shoes are liable to have their heel counters distorted by many thousands of strides. If one, or both, heel counters are mis-shapen inwards, they are showing signs of over-pronation.

An alternative assessment can be made by getting someone to draw two vertical lines on each of your legs with a felt-tipped pen, above and below the subtalar joint. One line, about two inches long, should be drawn on the lower end of the Achilles tendon, and the other on the heel bone, when both are in a neutral position. This should be done by lying face down on a bed or couch, with your feet sticking over the end, and the lines can then be drawn along a ruler to ensure straightness.

You can then run a short distance in bare feet (or, ideally, on a treadmill) while your colleague observes whether there is a marked inward angle on either leg between the two lines. If so, it is a sign of over-pronation. (If the resulting angle should be formed to a significant degree outwards, it is a sign of the much less prevalent over-supination).

Over-pronation can be treated by artificially restricting the excessive inwards movement through the insertion of rigid orthotic devices within the shoe. Orthotics can be purchased ready-made, and some of these can be slightly re-moulded to fit your own feet, since every case is different and the chances of a perfect solution being found ready-made in a packet at a sports shop are fairly slim. Professional medical help can also be sought in having your own orthotics custom-made, but this can be a rather expensive process, with no guarantee of success.

Self-help measures are rather limited. The purchase of training shoes which have been specifically designed to counteract over-pronation is one possibility. Another is to insert felt wedges in the heels of your training shoes, with a quarter-inch lift on the inside, tapering down to virtually nothing on the outer side of the heel. This may help to restrict the movement of the subtalar joint, but even if successful, the felt wedges will need to be regularly renewed, otherwise they will become flattened and less effective through continual use. Over-pronation needs to be carefully assessed because, unlike an injury, it does not 'get better'.

See also *Orthotics*, *Supination*.

Pulse

The pulse is an indicator of the heart rate, and as the blood is pumped away from the heart through the arteries, each wave of blood can be measured as a definite throb in arteries close to the skin surface. The most convenient is the radial artery of the wrist and by pressing the tips of two fingers of the opposite hand against the inside of the wrist (about one inch down from the base of the thumb) the pulse can be felt.

In an average adult the normal resting pulse is around seventy-two beats a minute at rest, although in a highly trained international distance runner it has been measured as low as thirty-two. The best time to take the pulse is when you are relaxed and at rest; first thing in the morning, before getting out of bed, is ideal. A resting pulse rate which falls over a period of some months is an indicator of improving fitness. But in a fit athlete, a resting pulse rate which is noticeably higher than usual may indicate an approaching illness or infection, or a state of over-training, and in such situations rest is required.

Q

Quadriceps

The quadriceps are a group of four muscles at the front of the thigh which work together, and are particularly important in hill running and sprinting; effectively, they are the lifting muscles of the leg. They cover the front and outer side of the thigh, along the length of the femur.

The muscles are the rectus femoris, the vastus lateralis, the vastus medialis (which is the bulky muscle just above the inside of the knee), and the vastus intermedius.

Additionally, the sartorius muscle, which extends from the hip bone diagonally across the front of the thigh to the inner side of the top of the tibia, and is the longest muscle in the body, helps the quadriceps to flex both the knee and hip.

The quadriceps work in complement with the hamstring muscles at the rear of the thigh, and maintaining a strength balance between the two groups is important. Strengthening the quadriceps independently, perhaps by weight training, but without paying similar attention to the hamstrings, could result in a torn hamstring when running at speed, as the weaker muscles are unable to keep up.

The quadriceps, the group of four muscles at the front of the thigh, are the lifting muscles

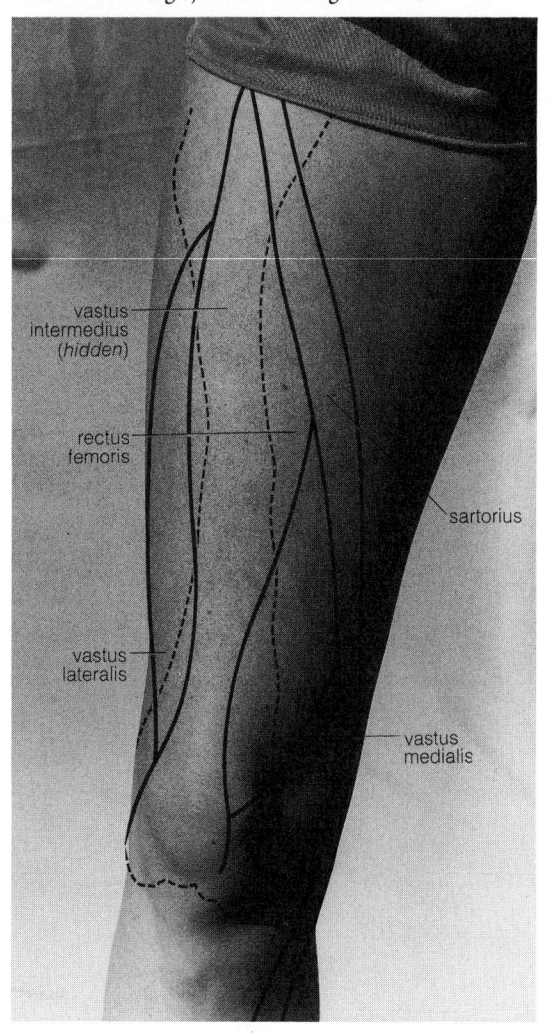

R

Resistance training

As a runner becomes fitter, so the training load needs to be gradually increased to maintain an improvement rate. Training is the adaption of the body to perform a specific task, so sometimes that task can be increased in difficulty by the introduction of some additional physical resistance.

Hill running, in which the gradient of the slope makes the body work harder, is the simplest form of resistance. But running in loose sand, and especially running uphill in loose sand, has been effectively used by many runners as a training aid, notably the Australian Olympic 1500m champion of 1960, Herb Elliott, whose preparation at the Portsea camp of his coach, Percy Cerutty, was a significant factor in his success. In Britain, the most frequently used sandhill facility is probably that at Merthyr Mawr in Wales, although Cornish sandhills have also been used to good effect. But a potential problem of sandhill running is Achilles tendon strain, which can occur if too much sandhill running is done in too short a time. In general, it is probably best used by runners who have regular access to the sand.

Other forms of resistance training include barefoot running in the sea up to calf level (although the surface beneath should be scrutinized at low tide for sharp objects), and running in heavy Army boots, although the value achieved through their additional weight is perhaps undermined by the often cumbersome running action which has to be adopted.

Harness training is favoured by some sprinters, in which they attempt to sprint while restrained by a harness around their waist held by a colleague who endeavours to hold them back, while walking or running behind. A variation involves wearing an Army-style belt, to the back of which is attached a rope which in turn is attached to a cement- or brick-filled

Former world indoor 400m record-holder Todd Bennett, watched by coach Mike Smith, demonstrates resistance running in sand

rubber motor tyre. The heavy tyre is then dragged, flat, by the runner along a set distance; the weightier the tyre, the more resistance it will provide.

There is no limit to the different and ingenious methods devised by runners and coaches over the years to add value to the training sessions by making them harder. One top 400m hurdler of recent years trained in a specially made weighted jacket, using hurdles that were three inches higher than in his race, and hurdling more of them in a single hard run than he would need to in competition. The reasoning behind resistance training could in some ways perhaps be aligned to that of the man who kept hitting his head against a wall 'because it will be so nice when I stop!'

See also *Hill Training*.

Rest

One of the most frequently overlooked components of a successful training programme is the value of rest. During training, muscle tissues are damaged, chemical waste accumulates, glycogen in the muscles is depleted, the blood sugar level drops and the runner may become dehydrated. So in order for the body to restore itself to a condition ready for another dose of hard training, some easing down between the longest and most draining sessions is needed.

If training was simply a matter of more and more running we would all be covering 500 miles a week. But, plainly, that would be too much. As the runner becomes fitter, he can indeed run further and faster for the same effort, but adequate recovery is still an important part of that continuing process of improvement.

The most serious runners train six or seven days a week, and while one complete rest day each week has a lot to commend it, mentally as well as physically, some runners can cope with everyday training. But volume and quality have to be varied during those seven days. To run flat out every single day would take the runner into a downward spiral towards over-fatigue.

When building up, a gradual increase in training volume (to a maximum of 10 per cent a month) can yield good results, but trying to do too much too quickly, or simply piling on more and more miles, can be counter-productive. Training can become obsessional, with the runner developing some deep-rooted fear that to miss a single day would lead to a dramatic drop in their fitness. In fact, physiologists estimate that there is no basic fitness loss for 5–7 days after stopping training, and that a day or two of rest can actually improve fitness by allowing the body time to regenerate and re-stock.

Ironically, runners at all levels often produce their finest performances after they have been prevented from training for some time by injury or illness (themselves frequently signs of over-training). Their bodies have simply responded to finally receiving the respite they had been seeking but were never granted, and the runner has been able to come closer to the form he sought but may have been inadvertently sabotaging.

So the belief that it is either a mental weakness, or a fitness-threatening action, to take an occasional day off training needs to be firmly eliminated from the runner's mind. Physical signs like over-use injuries, mouth ulcers, and insomnia (being 'too tired' to sleep) are other warnings that it is time to cut back, at least temporarily.

Methods to increase relaxation and promote recovery could include taking a sauna, a massage, or listening to music in the dark. Everyone has their own favourite way of relaxing. But the most important aspect is the genuine understanding that time spent in this manner once or twice a week is not time wasted which could otherwise have been spent on extra training. Instead, it is actually helping to improve the physical condition. And it is also a reassuring sign that the runner is in control of his body, rather than it being in control of him.

See also *Insomnia, Over-training*.

Restless leg syndrome

When a runner is covering high training mileage, particularly if he is unaccustomed to it, he may experience a night-time sensation in which, while trying to get to sleep, his legs seem to want to go on running. This reaction, which has become known as restless leg syndrome, has been attributed alternatively to having simply a local muscular cause, where metabolic reactions continue after exercise and cause spontaneous muscle movement, or to a neuro-muscular reaction, brought about by the mind continuing to run after the body has stopped.

It is different to cramp, as it rarely leads to painful muscle spasms, but the avoidance of possible dehydration by taking plenty of liquids at a time of heavy training (particularly during warm or humid weather) is a sensible precaution anyway, and may help to prevent the onset of either cramp or restless leg syndrome.

A more direct measure is to receive a simple but relaxing leg massage from a friend or partner, with particular concentration on the thigh muscles (quadriceps) and calf muscles, with the masseur always working with their thumbs in the direction of the subject's heart. A 5–10-minute massage on each leg after a run will help to calm the nerve endings and relax the muscles.

For a runner who has no access to massage, a self-help leg relaxation method is to deliberately contract each set of muscles for five seconds in turn while lying on a bed. During each contraction, the breath is held, then exhaled when the muscles are allowed to relax. The feet, calves, thighs and buttocks should be contracted in turn, and will normally be left

more relaxed than before the contraction.
See also *Cramp, Massage*.

RRC

The Road Runners Club (RRC), a national body, was founded following the inaugural London to Brighton road race, held in August 1951, to bring together 'all those interested in long-distance running, to serve their interests, and to act as a forum for all enthusiasts'. Its first meeting was held at the Regent Street Polytechnic on 30 June 1952, when it was addressed by Arthur Newton, the father of long-distance running in the UK, and among its original aims was to organize annually the London to Brighton road race. It still does so every autumn, but has subsequently expanded to cater for all aspects of road running activities at distances over ten miles. Its speciality is in marathons and ultra-marathon events.

During the fifties and sixties, road running was still considered to be a minority part of the athletics spectrum, but the RRC was vigorous then in campaigning for greater recognition and better organization, measurement and standardization of road racing. It also promoted a large number of distance running record attempts on road and track, developed its own race standards and insurance schemes, and publishes a comprehensive newsletter.

In recent years, the enormous boom in road running activities led to the formation, in 1985, of the AAA Road Race Advisory Committee, on which the RRC is represented. And while higher standards are indeed now being demanded of race organizers, who are often dealing with thousands of runners, the current interest is in many ways a legacy of the untiring, unpublicized but determined work of the RRC in its pioneering days, long before the sponsorship or televising of road races.

The RRC concentrates more on the serious side of distance running rather than the fun run. Its membership secretary is Peter Goodsell, 10 Honywood Road, Colchester, Essex, CO3 3AS.

See also *Ultramarathon*.

Runner's high

The feeling of euphoria which sometimes sweeps over a regular runner during a training run, creating an analgesic effect, has become known as 'runner's high'. It is sometimes described as the exercise-produced equivalent of a drug experience, sometimes even providing the runner with solutions to long-standing problems, or the writer or artist who runs with new ideas for creativity.

Only in recent years has this feeling of warm mental relaxation during a run been linked with a physiological cause. Scientists now relate 'runner's high' to an increase of brain chemicals known as endorphins, which are produced by the pituitary gland at the base of the brain. Running stimulates endorphin secretion, with researchers reporting blood endorphin levels measured several times higher after a long run.

Endorphins have a pain-reducing effect similar to morphine, and create the same physiological reactions when they come into contact with brain cells. Indeed, one theory is that they are also at least part of the cause of running addiction, where a runner may sometimes suffer a form of withdrawal symptoms if deprived of his daily run for too long. The very word endorphin is a marriage of endogenous (or growing from within) and morphine: literally, morphine from within. But endorphins are believed to be anything up to 200 times as strong as morphine, the parent chemical of heroin, although without the side effects of morphine or heroin.

Research is still continuing into endorphins, the effects of which only really began to be investigated following the Vietnam War, when an alarming number of US servicemen returned home with a heroin addiction. Federal funds were released to finance research into the cause of such addiction, and subsequent speculation over a possible link with running and 'runner's high' was almost incidental. Now the relaxed and enjoyable sensation which accompanies or follows a run can be ascribed to physiological reasons. But runners themselves did not need convincing of its existence.

See also *Endorphins*.

Runner's knee

More correctly called (though not that often!) chondromalacia patellae, this is a painful irritation of the undersurface of the kneecap (patella), where it rubs against the lower end of the thigh bone (femur), often causing a softening of the cartilage. It particularly affects older runners with some years experience of relatively high training mileage.

It is generally felt that an imbalance between the quadriceps muscles at the front of the thigh helps to create this condition. Three of the four muscles of the quadriceps group exert an upwards and outwards pull on the patella, while the fourth, the vastus medialis muscle, situated on the inside of the thigh just above the knee, is supposed to counteract this pull and keep the patella straight.

But the vastus medialis only contracts fully when the leg is completely straightened. This can be confirmed by straightening the leg, with the knee locked; the contracted vastus medialis can then be felt in the inner thigh, just above the knee.

In distance running, however, where there is considerable development of the other three quadricep muscles, the vastus medialis is often weakened because the leg is so rarely completely straightened. Distance runners tend to train with their legs bent practically all of the time, and thus the natural balance between the quadriceps muscles is disturbed, as the upwards and outwards pull of the three dominant muscles moves the patella too far; pain eventually results.

The best form of treatment is to try to rebalance the quadriceps by leg-straightening exercises, which will cause simple contractions of the vastus medialis, and holding the position for 10–15 seconds. They can be repeated up to ten times, with a brief recovery in between. Such an exercise can also be performed every hour if circumstances permit; it can be done sitting at an office desk, for instance.

But it must be appreciated that by no means all knee pain is caused by chondromalacia patellae. The knee is a complex joint, with a host of potential problems from the amount of shock absorption it is required to undertake in distance running. Torn cartilage, strained ligaments or osteoarthritis are other possible causes of knee pain, and expert medical advice is needed to positively identify and rectify such ailments.

See also *Knee*.

S

Sciatica

Pain down the back of the leg, particularly in the buttock or hamstring region, is often misdiagnosed as muscular in origin whereas it may well be referred pain, sometimes resembling a dull ache or numbness, from the sciatic nerve. This condition, quite common among distance runners, is known as sciatica.

The sciatic nerve emerges from the spinal cord between the lumbar vertebrae in the lower back, and travels down the full length of the rear of the leg. Thus, referred pain could extend right down the leg, even though it is more usually felt higher up.

The actual cause of the inflammation will normally be in the lower back itself, which may absorb a great deal of the shock generated by every footfall in training runs. This inflammation may be caused by a slipped disc, where one of the connective tissue rings separating the row of bony vertebrae which form the spine may have become slightly dislodged and protrude outwards, pressing on the sciatic nerve. Specific medical advice in this case will be required.

Sometimes the inflammation may be caused simply by a compression of the lower vertebrae through too much shock being absorbed in the back during long-distance running. In this case a form of gravity inversion treatment, reversing the process, has sometimes proved beneficial, as has relaxing massage of the lower back muscles to improve flexibility in the lumbar region. A switch to training shoes with greater shock absorption qualities, and where possible a choice of softer surfaces for training runs, can also help relieve the condition.

See also *Gravity Inversion, Hamstring*.

Second wind

The first two or three minutes of even a marathon may require somewhat harder breathing than is needed a little later in the race, when the runner has found his 'second wind'. In fact, so-called second wind is merely standard aerobic exercise, where the body is supplying oxygen at the same rate as it is being used. But the preliminary transitional stage (the first wind?), where the runner moves off from the start line, involves the body in coping with a sudden demand, causing a temporary rise in breathing rate until the higher oxygen requirements are met.

Sex

For years most of the speculation about the effects of sexual intercourse upon running performance revolved primarily around whether making love the night before a race would tire the runner out. In some sports there is still a mystique about it, with soccer managers and boxing trainers allowing their charges nothing more energetic than a game of cards on the night before a major competition.

But in running the general view now is that maintaining normality as far as possible, whether in eating, sleeping or sexual habits, is most likely to lead to a satisfactory competitive performance. Physiologically, sex itself may be no more tiring than a short, brisk walk, using up only 150 calories! But if it is preceded by the 'chase' after a partner, then the experience could prove detrimental, more from the physical and emotional drain of the chase, possibly involving, a short, late night, than from the sexual act itself. Given natural instincts, it is not a topic on which there can ever be a specific right answer. Racing performances have certainly been ruined on occasions through untimely diversions to matters of the flesh, but there are also instances like the international runner who broke four minutes for the mile for the first time in his life less than an hour after making love.

Relaxed love-making with a regular partner may actually prove beneficial to some runners in relieving anxiety about the forthcoming competition, and indeed as sex and anxiety are so closely entwined, there is probably a great deal of research which could be done about the relationships of sex, anxiety and running.

So far one of the most representative studies of the sexual attitudes of runners has been the survey carried out amongst its readers by the American magazine *The Runner* in May 1982. Although response was voluntary, the 3140 questionnaires reflected, according to a professional research company, a representative cross-section of its 205,000 subscribers. The average characteristics of the respondents were that 77 per cent were male, 65 per cent were married, and 67 per cent in professional or managerial posts. They trained on average six days a week, at an average volume of thirty-eight miles per week, and raced an average of eleven times a year. They also engaged in sex on average 2.9 times a week.

But when it came to the first question, 'If forced to choose between running and sex, which would you give up?', 65.6 per cent chose to give up running, and only 26.5 per cent to give up sex. A vast majority (60.6 per cent) felt that their sexual vigour increased when they attained their highest level of fitness, and 90 per cent did not abstain from sex just because they had a race the next day. Of these, most (73.2 per cent) felt that it still had no effect on the race at all, while 13.3 per cent felt it actually improved their relaxation.

In general terms, 95 per cent thought that running improved their appearance, while 80 per cent thought that the self-confidence instilled through running also carried over into sexual relationships. But nearly half (45.8 per cent) admitted that they sometimes felt too tired from running to make love. Indeed, one leading British distance runner has even jokingly described training hard for a marathon as being the best form of birth control in existence.

Runners are generally adept at finding out for themselves what is good for them and what is not, and it seems likely that the most potentially detrimental aspects of sex affecting running relate to the runner's mental state, through emotional upset and anxiety. But while running may be affected, it is rarely in itself the root cause. An exception might be in the case of a runner whose partner was a non-runner, but whose own obsession with training was placing a strain on their relationship.

Increasingly, though, running may become very much a shared interest which can actually enhance a relationship. According to 62.7 per cent of the respondents in *The Runner* survey, the perfect Sunday was 'a run, a shower with your mate, a bottle of wine and soft music'.

Shin soreness

A tight pain down one or both shins during or after running is known as shin soreness, or shin splints. It is usually caused by over-training, particularly if a runner is building up his mileage after a prolonged absence, as the anterior tibial (shin) muscles, which also support the arch mechanism of the foot, get used to hard training again.

Training shoes with inflexible soles may also contribute to the problem, as the shin then has to absorb an abnormal amount of shock on each stride. Similarly, training excessively in spikes, or getting back into spiked shoes after the winter, may also place a high stress on the shins as the lower heels of the shoes alter the mechanics of the leg.

If the shin soreness can be clearly traced to such a sudden change of running action, like a switch to spikes, or a new type of training shoe with a significantly different sole thickness, then a slight and temporary reduction in training volume will probably help the condition to ease.

But if it is caused by sheer volume of training,

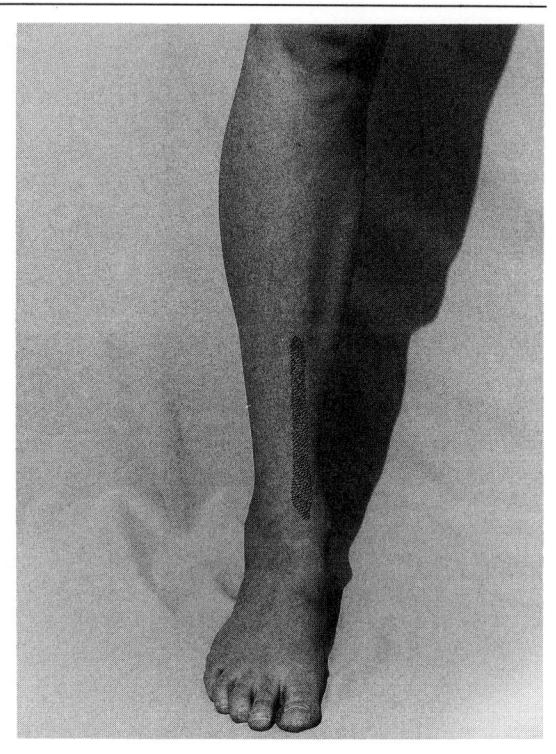

The cause of shin soreness has to be pinpointed, as continuing to train with the condition could cause a stress fracture

then a more permanent reduction may be required; otherwise the soreness may develop into a stress fracture of the tibia. This is often the consequence of trying to ignore shin soreness by training normally, and can lead to an enforced rest of around six weeks. But any reduction in training volume can be compensated by the addition of swimming or cycling sessions to maintain similar cardiovascular fitness.

Some relief of the shin soreness itself can be obtained by the application of ice packs to the affected area, while wearing anything which restricts the circulation in the lower leg, such as tight socks, should be avoided.

See also *Compartment Syndrome*.

Shoes

The average runner takes around 1000 strides in every mile, and on each one of those strides his feet hit the ground with a force nearly three times his bodyweight. Additionally, every runner has his own style and biomechanical peculiarities, which may even be different in his left and right feet.

So considerable time and evaluation has to be given to the choice of running shoes, which are items of substantial expense. Choosing a pair of shoes simply because the colour appeals, or because a particular athlete broke a world record in the same brand last week, is insufficient evaluation!

Running shoe manufacturing is now a multimillion dollar industry, with the commercial demands and rivalry making it necessary for each company to try to convince the running population that their shoes are better than anyone else's. In fact, among the leading brands there is probably not an enormous difference of quality, and the answer to which running shoe is the best really depends on your feet.

The research which has been carried out into such aspects as rear-foot motion control and shock absorption means that there is certainly a very wide choice available. But rather than make it easier for the runner to choose, it is now probably harder than ever, although much easier to accidentally buy a shoe which was never intended for you.

A shop which specializes in running shoes is the best place to buy them because the assistants will often be able to offer the greatest expertise, and are frequently runners themselves. They should be able to advise which of the frequently changing range of shoes have been designed specifically for (say) a heavy runner who pronates excessively, or a female runner who trains at a high intensity and has no excessive foot abnormalities.

Yet even twenty years ago, there was often very little choice. If the runner could find a training shoe in his size, that was probably as much as he felt he needed to consider.

The earliest shoes which could be said to have been made for running are probably those found in an Oregon cave in 1932 by archaeologist Luther Cressman. The shoes were sandals made of crushed sagebrush bark, and were some 10,000 years old. They would have been worn by a cave-dwelling hunter, whose only means of transport was running.

But the first specially made running shoes for sport only date back to the mid-nineteenth century, with a particular model known as the Spencer Shoe having been cited by running shoe expert Peter Cavanagh, PhD, as the beginning of the running shoe evolution. This pair of shoes, thought to have belonged to Lord Spencer, is on display at Northampton Museum and is dated around 1865. Each shoe has three spikes under the forefoot and one under the heel, and the design was probably evolved from early cricket boots of that period.

At the turn of the century, with the newly inaugurated marathon becoming more popular, distance runners wore rather cumbersome heavy boots or shoes which had leather uppers and soles, but very little flexibility. Magazine advertisements at that time also show high-cut boots described as 'long-distance running shoes', but photographic evidence suggests that most of the leading runners of the era perferred low-cut shoes. They also wore 'pushers', which were like lightweight inner slippers made of chamois skin, which covered the front of the foot when worn inside the leather shoes to reduce blistering. Runners of that time sometimes soaked their feet in beef brine for half an hour a night to toughen the skin.

The manufacturing of spiked and distance running shoes developed only slowly, although the introduction of rubber technology helped produce more comfortable and functional types of shoe. But the rivalry between two German companies from the late forties helped accelerate that development. The companies, Adidas and Puma, were actually founded by brothers Adolf and Rudolph Dassler, and through the fifties and sixties their intense rivalry, particularly in the area of track spikes, was legendary (see panel on p. 151).

The road-running boom, which began in the USA in the late sixties and spread worldwide, spawned a fast-growing market, because every one of the millions of new recreational runners, as well as the existing participants, needed a regular supply of training shoes. And it is a continuing market. For, from the moment a pair of running shoes is first worn, your need for another pair gets nearer. So what needs to be borne in mind when selecting running shoes?

* Take your previous pair of training shoes with you to the shop so that the assistant can see the patterns of wear, including any signs of over-pronation. This will make it much easier for him to suggest which particular models should most suit you.

* The best time of day to buy running shoes is during the afternoon, when your feet are likely to have fully expanded, as they will during a long run.

* Try on the shoes with the thickness of socks (if any) you normally wear for running, and do not be afraid to jog around the shop in them. After all, any potential problems are likely to show up during a run, not while you are sitting down. If they seem at all tight, try half a size larger until you are satisfied.

* However tempting, don't buy a shoe which is not absolutely right simply because the shop does not have your size in stock. Try to wait until they have, or go somewhere else.

* Do not feel embarrassed if you try on a dozen pairs of shoes and then do not buy any of them. The onus is on the shop to supply shoes suitable for your feet, not the other way round.

* If you over-pronate a great deal, look for a shoe with a particularly rigid heel counter (the reinforced section curving around the heel).

* Try to avoid shoes with heel tabs, the hump which rises above the heel counter and which can dig into the Achilles tendon on every stride, possibly causing injury. Fortunately, the trend is for fewer models to have this feature.

* Another feature to inspect is the toe box, at the front of the shoe, which should provide sufficient height and width to prevent the toes being cramped. Running in shoes which are too tight can be like kicking a brick wall.

* The inside of the shoes should have the absolute minimum of seams, which are potential causes of blisters.

* The eyelets for lacing should ideally be reinforced with several thicknesses of material; anything less could result in the fabric being torn. (The laces should be taken out and re-threaded every week to help spread the wear on them, and examined for potential breaking points. It always seems to happen at the most inconvenient moment, and spare laces should be kept handy at all times.)

With the manufacturing switch in recent years from leather uppers to nylon, running shoes need much less 'breaking-in' time than previously. But as every foot is different, it is still worthwhile walking around in new training shoes for several days before starting to run in them, to accustom your feet to them.

The weight of shoes can be somewhat misleading. There are some very light, thin-soled shoes on the market which are designed primarily for racing, but even within that context they are intended to be worn by good standard, light-framed runners. In any case, most runners wear the same shoes for training and racing, and such lightweight racing shoes will not stand up to heavy training mileage. Additionally, a male runner of slower standard than, say, two and a half hours for the marathon (which is still a very high level) will be absorbing more shock than necessary when his style begins to deteriorate in the closing miles by wearing such shoes. So shoes which provide substantial support are essential for the vast majority of runners, and the additional few ounces in weight which have to be carried are more than compensated for by the additional protection to the feet and joints which they provide.

The continual search for improved shoes goes on. The Nike company produced an Air-Sole, in which pockets of air were used in the soles of road shoes to help reduce shock and offer, it was claimed, an extra energy return.

In 1981 there was some excitement about a model of open-toed running shoe, developed by the Lydiard Shoe Company in New Zealand, and which seemed set to do away with problems such as black toenails and blistered toes. But although testers reported that their major concerns over scooping up items like

The Dassler Brothers

A feud between two brothers, which helped accelerate the development of running shoes during the fifties and sixties, would surely have formed a good plot for a soap opera.

Adolf and Rudolph Dassler were the sons of a local laundress in the small German town of Herzogenaurach, near Nuremberg, and in the twenties they set up a business called Dassler Brothers, manufacturing carpet slippers.

Adolf (known as Adi), the younger brother, was a keen athlete who enjoyed developing sports shoes. Soon they realized that there was a greater potential market in sports shoes than in carpet slippers.

Their first running shoes were made in 1925, and the business expanded, with Rudolph concentrating on sales and production, and Adolf on new developments. But after the war, the brothers had a major disagreement about their roles in the company. It was also said that Rudolph envisaged his son Armin eventually taking over the company, while Adolf hoped that his own son, Horst, would do so. It reached breaking point in 1947 when Rudolph stormed out to start his own business on the opposite side of the river Duke, which flows through the middle of Herzogenaurach. He called his new company Puma.

Meanwhile, Adolf changed the name of the existing firm at first to Addas, and then to Adidas (Adi-Dassler). Both Puma and Adidas quickly expanded internationally, and during the fifties and sixties their rivalry in the arena of international track and field athletics was intense. Both companies worked furiously to develop the best shoes, and to persuade the top athletes to wear them in major competitions, which they considered the best public endorsement of all.

Yet from 1949 until 1974, when Rudolph died, the brothers never spoke to each other again. In 1978 Adolf died, and was buried in the same cemetery as his brother, overlooking their little town of Herzogenaurach. Adidas and Puma, the companies formed by their bitter argument, remain.

On the death of Adolf Dassler, the Adidas company was taken over by his wife, Kaethe. Following her death in 1984 their son, Horst Dassler, became chairman, having spent some twenty-five years learning the business. He had in that time also became one of the most influential (if not *the* most influential) people in the world of international sport through his close friendships with many top administrators at the very highest levels. So his own death from cancer in 1987 at the age of 51 was another unexpected twist of fate in the story.

The late Horst Dassler with a portrait of his father, Adi, who founded Adidas, one half of the sports shoe rivalry

small stones into the shoe, and tripping (since there was no toe box to keep the tip of the shoe off the road), did not seem to present a problem, the shoes did not become widely available.

Perhaps with a view to the leisure rather than competitive marketplace, in 1985 Puma announced a computerized shoe with an electronic device in the heel which could be plugged into a personal computer after a run to assess the runner's expended calories.

Most runners, though, are constantly looking for a shoe which is comfortable, durable, and economically priced. And although the best way for the runner to discover that ideal shoe is through trial and error, logistically it would be impossible to try out all of the many models available. But through careful questioning in the running shop (and of fellow runners), and considered deliberation and inspection, it is at least possible to narrow down the candidates.

As the shoes you choose will be your only point of contact with the ground for many hundreds of miles, it is worth spending some time trying to ensure that they will help rather than hinder you.

See also *Barefoot Running, Blisters, Foot, Orthotics, Pronation, Socks, Supination, Waffle-soled Shoes.*

The running shoe

A typical road-running shoe, such as that in Figure 1, may have three different layers of shock-absorbing material under the heel to reduce the impact at the point where most runners make their initial contact with the ground on every stride. Looking at the chief characteristics from the ground up, the outsole (A) runs the whole length of the shoe and is its first line of defence. It is also designed to give the necessary traction or grip with the running surface by its varous combinations of ridges and studs. It is usually made of solid carbon rubber for maximum durability, or blown rubber (which contains tiny air bubbles) for extra cushioning. In some shoes, there may be a combination of both at different contact points, with carbon rubber at the hardest wearing sections.

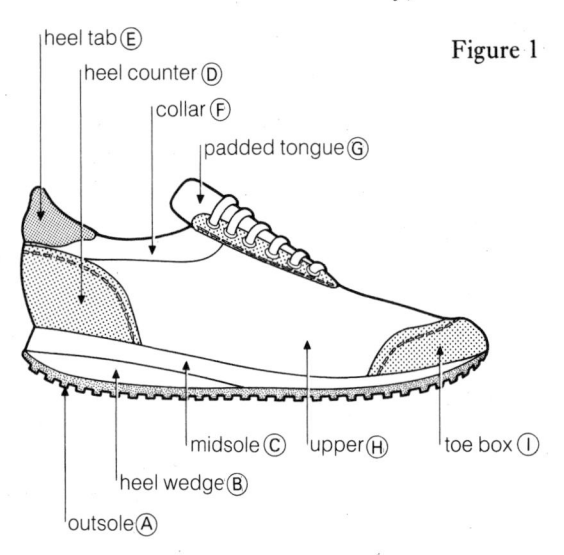

The heel wedge (B) is a wedge-shaped cushion which provides additional support between the heel and the arch, giving an extra lift to the heel and reducing the likelihood of Achilles tendon strain.

The midsole section (C) is the full-length shock-absorbing layer, usually made of EVA (ethylene vinyl acetate), a polymer which can have variable amounts of air bubbles within it. The more bubbles, the lighter and more cushioned, but less durable, the midsole section.

The heel counter (D) is usually made of thermoplastic, covered in suede (known as foxing), and provides additional control of the natural rearfoot movement in running. Even this rigid support is insufficient for some runners who over-pronate to a significant degree, and for them models of shoe with additional control devices are well worth considering.

The infamous heel tab (E) is supposed to protect the Achilles tendon, but for many runners does just the opposite, digging into the vulnerable part of the tendon on every stride. In such cases, and if all other aspects of the shoes suit the runner ideally, some careful surgery with a sharp tool, such as a Stanley knife, to slice off the tabs and level that section of the shoe with the collar (F), can relieve the problem. If necessary some zinc oxide tape can be used to cover the incision to prevent possible blistering from the freshly cut edge.

The collar itself, and the padded tongue (G), are both refinements of recent years to increase comfort around the foot and reduce the chance of blistering. The toe box (I) should be roomy enough to prevent blistering or black toenails. But in some runners, the toes may curl upwards on every stride causing toe nail bruising, or at least wearing a hole in the upper. This is a common occurrence, and affects world-record-breaking athletes as well as joggers. Although

Figure 1

unsightly, the worn holes in the toe area of the uppers (H) will not adversely affect the running action (and may even provide welcome ventilation!). Indeed, in the case of consistent bruising, a deliberate incision in the upper, at the point where the toe repeatedly strikes the inside of the shoe, may help relieve the problem.

In Figure 2, which shows the difference between the terms 'heel height' and 'heel lift', the flared design of some shoe soles is also clearly visible. The outsole and midsole are flared, so that the shock on heel strike is spread further, and stability is increased. But a disadvantage is that in runners with a somewhat bow-legged gait, there may be a tendency to catch the inside edge of this flared heel on the opposite calf, creating soreness or even an abrasion.

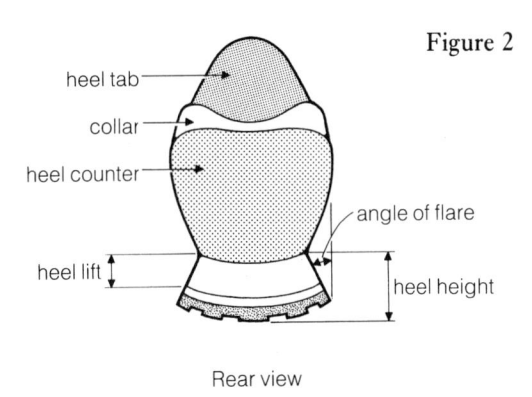

Figure 2

Rear view

Conventional, slip and combination lasting

Running shoes are constructed on lasts, which are special forms in the shape of human feet, using three main methods: conventional, slip and combination lasting. Conventional (or board) lasting entails a technique common with all types of footwear, where the upper material is pulled over the last and glued to the underside of a thin innersole board (see Figure 4). This board, which usually runs the full length of the shoe, provides a more rigid support and protection for the foot. For the runner with a very flexible foot, this traditional board-lasting technique gives additional stability.

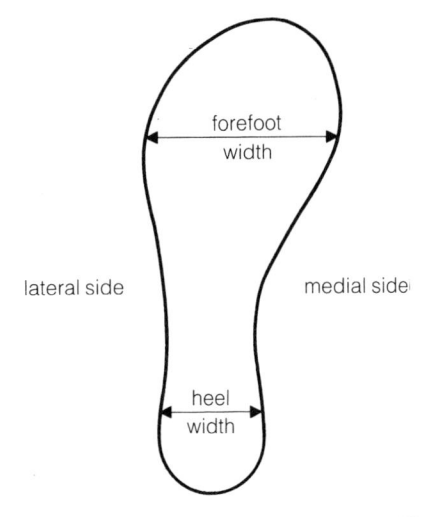

Figure 3

The second technique is slip lasting, which was developed to assist the runner in two major ways: lightness and flexibility. The upper material is not attached to a board, but instead is stretched right round and stitched to itself and, when it is put on the last, resembles a sock. The sole is then attached directly to this sock-like upper, producing a shoe which is both lighter and more flexible without the board innersoles of the conventional technique (see Figure 5). Runners with 'rigid' feet usually find this type of shoe to their liking, as long as there is good cushioning in the soles, for it allows a more natural running action.

As runners have so many individual quirks of style, some find they actually prefer the third type of shoe construction – a 'combination' lasting – which uses both the conventional and slip lasting techniques. A typical combination lasting could entail the conventional board for the rear two-thirds of the shoe, to provide maximum stability and protection, but then slip lasting in the forefoot area, with the board stopping short of the forefoot (see Figure 6). This has the advantage of still allowing maximum flexibility in that complex part of the foot which pushes off on every stride, while providing firm control under the rest of the foot.

As a simple assessment of which type of shoe would be best for you, look at your own bare

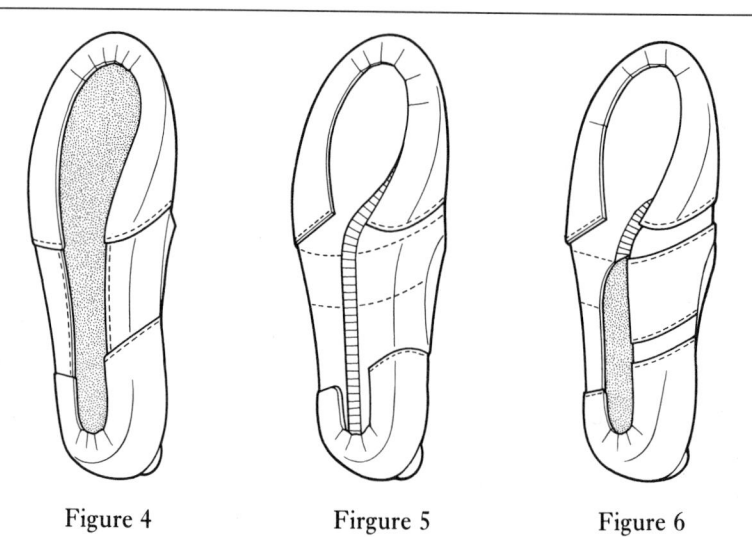

Figure 4   Firgure 5   Figure 6

footprint. If your heel and forefoot are distinctly separate, you have a high arch and should find slip-lasted shoes more suitable to your naturally rigid feet. But if your feet are over-flexible, the footprint will appear flat with little, if any, arch showing. In that case, board-lasted shoes will probably be more suitable.

A clearly defined arch means that your feet are 'normal', and you may find combination last shoes the most effective and comfortable.

Curved and straight lasted shoes

As well as the different methods of construction, the shoes may be made on curved or straight lasts (see Figure 7). The majority of runners have feet which curve slightly inwards, but some have a straighter foot shape. In that case, their toes will not fit cleanly into a shoe made for a curving foot, and instead they will need a straight-lasted shoe. Conversely, the toes of a runner needing a curve-lasted shoe will feel uncomfortable in a straight-lasted shoe. In both cases, the test is whether there is room in the toe box for the longest toe to move forward without hindrance from the shoe during the normal running action.

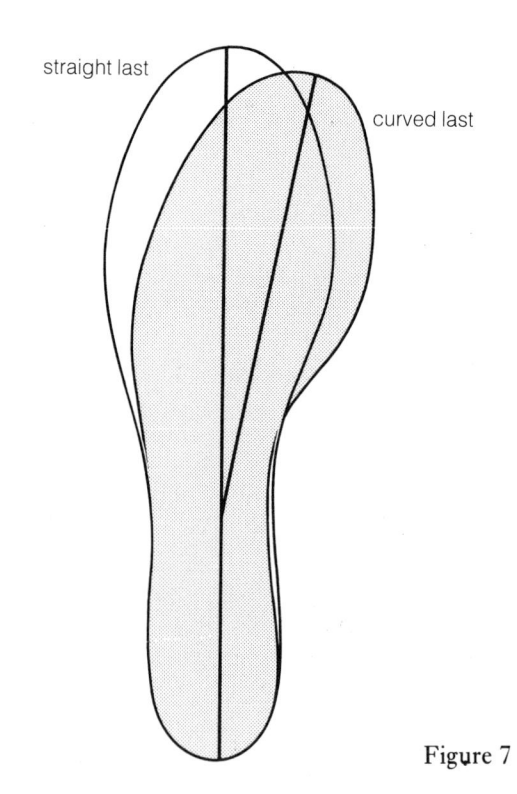

A straight-lasted shoe also gives more support to the medial (inside) edge of the foot and so for severely pronating runners, or for those who run at a slow pace, they can provide extra help. For faster running, or for those who naturally run on the outside of their feet, the curve-lasted shoes will usually be more beneficial.

straight last

curved last

Figure 7

Sleep

To maintain a hard training routine, usually in conjunction with a full job and social life, demands careful pursuit of adequate sleep to assist the recovery process. Most people (runners or not) sleep in the region of eight hours a night, and while there are some individuals who can train hard on less, most distance runners admit they would prefer to have even more sleep if circumstances allowed.

Sleeping only six or seven hours a night is not life-threatening, but some runners who meticulously examine every other aspect of their training routine, including diet and running shoes, may overlook an area which could be undermining the real value of everything else. If a runner feels constantly tired, even when training lightly, and seems to fall prey to every infection near him, then adjusting the daily routine to enable an extra 30-60 minutes sleep a night could make a significant difference. This may mean training earlier, because the exercise itself, followed by a shower or bath and then an evening meal, may for some people prevent a rapid descent into sleep. For others, it may actually accelerate it. But most runners find their normal routine through a combination of trial and error, and family and working commitments. Even so, there are those who can run quite happily early in the morning, and others who can barely put one foot in front of the other before 11 a.m.!

Some international-level athletes who are training twice or even three times a day find an hour's afternoon nap helpful, but it is a luxury beyond the reach of the vast majority of runners. In any case, such naps are only really valuable as long as they do not adversely affect the night's sleep.

Nervous apprehension often inhibits sleep the night before a major competition, but if that insomnia continues during normal training periods, other factors, such as over-training and even anaemia, have to be considered as possible causes, and treated accordingly.

It is usually considered that sleep the night before the race matters less than the night before that. But as yet there is no firm scientific evidence to support this theory. Instead, the view might be expressed as 'if you are mentally too active to sleep properly the night before a race, then at least try to ensure a good sleep the night before that'. The true benefit of sleep to the runner comes from obtaining a sufficient amount regularly and not trying to catch up in a hurry.

See also *Insomnia*.

Smoking

Quite apart from the undoubted long-term health risks related to smoking, cigarettes have short-term negative effects on an exercise like running, which is so dependent on the efficiency of the lungs and oxygen utilization.

The burning of tobacco produces nicotine, tar and carbon monoxide. The nicotine, acting as a stimulant, raises the blood pressure, constricts blood vessels and slows down the rate at which the blood returns to the heart. It also delays the digestive processes.

The tar, in tiny particles, is deposited on the bronchioles and the lungs, curtailing their efficiency, and in time frequently causing chronic lung disease.

The third product, carbon monoxide gas, reduces the oxygen-carrying power of the haemoglobin in the blood by 10-15 per cent, limiting in turn the body's ability to function at its peak ability. Even disregarding for a moment the strong links with the causes of cancer, heart disease and bronchitis, for a runner there could be few less helpful things in improving fitness than cigarettes. At best, smoking is a dangerous (and expensive) handicap. It also kills.

Snow

Once the initial novelty of a heavy snowfall has worn off, it becomes a hazard and a menace to most runners. While it is still soft, snow provides a little resistance training, but once it has become packed down on the pavements it becomes a potential bone-breaker to the unsuspecting runner, especially when the sun goes

Snow provides an additional hazard for the cross-country racer and the casual trainer alike

down and it takes on a grey, shiny quality on which it is easy to slip.

So when snow is on the ground, it is best to stay on tried and tested training routes, where at least the surface underneath is predictably safe. Unfamiliar cross-country routes in snow may be visually pleasant, but all manner of potentially ankle-twisting stones and ruts remain in wait.

Whenever possible, the runner should try to run on cleared paths and roads, but without putting himself, or motorists, at risk. The traditional light-coloured clothing at night needs to become something more vivid against the surroundings, like bright yellow or orange.

Shoes with good grip are essential, and runners can expect to experience some aches and stiffness in the leg muscles and joints after running because the need to retain balance will often cause a slightly tense and unaccustomed action, as if the legs are prepared to take evading action on every stride in case of a fall. As the snowy conditions sometimes set in for several weeks or more, it is advisable at least to aim to retain existing fitness if it becomes impossible to improve it. As a break from sliding around on the roads, a switch to swimming, riding a stationary cycle, or even running on a treadmill (the way in which Ingrid Kristiansen has successfully overcome the Norwegian snows) could provide a safer method of retaining cardiovascular fitness.

Socks

Socks help to reduce the blister-causing friction between your foot and the inside of your shoe, to absorb sweat, and to cut down the shock as your foot hits the road. For long training runs, there can even be a certain psychological reassurance about having thick socks with reinforced soles, but in races some runners prefer thin, lightweight socks, or no socks at all. Experimenting to decide which suits you best should always take place in training, though, and not in a race.

Socks should be kept clean because dried 'sweaty' socks may have sharp crinkles in them which may then cause the very blisters they are supposed to prevent. Once a running sock has a hole in it, it should be thrown away, because darns can also cause blisters.

If you do choose to run without socks, which some runners find cooler and psychologically lighter, as a precaution rub petroleum jelly, such as Vaseline, on parts of the foot which may be susceptible to blistering, particularly the prime areas of vulnerability, the tops of the toes, the arches, and around the back of the heels. Some runners find a thin piece of sponge inserted between the heel and the back of their shoe can prevent heel blisters, but beware of inadvertently making the shoes too tight. Avoid socks which are tight around the ankle, or are of knee length, because in both cases the circulation may be restricted.

If you normally wear thick running socks (ladies, particularly), remember to take them with you whenever you buy new running shoes, to ensure a good fit.

Spikes

On track and cross country, spiked shoes afford better grip, although the wide range of ridged and waffle soles now available on many training shoes usually means that they too are quite adequate on all but the muddiest surfaces. Indeed, many distance runners prefer the additional support they get from training shoes and wear them anyway.

Spiked shoes tend to be made as light as possible which, for sprinting and middle-distance running (say, up to 1500m) can be advantageous. But at longer distances, even on the track, the slight additional weight of training shoes may be more than compensated for by the comfort and familiarity of the shoes, and a normal running action. Running too far in unfamiliar spiked shoes with their lesser heel support can lead to Achilles tendon strain, as can jogging too many recovery runs during an interval training session.

If you decide to wear spiked shoes, try to become used to them over a period of weeks first, gradually increasing the proportion of a training session for which you wear them rather than executing a full session in them straight away.

Distance runners buying spiked shoes will probably find those models with the deepest heel wedge the most suitable. Models with virtually no support under the heel are primarily meant for sprinters, who tend to run on their toes. In longer events, the heel normally comes down first, even though the spikes are traditionally situated in the sole. The logic for this is not entirely clear, and in cross-country running spiked shoes which combine a well ridged sole with spikes are best, for it is that unspiked part of the shoe which lands first on often slippery surfaces. In fact, IAAF rules do allow for two heel spikes (and four for javelin or high jump), but running-shoe designers rarely include this facility.

The IAAF rules also limit the number of spikes in the sole of each shoe to a maximum of six, and if you wonder why there are usually seven holes in this part of the shoe, this is to allow you to alter the pattern of the six spikes to suit your own preference. A 'blank' is supplied to fit into the unused hole so that it does not become clogged with mud. The spikes themselves are screwed firmly into place with a special tool known as a spike spanner or spike key, and they should be tightened before every race or training session.

Before major championship track events, an official usually checks the athletes' spikes to ensure the limit of six on each shoe sole is observed. In the late sixties, a shoe was developed which actually had row upon row of tiny spikes, like a brush, and was indeed known as the 'brush spike'. But it was quickly banned as providing unfair assistance.

On today's synthetic track surfaces, a very sharp running spike of 6mm is usually considered the maximum length either desirable (to limit damage to the track) or necessary. But on cinder tracks, which may offer a less stable surface, 9mm or even 12mm spikes may be required, while in cross-country events spikes as long as 15mm can prove their worth in the heaviest going. Most runners keep a small box of different length spikes with their shoes together with the necessary tools to make last-minute changes if necessary. A pair of pincers is a useful accessory in case any of the installed spikes proves difficult to unscrew.

Spiked shoes are often worn without socks, and bought in a slightly smaller size than road shoes. A dusting of talcum powder or smearing of Vaseline on the feet before putting them on can ensure a snug fit. But they are no longer the indispensable part of a runner's equipment that they were once considered.

Sprinting

Although sprint races are completed in just a fraction of the time of distance races, just as much training preparation has to go into the explosive action. But it is a different type of training.

For instance, the sprinter can win or lose a race through poor starting technique, something unthinkable to a marathon runner. So frequent work using starting blocks is essential. When the runner is given the command 'Take your marks', he walks up to the line, and backs into the blocks. In the crouch position, most of the weight is taken on the rear knee and by the fingers and thumbs which are placed right up to the nearside edge of, but not on, the starting line. The hands are almost directly under the shoulders, as the runner sets his gaze about 5–10m down the track.

At the command 'Set!', the hips are raised, the rear knee comes off the ground, and the weight is moved forward on to the fingers. This is an uncomfortable position, which cannot be held for long, but the starter will not fire the gun until all the sprinters are motionless in this position. Usually it is held for 1–2 seconds at the most. If it takes longer, he will probably ask the runners to stand up and begin the whole procedure again.

As the gun fires, the sprinter first lifts his hands off the ground, but to avoid toppling

Top: Typical spiked shoes showing (left) the seven optional spike holes and (upper right) a heel wedge suitable for a distance runner

Below: A selection of spike keys used to screw the different length spikes in and out of the shoes

The 1986 European 100m champion Linford Christie (5) beats international teammate John Regis (18) in an indoor 200m at Cosford: a hundredth of a second can make all the difference in sprinting

forward almost simultaneously has to give himself a firm drive off the blocks, with the rear leg coming through first while the front foot gains maximum momentum from pushing against the front block. The first 30–40m in a sprint is the acceleration phase, where the body gradually becomes upright from its natural forward lean at the start, and the strides are rapid but at less than full extension.

This starting routine has to be rehearsed again and again, until the sprinter can reduce his reaction time to its minimum, and obtain a fast clean start, without anticipating the gun. To do so in a race, or to topple out of the 'Set' position, would be charged as a false start, and a second such offence by the same athlete would result in disqualification.

But while a good start is vital, conditioning is also an important aspect of sprinting, to ensure that the top speed, reached after about six seconds of running, can be maintained to the finish. A dynamic arm action, which in turn affects leg speed as they work together, is an important element of successful sprinting, with athletes spending a great deal of training time on upper body strengthening exercises, such as weight training and punching a boxer's speedball. These sort of activities would be largely unnecessary to the marathon runner, who uses his arms primarily as balances.

Sprint drills, a series of repeated exercises which concentrate on very specific aspects of the sprinting action, also form part of the sprinter's training to try to make them second nature. For in just ten seconds of sprinting time, everything has to happen simultaneously and subconsciously.

Hill training and resistance training are also

likely to be included in the sprinter's build-up, as he seeks to develop explosive power and strength, but allied to the relaxation which allows muscles to work more efficiently.

The finishing technique also has to be perfected; the correct timing of the 'dip', which can ensure the runner's torso is first across the line in a close fought race, is crucial.

See also *Starting Blocks*, *Wind Gauge*.

Staleness

The word staleness does not refer, in the running sense, to unwashed socks, but to a temporary and severe waning of enthusiasm for training and racing. In some runners enthusiasm can develop into sheer obsession, and too much unrelieved obsession can in turn lead to a state where the body is extremely fit, but the mind is beginning to wander. To put it another way, the flesh is willing but the spirit is weak.

Too much continual high-level training, especially if it is at the expense of other enjoyed pursuits, can lead to a situation where even the normally dedicated runner looks upon the prospect of yet another training run with disinterest. It particularly applies to the competitive runner who has had a great many races in a short time, when the thought of another fails to produce the nervous feeling usually required for the best performances.

In such circumstances, a break from training, even for just a few days, is essential. Using the opportunity to catch up on social life, films, theatre, or other interests, can actually restore the appetite for running, simply through the change of scenery.

Most top-level runners tend to divide their training into sections, comprising a set period of high-level training, followed by a spell of reduced training in between serious racing, and a recuperative phase of rest. Then the steady build-up towards the next high volume training begins again. The whole cycle may take six months or a year each time, but it follows the same pattern, like summer follows spring.

A sprint race can be won or lost in the opening strides, where starting blocks are crucial

Trying to train and race at the same unrelieved level for too long can result in the mental fatigue which affects both attitude and performance, and is known as 'getting stale'.

Starting blocks

For competitors in events up to and including 400m in length starting blocks are compulsory in competitions held under IAAF Rules, and can be fitted with apparatus which detects a false start, where the foot has left the block before the starter's gun has fired.

The starting blocks consist of two rigid plates attached to a metal frame, which is firmly fixed to the ground by pins. The sprinter can adjust the plates in angle and position to his own requirements to ensure a reliable surface against which to push his feet at the start.

The blocks are not compulsory in domestic competition and, ironically, were only authorized at all by the IAAF in 1938. Prior to that sprinters in major competitions (including Jesse Owens in his memorable Berlin Olympic performances in 1936) had to dig foot holes in the cinder track surface with trowels.

Starting blocks were developed in 1927 by two Americans, George Bresnaham and William Tuttle, and from their experiments they assessed that the benefit to a sprinter using

Jesse Owens had to dig holes in the cinder track with a trowel before his historic performances at the 1936 Berlin Olympics

blocks in a 100-yard race averaged 0.34 seconds. At the American National Collegiate Championships in Chicago on 8 June 1929, George Simpson became the first man to sprint 100 yards in 9.4 seconds, but the mark was not ratified as a world record by the IAAF because of his use of starting blocks. When the IAAF did allow starting blocks from 1938 it was not because of the help they offered athletes, but rather because they speeded up proceedings at athletics meetings and protected the track.

Blocks are not allowed in events longer than 400m (apart from the lead-off runner in 4 × 200m and 4 × 400m relays). But at all distances, including the marathon (although it rarely happens), an athlete is allowed only one false start. Disqualification follows a second offence, except in the decathlon and heptathlon running events, where two false starts are allowed, with disqualification on a third offence.

Steeplechase

Not an event for the fainthearted, with its solid timber barriers and water jump, the steeplechase has its historical roots in the nineteenth century, when the horse-racing version was already well established.

The traditional story is that in 1850 an undergraduate of Exeter College, Oxford, named Halifax Wyatt, was complaining to some friends that he would rather run the steeplechase course himself than ride it again on the horse which had just thrown him in a race. From subsequent conversations, a human steeplechase was organized at Binsey, near Oxford, later that year, and the first man home on the two-mile course with its twenty-four jumps was Wyatt himself.

In fact, there are reports of a steeplechase having been held as early as 1828 in Edinburgh. But the event was certainly included in the Oxford University sports for a few years from 1860, and a track steeplechase was included in the English championships in 1879.

It was introduced into the Olympic Games in 1900, but at two different distances, 2500m and 4000m and consisted of stone fences, a water jump, hurdles and other obstacles. The Olympic distance varied until the adoption of 3000m in 1920, when it was won by Englishman Percy Hodge in 10:0.4. It has remained that length internationally ever since, although in the 1932 Olympic Games the competitors ran a lap extra because of an official's error; the result was allowed to stand.

The sheer fatigue caused by running 3000m, plus the need to hurdle solid barriers on each lap, has made it a spectacular event. The fall of American Henry Marsh at the last barrier in the 1983 World Championships, just as he was challenging Patriz Ilg for the gold medal, is typical of its drama and unpredictability. And when Chris Brasher unexpectedly won the Olympic gold medal for Britain in 1956 he was at first disqualified for bumping an opponent on the last lap, and had to wait three hours before the jury of appeal agreed it was accidental and reinstated him.

One of Britain's best steeplechasers, Colin Reitz, (5), drives out of the water jump

The competitors have to negotiate twenty-eight hurdles and seven water jumps in the course of the race (for which there is a junior version of 2000m, involving eighteen hurdles and five water jumps). Each barrier is three feet high (0.914m), at least 13 feet (3.96m) in width, and weighs between 80 and 100kg. The water jump is also three feet high, with a length of 12 feet (3.66m). The runners put one foot on the top of the water jump, and usually hurdle the other barriers simply for speed; but they could stop and climb over them if they wished.

At present the event is confined to male athletes, but the IAAF Women's Committee is investigating the possibility of a steeplechase suitable for women.

Stitch

Although most people associate stitch with their schooldays, when they had a sharp pain in their side during a run and had to stop and walk, it can affect even Olympic athletes.

Its occurrence is often related to trying to take prolonged exercise too soon after a meal, with one theory being that the pain comes from internal organs, such as the spleen and liver, as the blood flow is urgently redistributed from digestion to exercise. At least three hours should be allowed after a meal before running long distances, and so perhaps the school dinner-hour and games period often come too close together for Nature!

Even when international athletes allow their normal three-hour gap between eating and running, they may still suffer stitch in major races, because their increased anxiety over the event may in turn slow down the digestive process. Thus, allowing an extra hour for digestion before an important race could help ward off the risk.

While science still has no foolproof remedy, practical relief may be found while running by increasing the angle of forward lean, or by lifting the body from the waist to stretch out any possible cramp-like spasm in the diaphragm, or by gripping a hard object, like a stone, in the hand. If all else fails, stop and walk!

Stress fracture

The stress fracture, which is particularly associated with distance runners, usually manifests itself first as a sharp pain in the lower leg or midfoot, and is the result of a considerable volume of repetitious training, not necessarily at great speed. The most vulnerable areas for the runner are in the two lower bones of the leg – in the upper two-thirds of the tibia (shin bone), or just above the outer ankle in the fibula – and in the second, third and fourth metatarsals, which are the mid-foot bones leading back from second, third and fourth toes.

Although these bones are of contrasting sizes, their basic shape (long and narrow) is similar, and it is repeated stress across these bones which finally causes a painful, if medically almost imperceptible, crack.

The initial symptoms are recurrent pain in these areas while running, although sometimes the pain will deceivingly wear off after a mile or so, only to recur after the run. Runners who have considerably raised their training mileage in a relatively short time, or run a very high mileage, may be particularly vulnerable. Pressing the affected bone and discovering one specific, localized area of pain can indicate the strong possibility of a stress fracture, particularly if it is accompanied by some swelling.

Although too much running on the road is often blamed as a cause, some sport injury experts simply blame too much running on any surface, since it is the continual action of the muscle pulling across the bone which causes the crack, like the stresses which can cause fatigue cracks in an aircraft wing, or the way in which constantly bending a paper clip will eventually cause it to break.

If a stress fracture is suspected, confirmation is often difficult to obtain, as standard X-rays rarely show up anything until after the bone has healed, some 4–6 weeks later, when a tiny ridge may have formed.

A bone scan is the most effective method of quick confirmation, as it will show the activity in the bone where Nature is repairing the crack, but such scans are expensive and difficult to obtain. Many doctors feel that a runner with a possible stress fracture should not come high on the list of priorities for a bone scan.

Usually a combination of the symptoms, the site of the pain, and any incidence of a major change in training load will be sufficient to convince the experienced runner or coach that it is almost certainly a stress fracture. Some runners have a particular susceptibility to them.

The treatment is just to allow Nature to complete the healing process, but although this means no running in the first 3–4 weeks of recovery, it need not mean no exercise. Regular swimming and cycling help the cardiovascular system retain a considerable degree of fitness if the pulse can be raised and maintained at an aerobic level for periods similar to running sessions. These exercises, which should place no weight-bearing stresses on the affected leg or foot, are suitable substitutes until running can recommence. Indeed, runners who suffer from stress fractures are often advised to retain at least one swimming and one cycling session in place of running on their return to normal training as a way of trying to prevent a recurrence of the stress fracture.

The bones adapt and strengthen gradually to accommodate the forces demanded of them in training, and it is when the volume of training increases at a greater rate than adaption of the bone that the fracture can first occur. An extreme example of this is the 'march fracture', which refers to a crack in the third metatarsal, and is so-called because it is frequently suffered by soldiers suddenly put on long route marches.

So the return to training should be carefully graduated, since in the 4–6 week recommended minimum period away from running while the fracture heals, the other bones may have softened slightly without their regular training dose of stress. Thus, the runner is at a vulnerable stage on his return, and those who suffer a series of stress fractures in quick succession, and are considered unlucky, are more usually victims of trying to get back to full training again too quickly.

If the original pain has not subsided on return to training, despite a 4–6 week lay-off from running, further medical investigation may be required.

The importance of good, supportive and well-cushioned footwear at all stages of a runner's career cannot be over-emphasized, particularly when returning from a stress fracture. Road training cannot be avoided, but the occasional venture on to softer surfaces will at least help to alter the repetitive stresses.

A higher than average level of stress fracture has been reported among female runners who are amenorrhoeic (i.e., whose periods have ceased), and there is now thought to be a link between this and the subsequently reduced levels of the hormone oestrogen, which affects the calcium content in the bones. A prolonged cessation of menstruation may therefore slightly weaken the bones, and make the hard-training female athlete more at risk to a stress fracture than the female who experiences normal menstruation. Calcium supplements in the diet may help to counteract this, although research is still continuing, and indeed added calcium may assist any athlete, male or female, to reduce the possibility of a stress fracture.

Stride

In the same way that we all have different fingerprints, so we all have different stride lengths. There is no chart which can tell you by age, height, best performance or resting pulse rate what your correct stride length should be. You will find it simply by running, and as you become fitter and stronger, so your stride length will automatically adjust.

The runner who needs most help on stride length is often the one who is trying to copy the style of someone else (usually a top international) to the detriment of their own economic running. Or else they have read that the two factors governing running speed are, quite correctly, stride-length and stride-frequency. So they estimate that if their own normal stride length is two metres, and they try to increase it to 2.25m and keep the same frequency, then they will surely cover the ground faster. But what actually happens is that they over-reach themselves biomechanically in trying to find the other 25cm on every stride, their natural style disintegrates, they soon become disjointed and, ironically, less efficient.

The best way to naturally improve the stride length is just to use normal training methods (like LSD, fartlek, interval and resistance) with a normal, comfortable stride. Then, as the legs become stronger and more efficient, so the stride length and frequency will improve surely, but almost imperceptibly. Like so many other aspects of running, the desired improvement can be earned simply through regular training and patience. Attempted short-cuts rarely pay dividends.

Sunday Times National Fun Run

Britain's biggest annual participatory running event is not the London Marathon, but the *Sunday Times* National Fun Run in Hyde Park, which pre-dates the marathon by two and a half years and was first held on 1 October 1978. At the end of September each year around 30,000 people of all ages, shapes and levels of fitness take place in a series of runs divided into age and sex categories.

The concept is based on a similar event held in the Bois de Boulogne in Paris each year, the Cross du Figaro, which began in 1961 and succeeded in putting the fun back into running for thousands of French families.

The idea was developed in London by *Sunday Times* sports editor John Lovesey and leading sports writer Norman Harris, an accomplished marathon runner (2hr 40min 21sec in the 1965 AAA Marathon), who has been the National Fun Run director since its

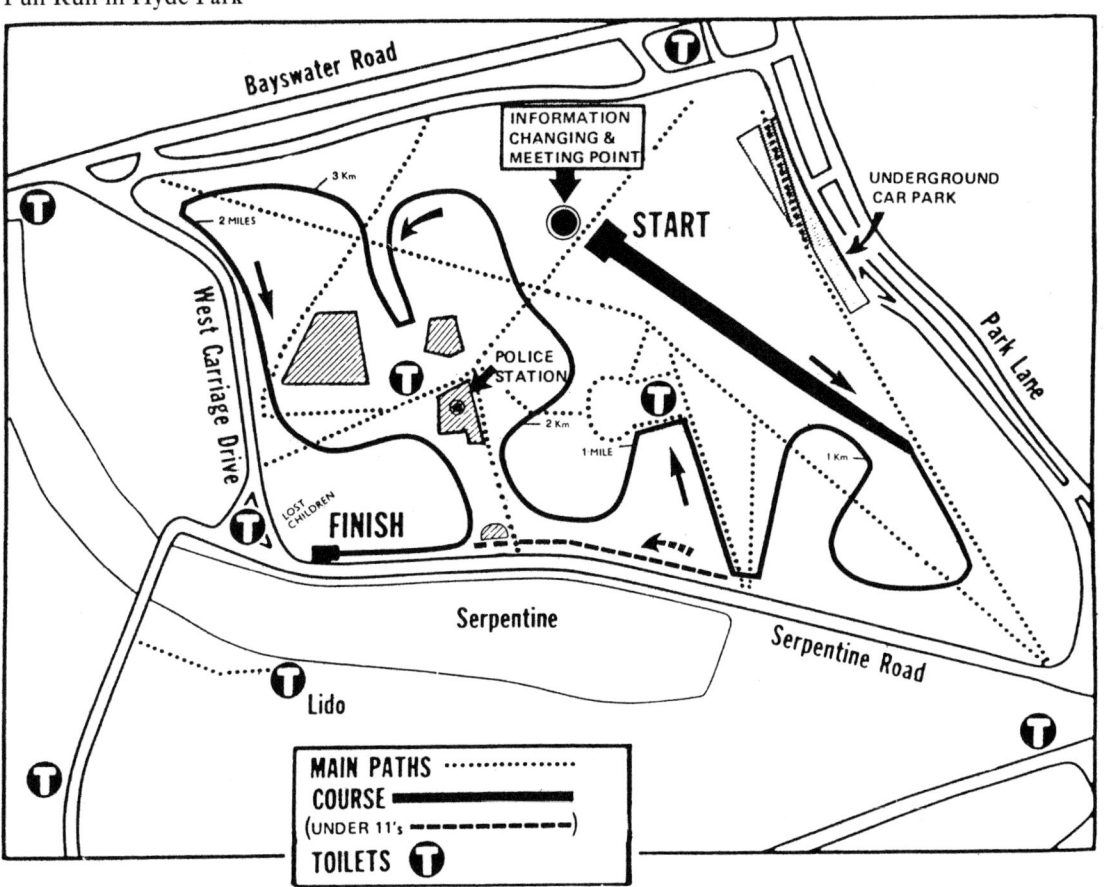

A map of the winding 2½-mile course used each year by 30,000 runners in the *Sunday Times* National Fun Run in Hyde Park

inauguration. At Hyde Park all events, apart from an under-11s 2km (1¼ miles), cover the same flat grassland course of 4km (2½ miles), and while a finishing order is established, counting towards an overall team competition, there are no prizes. Instead, every runner who completes the course receives a categorized certificate of gold, silver or bronze, according to how well they did in their particular event. There are also separate category overall placings for the leading couples, two-generation and three-generation family teams, as well as for group teams from businesses, pubs, sports clubs, schools, universities, the media, government, medical groups, fitness clubs and groups of friends.

In 1986 nearly 2000 teams took part, although individuals are equally welcome, and money from the entry fees is donated to a designated charity each year. The events take place in quick succession, yet the day's activities still last from 10 a.m. to around 4.30 p.m., and are climaxed by a mass jog in which thousands of participants jog round the course together in a celebration of running.

Each year the event is oversubscribed, and early entry is essential; details of entry procedure appear each year in the *Sunday Times* during early summer. And while the concept attracts leading runners in fund-raising efforts for charity (Dave Moorcroft and Wendy Sly broke the course records for men and women in 1986 while running for their own nominated charities), the aim is to get as many people as possible, of all standards, to take part in what is essentially the ideal family picnic day if you enjoy running and the company of runners.

Total number of entrants by year –

Year	Entrants
1978:	12,000
1979:	15,000
1980:	18,000
1981:	27,000
1982:	27,000
1983:	29,000
1984:	30,000
1985:	30,000
1986:	30,000

Supination

Each time the heel hits the ground during a run, a side-to-side stabilizing movement of the foot occurs at the subtalar joint, which is just below the ankle joint. This helps to absorb some of the shock which is sent through the foot and up the leg, with the movement inwards being known as pronation, and the follow-up movement outwards, before the heel lifts off the ground again, being known as supination.

These are perfectly natural actions, but in some runners an excessive pronation inwards can lead to injury, while the corresponding supination movement on each stride occurs only minimally, if at all.

But while over-pronation is fairly common, there are also cases of over-supination. These can occur if the foot is too rigid, and the predominant tendency of the foot is to move outwards at the subtalar joint on each stride. The result is that its natural shock-absorbing quality is severely reduced, as it tends to land with a rigid slap, and the fluid movement with which the foot is designed to dissipate shock is lost.

While excessive supination can be detected by the same methods as excessive pronation (see page 140), there is no actual cure. But its effects can be minimized by the insertion of shock-absorbing material in the shoes. Excessive supination usually occurs in runners with high arches, and if orthotics are needed in the shoes, the semi-rigid type are preferable, since they act as additional shock absorbers.

See also *Orthotics, Pronation*.

Sweating

The control of body temperature during hard exercise is essential, because the heat generation during an activity like running is considerable. If its effect on the body were to go unchecked, vital organs like the kidneys and liver would not be able to cope. One estimate shows that the effort of running a marathon without the benefit of any heat-loss mechanism would almost double the temperature of the body.

Sweating is more important than the other major heat-loss mechanisms of the body, convection and radiation. (For convection and radiation, see also *Heat*.) When the body temperature rises, the brain sends nerve impulses to the sweat glands, stimulating them to secrete their water and salt (mainly sodium chloride) on to the skin. There are between three and four million sweat glands on the human body, and they are particularly abundant on the soles of the feet, palms of the hands, armpits and forehead.

But the simple secretion of sweat does not, in itself, cause heat loss. Instead, the sweat absorbs heat from the skin (to where it has been brought from the muscles by the blood), which causes it to evaporate. It is this transformation of sweat into water vapour, using the body heat, which is the actual process of temperature regulation.

However, this evaporation becomes more difficult in conditions of high humidity, where there is already a considerable percentage of moisture in the atmosphere. Characteristically, the runner becomes increasingly soaked with sweat, as it is unable to evaporate and perform its body-cooling task, and as the exercise continues so the body goes on producing sweat copiously in a desperate effort to lower its temperature.

The eventual result would be a spiral into dehydration unless the runner is able to replace the lost fluid quickly. So before a race on a hot, humid day the distance runner should ensure he is fully 'hydrated' by taking frequent drinks, and supplement them by taking in further liquids from the earliest available moment in the race, rather than waiting until he is thirsty.

Runners who are used to training frequently tend to have the most efficient and easily stimulated sweating systems. But females tend to sweat considerably less than males, with no apparently diminishing effect on their temperature regulation, for reasons which are, as yet, not clearly understood.

After heavy training the replacement of fluid may need to continue for a considerble time, and some runners find they need to stand 1–2 glasses of water beside their bed to cope with night thirst.

See also *Heat, Humidity*.

T

Tibia

Sometimes known as the shin bone, it is the tibia you can feel just below the skin surface at the front of the lower leg, from the knee down to the ankle. This is the main weight-bearing bone of the lower leg, although it works in conjunction with its partner, the more narrowly defined fibula, which is situated on the outside of the leg.

The area of the shin may give rise to a number of painful conditions attributable to running, notably simple shin soreness, a stress fracture of the tibia, or anterior compartment syndrome. Additionally, if the bony lump situated just below the knee, at the front of the tibia and known as the tibial tuberosity, is particularly tender or painful to touch, especially in the case of a hard-training teenager, then Osgood Schlatter's disease must be considered as a potential cause. In such cases rest is the only treatment, as the bone is allowed to complete growth.

See also *Fibula, Osgood Schlatter's Disease, Shin Soreness, Stress Fracture*.

Topless running

In the United Kingdom runners have to wear at least a vest and shorts during competition. But in the USA, some male athletes compete in road races on warm days wearing just shorts, which has the physiological advantage of exposing a greater area of skin to assist in heat dissipation.

However, the first recorded instance of a female athlete finishing a race topless also occurred in the USA, at the Evergreen 10km in Evergreen, Colorado, on 2 August 1980. An unidentified female competitor among the thousand-strong field shed her T-shirt in the last half mile and crossed the finishing line topless to a standing ovation, and with excellent heat dissipation.

Track etiquette

When using a running track on which a number of athletes are training it is important to observe a certain universal track etiquette to minimize the risk of accidents.

All running should be in an anti-clockwise direction around the track. In general, the two inside lanes are assumed to be used by athletes running hard, and all other running, such as warming up, warming down, or steady-paced jogging, should be performed in the outer lanes, whether you are a beginner or an Olympic champion.

Similarly, everyone has the right to use the inside lanes for hard running, even if your flat-out pace is fairly modest. When you want to run hard yourself, wait until the inside lanes are clear near you, then move on to them, complete your run – it might be 400 metres – but then as soon as possible afterwards step on to the infield, or into an outer lane. Don't stand in the inside lane with your hands on your knees, gasping; it's the equivalent of stopping in the fast lane of the motorway to wipe your windscreen.

If you are running flat out, and someone comes up fast behind you, don't feel you have to move out in that case; they will expect to overtake you. But if an athlete who is running hard suddenly finds someone standing, walking or jogging slowly in the inside lane, he will usually shout out the single word 'Track!', which is the equivalent of the motorists' horn. It is the hard-running athlete's right of way, and those who are blocking the path are expected to step sharply on to the infield or into an outer lane. Getting off the track is preferable, because moving outwards (especially if the runner decides he has to overtake) can still cause a collision.

Alternatively, if a runner travelling at speed is forced suddenly to brake, swerve or stop a serious muscular injury may result.

Thus, it is important to always check for the approach of runners before crossing the track, especially on all-weather tracks which do not give you the tell-tale crunchy footsteps of a cinder circuit. Similarly, remember that running tracks are also used by field events athletes who may throw the javelin, hammer, shot or discus from some way away, and once it is flying through the air they can do nothing if you step in its path.

Some runners feel that if they are away from the roads and the traffic, then they are free from potential hazards when running. In fact, on a running track there may still be hazards. If you are not careful, you could even be one of them!

Tracksuit

Although the tracksuit has been looked upon in many ways, from standard sporting equipment to status symbol to high fashion and back, its use, whatever its colour combination or sprinkling of badges, is simply to keep the body warm before and after training or competition.

In fact, the standard two-piece tracksuit has been widely replaced by any combination of fleecy-lined top and trousers which will allow maximum movement and comfort, and which is easy to get on and off over shoes. Most runners tend to settle on a group of favourite clothes which form their 'track suit', and through practical experience will discard any which are not really suitable. A pair of leg-hugging tights, for instance, may keep you warm, especially as a secondary, inner layer, but adequate time has to be allowed to take them off and re-tie your shoes comfortably.

Once the body has started hard, continuous exercise in the form of a race or training run, it needs to be able to lose the heat it generates very quickly, so the tracksuit would interfere with that process. But until then it is needed, because although there is some body heat produced during the pre-race warm-up, it is not a continuous hard activity, and may be punctuated by stopping to perform exercises, or walking or jogging.

If the runner has warmed up sufficiently, taking off the tracksuit should not create major discomfort unless he does so too early. But timing the warm-up correctly is crucial, particularly in races with large fields. At a track event with perhaps only a dozen competitors, the starter will usually wait, within reason, for you to be ready. But in a field of some hundreds, the gun goes, ready or not.

At the start of some major mass marathons, tracksuits have to be removed so early to get everyone on to the start line that runners may face half an hour stripped off in sometimes poor weather conditions. But the temporary adoption of plastic bin liners as a cheap, effective and disposable method of retaining some body heat has been widespread in races like the New York and London marathons. In New York many runners also retain some items of old clothing until the last minute, then throw them off before the gun, never expecting to see them again. The organizers actually collect and sort this gear, and anything usable is washed and donated to charity.

Whilst some of the smartest current tracksuits are expensive and well made, they sometimes do not offer the fleecy warmth needed at the end of a hard road run, when your body is beginning to become cold, and you need such a layer next to your skin. Often a simple hooded top is the best item of clothing to put on first after a race, to keep your body and arms warm while you get the rest of you dressed.

At mass participation events, where it sometimes takes time to find your discarded clothing afterwards, even in labelled bags, it may be worth ensuring that a second set of dry, warm clothing can either by collected from a friend who is specifically looking after you, or is left in a predetermined place. Sometimes even the

European indoor 3000m champion Yvonne Murray wearing a tracksuit for training on a cold day

best-organized systems of shifting clothing from start to finish go awry, and if you have a spare set available you can then get warm first and go in search of the missing gear afterwards. At the end of marathons, losing your tracksuit and shivering with cold is no joke.

Whatever a tracksuit, or its substitute, looks like or feels like, its primary function is always to help regulate the body temperature. You wear it to reach a level of pre-competition or training warmth, and you put it on afterwards to prevent unnecessary heat loss as your body cools. But, particularly among young athletes, its use is still occasionally confused with that of a kind of status symbol. One boy once asked another: 'Why do you need a tracksuit? You're not a very good runner.'

'I may not be very good,' answered the other boy, 'but I still get cold.'

See also *Hypothermia, Warming Up.*

U

Ultramarathon: a tale of two races

For those rugged individuals for whom a mere marathon is just a warm-up, the ultramarathon, which can be anything from a 30-miler to a six-day race, provides the ultimate challenge. In the late 19th century in particular, six-day endurance races were popular spectator events on both sides of the Atlantic, with large crowds packing indoor arenas to watch (and bet upon) runners circling the cramped 220-yard tracks. The drama of the race, as well as the sometimes unscrupulous off-track activities, later formed the colourful basis for a number of books, both fictional and factional.

Some of the performances were quite astounding, considering the lack of modern training knowledge and back-up. Or are we softer now? In 1888, for example, a Briton, George Littlewood, covered 623 miles 1320 yards (1003.832km) in six days at Madison Square Gardens, New York City. Although the event was to fade from popularity for a while, it was not until July 1984, nearly a century later, that Yiannis Kouros of Greece bettered that record, with 635 miles 1023 yards.

The two current annually contested classic ultramarathon races are the London to Brighton (53 miles 450 yards/85.7km) and the Comrades Marathon between Durban and Pietermaritzburg (54 miles 1100 yards/87.9km) in South Africa. The latter, of course, is no longer the international event it once was because of the expulsion of South Africa from the International Amateur Athletic Federation in 1976. This means that no runner from any member nation of the IAAF can take part in events staged in that country.

Of the two classic races, the Comrades event is considerably older, having first been held in 1921. It was founded by a railway engineer named Vic Clapham, who was a member of a South African ex-servicemen's association named the Comrades of the Great War. Many of the participants in the early years of the race were former infantrymen, and in many ways it was similar to the type of route marches they had endured.

In 1922, its second year, it was won by a man who was to become known, ironically, as the father of long-distance running in the UK: Arthur Newton. He was born in 1883, the son of a Norfolk clergyman, and settled in South Africa in 1901, later buying a farm which produced first-grade cotton and tobacco. Newton seemed set for a prosperous life as a farmer until a change of government put the land he owned and had developed into a 'native territory' belt in 1922, ending his farming career without compensation. Searching for a method of getting into the public eye, and hoping to bring some attention to his situation, he spent five months carefully preparing to compete in the Comrades Marathon, even though he had no previous background in running.

Nevertheless at the age of 39, and a complete novice, he won the race and retained the title for the next three years. His sharp, reasoning mind helped him to plan his training, and although it did not help his farming situation, he moved quickly to the forefront of the world's long-distance runners. In 1924 Newton returned to England and set a world 50 miles best (5h 38:42) on the London to Brighton road, long before a race existed, and his continued road-running successes in both England and South Africa were only halted when he took part in a professional 1928 Trans-America race, forfeiting his amateur status.

In South Africa, meanwhile, the Comrades Marathon was becoming established as an annual event, with the distinguishing feature of being run in opposite directions in alternate years. In 1921 it was run from Pietermaritzburg down to Durban on the coast, which involves an overall drop of 2500 feet (762.5m) to sea level, while in 1922 it was run in the 'up' direction, from sea level at Durban to the altitude of Pietermaritzburg. It has alternated ever since.

For many years, though, while it remained a popular spectator event, the actual number of participants remained below 100. Only in the sixties did the field begin to swell, and by 1971 topped 1000. With the subsequent running boom, and the official inclusion of non-whites and women in 1975, the entry continued to soar towards its current mark of nearly 11,000. The event proudly claims that it is now totally integrated (although its society, sadly, is not). It is held each year in late May, on the national holiday of Republic Day, and attracts enormous attention, stimulated by live television coverage.

The current Comrades Marathon hero is Bruce Fordyce, who in 1987 achieved a record

Bruce Fordyce (right, number 1), the South African-based runner who has managed to win both the London to Brighton and Comrades races

London to Brighton Winners

NB. The course has varied in exact distance over the years, from 51¾ miles in the earliest races, to its longest of 54 miles 460 yards (87.325km) in 1979 and 1980, when the route was diverted at Horley to avoid roadworks at Gatwick Airport. The current course is 53 miles 450 yards (85.706km).

Record: Although Alastair Wood's 1972 run of 5:11.02 is the fastest to date (an average pace of 5.89 minutes per mile for the 1972 course), former European & Commonwealth Marathon champion Ian Thompson averaged 5.81 minutes per mile for the considerably longer 1980 race.

Year	Winner	Time
1951	Lew Piper (Blackheath H)	6:18.40
1952	Derek Reynolds (Blackheath H)	5:52.22
1953	Wally Hayward (South Africa)	5:29.40
1954	Bill Kelly (Reading AC)	5:39.47
1955	Tom Richards (South London H)	5:27.24
1956	Ron Hopcroft (Thames Valley H)	5:36.26
1957	Gerald Walsh (South Africa)	5:26.20
1958	Mike Kirkwood (Haltemprice)	5:47.44
1959	Fritz Madel (South Africa)	5:43.58
1960	Jackie Mekler (South Africa)	5:26.56
1961	John Smith (Epsom & Ewell H)	5:37.43
1962	John Smith (Epsom & Ewell H)	5:35.22
1963	Bernard Gomersall (Leeds Harehills)	5:47.55
1964	Bernard Gomersall (Leeds Harehills)	5:39.44
1965	Bernard Gomersall (Leeds Harehills)	5:40.11
1966	Bernard Gomersall (Leeds Harehills)	5:32.50
1967	John Tarrant (Salford H)	5:41.50
1968	John Tarrant (Salford H)	5:37.27
1969	Dave Bagshaw (South Africa)	5:28.53
1970	Joe Clare (Blackheath H)	5:41.08
1971	Dave Levick (South Africa)	5:21.45
1972	Alastair Wood (Aberdeen AAC)	5:11.02
1973	Joe Keating (Ealing/Southall AC)	5:11.30
1974	John Newsome (Wakefield H)	5:16.07
1975	Cavin Woodward (Leamington CAC)	5:12.07
1976	Tom O'Reilly (Small Heath H)	5:23.32
1977	Don Ritchie (Forres H)	5:16.05
1978	Don Ritchie (Forres H)	5:13.02
1979	Allan Kirik (USA)	5:32.37
1980	Ian Thompson (Luton United H)	5:15.15
1981	Bruce Fordyce (South Africa)	5:21.15
1982	Bruce Fordyce (South Africa)	5:18.36
1983	Bruce Fordyce (South Africa)	5:12.32
1984	Barry Heath (Royal Marines)	5:24.15
1985	Hoseah Tjale (South Africa)	5:31.26
1986	Terry Tullett (Brighton/Hove AC)	5:53.10*
	*(Daniel de Chaumont, South Africa	5:51.57, disq.)

WOMEN

NB. Dale Greig (Paisley) completed the course as an unofficial female participant in 1972 in 8:30.04, and Leslie Watson (London Olympiades) led home three unofficial women finishers in 1979 in 6:55.11. Women were officially included from 1980.

Year	Runner	Time
1980	Leslie Watson (London Olympiades)	6:56.10
1981	Lynn Fitzgerald (Highgate H)	7:47.28
1982	Ann Franklin (Mynyddwr de Cymru)	7:01.51
1983	Ann Franklin (Mynyddwr de Cymru)	6:37.08
1984	No finishers	
1985	Sandra Kiddy (USA)	7:02.37
1986	Eleanor Adams (Sutton/Ashfield)	6:42.40

seventh consecutive victory in the race. Although based in South Africa, he was born in Hong Kong, part educated in England, and holds a British passport. Through this, he also managed to enter and win the London to Brighton race three times from 1981–3, although the close historic links between the two races have proved something of an embarrassment to the governing bodies of the sport in recent years. Fordyce, for example, had to be advised that while he could compete in either England or South Africa if he wished, he could not run in both. He chose South Africa.

Initially, the links between the two events had been established through Arthur Newton. When he moved back to England, Newton stimulated a great deal of interest in ultra-distance running through four books he had authored and countless magazine articles he had written in the forties and fifties. A great many distance running enthusiasts used to gather at his Ruislip home to talk about the sport, and from such informal discussions the possibility was born of creating a road-running race from London to Brighton. The idea reached Ernest Neville, an athletics official who had long experience of organizing walking races on the London to Brighton route, and on 11 August 1951 Neville organized the first annual running race on the course, as part of the Festival of Britain celebrations and sponsored by the now defunct *News Chronicle* newspaper.

Forty-seven runners started, thirty-two reached the finish at Brighton Aquarium after running 52 miles 394 yards through wind and rain. Lew Piper (Blackheath Harriers) won that inaugural race in 6hr 18min 40sec, and subsequently a new body, the Road Runners Club (RRC), was founded with the primary object of promoting the event annually. The inaugural meeting of the RRC was held at Regent Street Polytechnic, London, on 30 June 1952 and was addressed by Arthur Newton, who lived to see the race grow from strength to strength before his death in 1959 at the age of 76.

The exact distance of the race, which winds through Croydon, Redhill, Horley, Crawley, Bolney and Pyecombe and takes in three waves of hills, has changed over the years because of roadworks and diversions on the A23 which is extremely busy, but the current course is 53 miles 450 yards (85.7km).

Unlike the Comrades Marathon, the London to Brighton race retains a compact entry, all of whom have to show proven ability at long-distance running to qualify. Usually around 150 runners toe the traditional starting line on Westminster Bridge at 7 a.m. on a Sunday in late September or early October. From 1980, women were officially included in the race.

The London–Brighton and Comrades races had become 'twin' events over the years, pinnacles for the ultra-distance exponents. Winning both became a major ambition for runners whose talents lay beyond the range of normal Olympic events. South Africans Wally Hayward and Jackie Mekler, who both won the Comrades race five times, also won the

The programme cover for the first London to Brighton road running race, held in 1951

'Brighton': Hayward in 1953, and Mekler (the 1954 Commonwealth Games Marathon silver medallist) in 1960. The South African-based native Yorkshireman Dave Bagshaw also won the London–Brighton in 1969 and the Comrades race three times, from 1969–71. Fordyce is the latest (and, for the time being anyway, presumably the last) winner of both races.

Britain provided the winner of the Comrades event on three occasions: in 1962, John Smith of Epsom & Ewell H, who also won the London–Brighton in 1961–2; in 1965, Bernard Gomersall of Leeds, who won the London–Brighton four times from 1963–6; and in 1972 Mick Orton, who led Tipton Harriers to a distinguished team victory.

The IAAF ban on South Africa in 1976 meant that the last official and serious UK challenge in the Comrades Marathon came from Cavin Woodward of Leamington, who was runner-up that year. But the continuance of South African qualified runners appearing in the London to Brighton race in succeeding years created some embarrassment for the IAAF member body, the British Amateur Athletic Board.

While the 'Brighton' organizers were apparently reluctant to end their long-term links with the 'Comrades', the BAAB had little choice but to uphold the IAAF rules. Even after Bruce Fordyce's three Brighton wins, there was a major row when two other South Africans, Hoseah Tjale from Johannesburg and Derrick Tivers from Durban, finished first and second in the 1985 London to Brighton event, and race organizer Ian Champion (who maintained they had run as individuals, not representing their clubs or country) was suspended from organizing races for two years.

Only the following year further embarrassment was heaped upon the BAAB (and the Road Runners Club) when it turned out that the 1986 winner, Daniel de Chaumont, who had entered as a Frenchman and was unknown to the organizers, was actually South African too. He was subsequently disqualified by the Road Runners Club Council, and the runner-up, Terry Tullett, was awarded the race. But it seemed that the long-standing links between the two events were indeed harder to shake off than anyone could have imagined.

Comrades Marathon Winners

a = Pietermaritzburg to Durban
b = Durban to Pietermaritzburg

Year		Winner	Time
1921	(a)	Billy Rowan	8:59.00
1922	(b)	Arthur Newton	8:40.00
1923	(a)	Arthur Newton	6:56.07
1924	(b)	Arthur Newton	6:58.22
1925	(a)	Arthur Newton	6:24.45
1926	(b)	Harry Phillips	6:57.46
1927	(a)	Arthur Newton	6:40.56
1928	(b)	Frank Sutton	7:49.07
1929	(a)	Darrell Dale	7:52.01

Year		Winner	Time
1930	(b)	Wally Hayward	7:27.26
1931	(a)	Phil Masterton-Smith	7:16.30
1932	(b)	Bill Savage	7:41.58
1933	(a)	Hardy Ballington	6:50.37
1934	(b)	Hardy Ballington	7:09.02
1935	(a)	Bill Cochrane	6:30.05
1936	(b)	Hardy Ballington	6:46.14
1937	(a)	Johnny Coleman	6:23.11
1938	(b)	Hardy Ballington	6:32.26
1939	(a)	Johnny Coleman	6:22.05
1940	(b)	Allan Boyce	6:39.23
1941–45		Not held	
1946	(b)	Bill Cochrane	7:02.40
1947	(a)	Hardy Ballington	6:41.05
1948	(b)	Bill Savage	7:13.25
1949	(a)	Reg Allison	6:23.21
1950	(b)	Wally Hayward	6:46.25
1951	(a)	Wally Hayward	6:14.08
1952	(b)	Trevor Allen	7:00.02
1953	(a)	Wally Hayward	5:52.30
1954	(b)	Wally Hayward	6:12.54
1955	(a)	Gerald Walsh	6:06.32
1956	(b)	Gerald Walsh	6:33.35
1957	(a)	Mercier Davies	6:13.55
1958	(b)	Jackie Mekler	6:26.26
1959	(a)	Trevor Allen	6:28.11
1960	(b)	Jackie Mekler	5:56.32
1961	(a)	George Claassen	6:07.07
1962	(b)	John Smith (UK)	5:57.05
1963	(a)	Jackie Mekler	5:51.20
1964	(b)	Jackie Mekler	6:09.54
1965	(a)	Bernard Gomersall (UK)	5:51.09
1966	(b)	Tommy Malone	6:14.07
1967	(a)	Manie Kuhn	5:54.10
1968	(b)	Jackie Mekler	6:01.11
1969	(a)	Dave Bagshaw	5:45.35
1970	(b)	Dave Bagshaw	5:51.27
1971	(a)	Dave Bagshaw	5:47.06
1972	(b)	Mick Orton (UK)	5:48.57
1973	(a)	Dave Levick	5:39.09
1974	(b)	Derek Preiss	6:02.49
1975	(b)	Derek Preiss	5:53.40
1976	(a)	Alan Robb	5:40.43
1977	(b)	Alan Robb	5:47.09
1978	(a)	Alan Robb	5:29.14
1979	(b)	Piet Vorster	5:45.02
1980	(a)	Alan Robb	5:38.25
1981	(b)	Bruce Fordyce	5:37.28
1982	(a)	Bruce Fordyce	5:34.22
1983	(b)	Bruce Fordyce	5:30.12
1984	(a)	Bruce Fordyce	5:27.18
1985	(b)	Bruce Fordyce	5:37.01
1986	(a)	Bruce Fordyce	5:24.07
1987	(b)	Bruce Fordyce	5:37.01

WOMEN

Year		Winner	Time
1977	(b)	Lettie van Zyl	8:58.00
1978	(a)	Lettie van Zyl	8:25.00
1979	(b)	Jan Mallen	8:22.41
1980	(a)	Isavel Roche-Kelly	7:18.00
1981	(b)	Isavel Roche-Kelly	6:44.00
1982	(a)	Cheryl Jorgenson (USA)	7:04.00
1983	(b)	Lindsay Weight	7:12.56
1984	(a)	Lindsay Weight	6:46.35
1985	(b)	Helen Lucre	6:53.24
1986	(a)	Helen Lucre	6:55.15
1987	(b)	Helen Lucre	6:48.22

W

Waffle-soled shoes

The waffle-soled running shoe, with its dozens of small rubber studs, owes its name to its inventor, Bill Bowerman, the distinguished University of Oregon track coach from 1948 to 1973. For in addition to being a successful coach, Bowerman also had a particular interest in the development and manufacture of running shoes, and was closely involved in the foundation of the Nike company in the USA in 1972. He wanted to develop a light running shoe with a sole which could be worn with equal effect on road, grass or track, and one morning began to study the distinctive squared pattern on the breakfast waffles made by his wife.

In an experiment to try out the gripping properties of a shoe with that pattern, he actually put pieces of urethane into his wife's waffle iron in the kitchen, and managed to produce not only a dreadful smell but also the prototype material for the sole design he eventually patented. Although the design changed somewhat over the years, and was adapted by other shoe

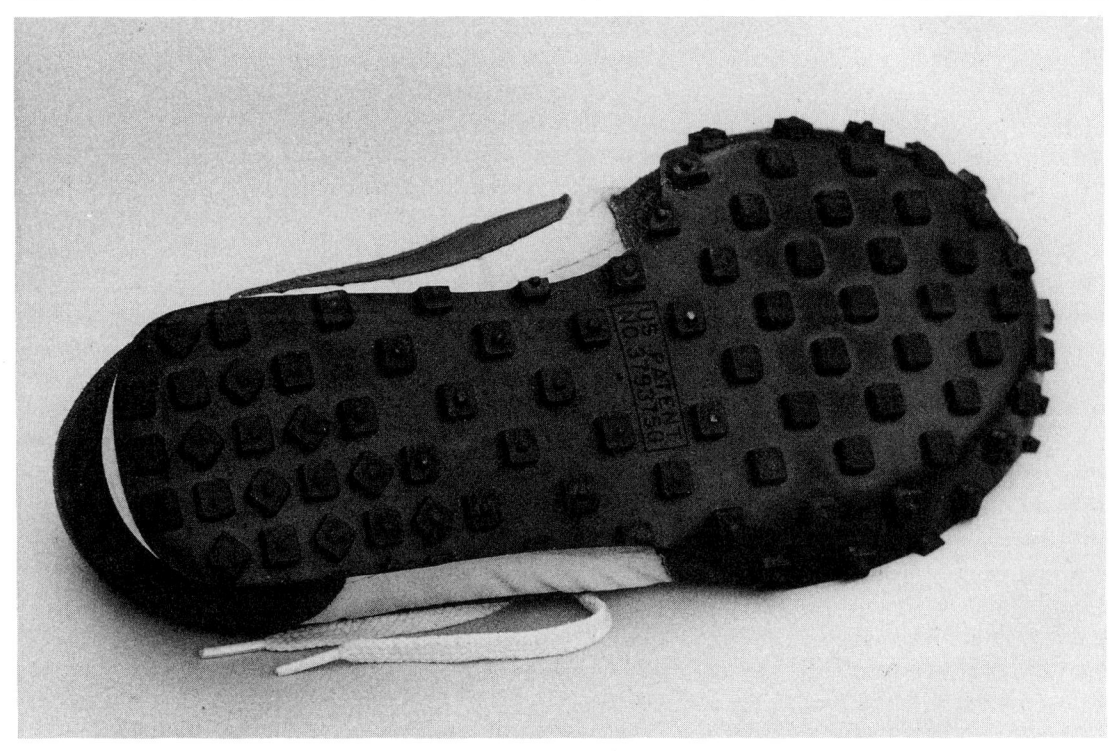

The multi-purpose waffle-soled shoe, which offers an alternative to spikes and studs

manufacturers, the name for the studded rubber soles as 'waffles' stuck – as did bits of melted urethane in his wife's ruined waffle iron.

Warming down

Following a strenuous training session or race, warming down should be the inevitable 'signing off' routine which not only allows a mental unwinding process, but will physiologically help the body recover from its efforts by clearing out the exercise waste products which could otherwise remain in the muscles and cause stiffness the following day.

If the runner finishes a race or final run in an interval session with a great volume of lactic acid in his muscles, but then does not run another step that day, the remnants of that lactic acid will take a great deal longer to clear than if he jogs for 10–15 minutes after recovery. Similarly in road and cross-country races, a gentle post-race jog can help the runner to return to normal training more quickly.

In a situation where a track athlete may have to run a semi-final or a final relatively soon after a qualifying round, a thorough warm-down after each race is more important even than another warm-up.

See also *Lactic Acid*.

Warming up

A routine of jogging, stretching and striding should be part of every runner's preparation before a fast training session, such as interval or hill training, and before a race. This warm-up performs the same function as switching on a car ignition, and getting the engine to gently accustom itself to being in action; no one comes out of their garage at 60 m.p.h.

In human terms, the warm-up stretches muscles, mobilizes joints, and sets the heart–lung system into greater levels of activity in preparation for a hard effort to come. Potential injury in muscles which are still tight from a previous training session is reduced by allowing them time to relax (and if they do not relax, serious thought should be given to training hard anyway).

The shorter, faster and more explosive the running to be performed (such as sprinting or hurdling), the longer and more thorough the warm-up should be. International athletes in these events often spend an hour or more just warming up.

For the longer events, such as the marathon, the warm-up is less important, as the early miles will perform the task. Some stretching of all the leg muscles and joints is advisable, but much of the marathon runner's pre-race preparation will often revolve more around measures designed to prevent chafing, blisters or dehydration later in the race. Before a training run, the distance runner should perform some stretching exercises, especially if he has had some muscle injury, but frequently distance runners are content (if not always best advised) to go straight out of the front door and into their run.

Warming up before training usually raises no timing difficulties. But the racing warm-up has to be carefully timed backwards from the advertised start of the event, to allow all the components of the routine to be included in an unhurried fashion, to allow extra visits to the toilet because of nerves, and to ensure that the athlete is ready when his event is called up by the marksman. Conversely, the warm-up should not take place so early that all the beneficial effects have worn off by the time the athlete actually competes. Timing is often as important as the actual warm-up.

Road and championship track races tend to be punctual, but there are two particularly awkward situations for the distance runner trying to judge a race warm-up. The first is at a track meeting where there are either a considerable number of heats or graded age-group races of an event like the 1500m. It has been known for eleven heats of a 1500m to be required at a Southern Counties championship meeting, with the luckless runners drawn in Heat 11 trying to remain warmed up for a full hour after Heat 1 had been run. Worse, the athletes rarely know the draw in such circumstances until just before the heats start, so they have to warm up as if they are in Heat 1.

The second difficult situation can occur at cross-country meetings where there are a number of age-group events, and the programme specifies a starting time for the first race, followed only by the order of succeeding events. This is a very inconsiderate habit of some meeting organizers, and should be discouraged in favour of a system of at least announcing approximate starting times for each event (in case the previous one has not quite finished) rather than putting the onus on the athlete to keep an eye on other events and try to judge their own warm-up. But while this unsatisfactory situation still occurs at some events, it is best to be aware of it.

A typical warm-up for a track race or training session might consist of 1–2 miles jogging at a gradually increasing pace, followed by a series of stretching exercises taking 10–15 minutes. Then spiked shoes, if worn, should be put on, and a series of 3–4 runs of approximately eighty metres performed at a faster pace, with an exaggerated stride to stretch the legs fully. This final ritual is usually known as 'strides'. In a perfect warm-up, the final stride would be completed about two minutes before the marksman called for the competitors to take off their tracksuits.

At a high level of middle-distance track competition, a preliminary warm-up run earlier in the day often helps: a steady mile, followed by a hard mile, then another steady mile, for example, at least 4–5 hours before the race, can assist the actual race warm-up to be more effective. And prior to longer track races, and some road races, a great many top level runners will run a steady 3–5 miles on the morning of the race for, as they sometimes quaintly call it, 'a cough and a spit'!

Wind chill factor

A cold temperature may become far more uncomfortable, and even lethal, when a wind is blowing. The wind chill factor, as it is known,

Wind chill factor

aggravates the actual temperature shown on the thermometer, and even a wind of 10mph blowing at freezing point (0°C, or 32°F) will cool the face twice as quickly as still air at the same temperature. The direction of the wind is also a crucial factor, because a head wind has far more impact than a side wind in lowering the runner's temperature, and possibly in extreme cases causing hypothermia. The following table shows an approximate equivalent Fahrenheit temperature taking into account the wind speed.

Estimated wind speed (mph)	Actual thermometer reading (°F)						
	50	40	30	20	10	0	−10
	Equivalent temperature (°F)						
calm	50	40	30	20	10	0	−10
5	48	37	27	16	6	−5	−15
10	40	28	16	4	−9	−24	−33
15	36	22	9	−5	−18	−32	−45
20	32	18	4	−10	−25	−39	−53
25	30	16	0	−15	−29	−44	−59
30	28	13	−2	−18	−33	−48	−63
35	27	11	−4	−20	−35	−51	−67
40	26	10	−6	−21	−37	−53	−69

See also *Cold, Hypothermia*.

Wind gauge

In sprint and hurdles events up to 200m, the wind velocity during the race is measured by means of a wind gauge, a funnel mounted on a tripod, which is situated halfway along the home straight, no more than two metres from the track.

The velocity is measured from the start of the race for ten seconds in the case of the 100m, for thirteen seconds in the case of the 100m hurdles or 110m hurdles, and for ten seconds after the runners enter the straight in a 200m event.

A following wind speed in excess of 2.0 metres per second (4.47 m.p.h.) will rule any performances in that event ineligible for record recognition (except in the case of the heptathlon and decathlon, where wind speeds up to 4.0 metres per second are permitted for record ratification).

The original rules on wind speed were accepted by the IAAF in 1936, following a lengthy report on assistance from wind velocity by the German Federation, presented by Dr Karl Ritter. It claimed that the highest following wind velocity which did not improve a runner's time was 0.7 metres per second (or 1.0m/sec in the case of a side wind). Already countries such as the USA were rejecting record performances with a following wind of more than 1.34m/sec (or 3 m.p.h.) in their own domestic competitions.

But the rules accepted in 1936 allowed a following wind of 2.0m/sec, well in excess of Ritter's recommendation. Forty years later, after some more research at London's Imperial College of Science and Technology had suggested that 100m sprint times could be improved by 0.1sec with as little as 0.42m/sec following wind, the 1976 IAAF Congress in

Montreal was asked to reconsider the rules by the British delegate Harold Abrahams, the Olympic 100m champion of 1924. He argued that the existing rule of 2m/sec could make wind assistance worth almost half a second allowable. But no changes were made in the rules, and the wind assistance limit which was decided upon in such an arbitrary fashion half a century ago remains the official limit to the present day.

Women

Although women are drawing closer to men in terms of athletic records, it is unlikely, for physiological reasons, that they will ever catch up completely. Much of the progress has been due to the comparatively recent acceptance of women in events like the marathon, which men have been racing seriously for almost a century. And while the best women runners may still be able to beat a considerable number of men, it seems unlikely that they will ever be able to beat the *best* men.

This is not a sexist view, but one put forward by scientists who point out that women have smaller hearts relative to their body size and smaller lung volumes. The percentage of red, oxygen-carrying cells in their blood is lower (around 42 per cent, compared to the 47 per cent in the male), and the actual volume of blood in the female body is approximately 4–$4\frac{1}{2}$ litres, compared to 5–6 litres in the male.

It has been estimated that during a steady run a woman has to transport some nine litres of blood around the body to deliver one litre of oxygen to the muscles, whereas a male need only transport eight litres of blood for the same amount.

Women also have a higher body fat content than men, and although with this source of energy fuel in endurance events they could be said to be better equipped than men, it still has to be carried as additional weight. Physiologists report that whereas male endurance-trained athletes may have as little as 3–4 per cent body fat, in the equivalent female it is likely to be 10–12 per cent. But there are sporting occasions in which this is a positive advantage, as in Channel swimming, where the additional buoyancy and insulation afforded by the higher body fat (as well as potential energy source) have helped women to almost literally rule the waves.

The greater participation of women in running events worldwide has also highlighted particular phenomena, such as the relatively frequent instances of amenorrhoea (cessation of periods) among hard-training female runners. In general, the health and fitness enjoyed by female runners allows them to cope more efficiently with the regular physical discomforts to which women have to adapt, and when giving birth, trained runners tend to do so more easily and quickly.

The wider pelvis of the woman does, however, sometimes present running complications in that it causes the femur (thigh bone) to come into the knee at an angle, and may cause extra stress on that joint.

Historically, women's athletics only began to be organized seriously in the 1920s, but the first meetings for women only were probably those at Vassar College, Poughkeepsie, New York State, from 1895. Performances there, such as a 36.25sec 220 yards by a Ms Haight, were modest but significant in their own way.

In 1917 the Fédération Féminine Sportive de France was formed by Alice Milliat, and in 1921 she went on to form the Fédération Sportive Féminine Internationale (FSFI) in Paris, following a match between France and Britain. There were six original members, including Britain and the USA, but a request from the newly formed organization to include women's events in the 1924 Olympics was turned down by the IOC. So instead, the FSFI held its own 'Women's Olympics' in Paris in 1922, and subsequently every four years until 1934 staged a women's World Games which, eventually, nineteen nations were attending.

In the meantime, the IOC had tentatively allowed a selection of five women's events into their 1928 Amsterdam Olympic Games, after a 12–5 vote and despite particular opposition from Finland.

But the collapse of several undertrained competitors in the women's 800 metres at Amsterdam unfortunately created the wrong impression, and the event was considered too strenuous for women at the Olympics; they were not allowed to run anything further than 200 metres again in the Games until 1960.

From that time (and with the FSFI having merged with the IAAF in 1936), women's athletics was gradually given greater status. The 800m was returned to the Olympic programme in 1960, the 400m added in 1964, the 1500m in 1972, the 3000m and the marathon in 1984, and the 10,000m in 1988.

The IAAF now has its own women's committee to supervise the development of their side of the sport, and in December 1983 the IAAF held its first Women's Athletics Congress

Left: Joan Benoit, winner of the first ever Olympic women's marathon, at Los Angeles, 1984

Below: Thousands of women are enjoying the wider range of competitive and recreational running opportunities now open to them

in Mainz, West Germany. Not only are women now encouraged to take part in distance running, but they may soon be competing at championship level in other previously all-male preserves like hammer-throwing, triple jumping and pole vaulting.

Z

Zatopek, Emil

In terms of Olympic achievement, the Czech runner Emil Zatopek remains the only athlete to have won the 5000m, 10,000m and marathon at the same Olympics (Helsinki, 1952). But in the history of running it was his courageous self-experiments in training which marked him out as an individualist who, like so many other innovators, was at first considered crazy.

Zatopek, who was born in Koprivnice, Northern Moravia on 19 September 1922, and worked in a local shoe factory after leaving school, did not start competitive racing until he was 19 years old, in 1941. But, self-coached, his career only really began to develop after the war in 1945, when he adopted the Swedish training method of fartlek after a visit to Czechoslovakia by Arne Andersson. He took the sessions to much greater lengths, and added interval training of high quality and even higher quantity.

Zatopek wanted to find the limits of his body, and sometimes even held his breath until he almost blacked out, just to see how long he could do so. He felt that it was possible to absorb far more training than had been previously believed, and after he was conscripted in the Army in 1945 he began to perform mammoth interval sessions round and round a 400m track. Sometimes he alternated sixty- and ninety-second laps up to 50 times, making it even harder by running in heavy basketball boots or, on occasions, his Army boots!

He explained this philosophy thus: 'I will run more, and maybe I will run faster.' Another typical training session was 5×200m in 38–40sec each, and 15×400m in 80–90sec, just as a warm-up, then 15×400m in 70–72sec, 10×400m in 80–90sec, and finally 5×200m flat out, at around 30sec each. Each run was separated by a jog of just 200m, or even 100m.

Combined with his steady-paced running, he was covering some 800km a month at the peak of his career – equivalent to around 25km (or 15 miles) a day, much of it at speed, and some of it in heavy footwear. In that immediate post-war era some people thought Zatopek would kill himself, especially as he raced and trained with an agonized expression, his tongue sometimes hanging out ('It is not gymnastics or ice skating, you know,' he explained).

Although it was not textbook style, his unique approach was successful. He was fifth in the 1946 European 5000m Championships, which encouraged him to step up his training even more, with track sessions like 40×400m, with 250m jog recovery. In June 1948, in only his second-ever 10,000m, he missed the world record, held by Finland's Viljo Heino, by just 1.6 seconds with 29:37.0. Then six weeks later he burned off Heino himself to win the Olympic title at Wembley Stadium in 29:59.6.

Zatopek's world dominance at the event was such that he was to win thirty-eight consecutive 10,000m races between May 1948 and July 1954 (including eleven in 1949 alone), before succumbing to the sprint finish of the little Hungarian Jozsef Kovacs in a close race in Budapest on 3 July 1954.

He also broke the world 10,000m record five times between 1949 and 1954, effectively improving it by over forty seconds. And in the meantime he had won the 1948 and 1952 Olympic titles, as well as the 1950 European title, and won the 1954 European title (gaining revenge over Kovacs this time), in August 1954. He was nicknamed 'the human locomotive'.

At 5000m he was almost as successful, winning the 1950 European title and the 1952 Olympic title, remaining undefeated at the distance from October 1948 to June 1952, and setting a world record of 13:57.2 in 1954. In all,

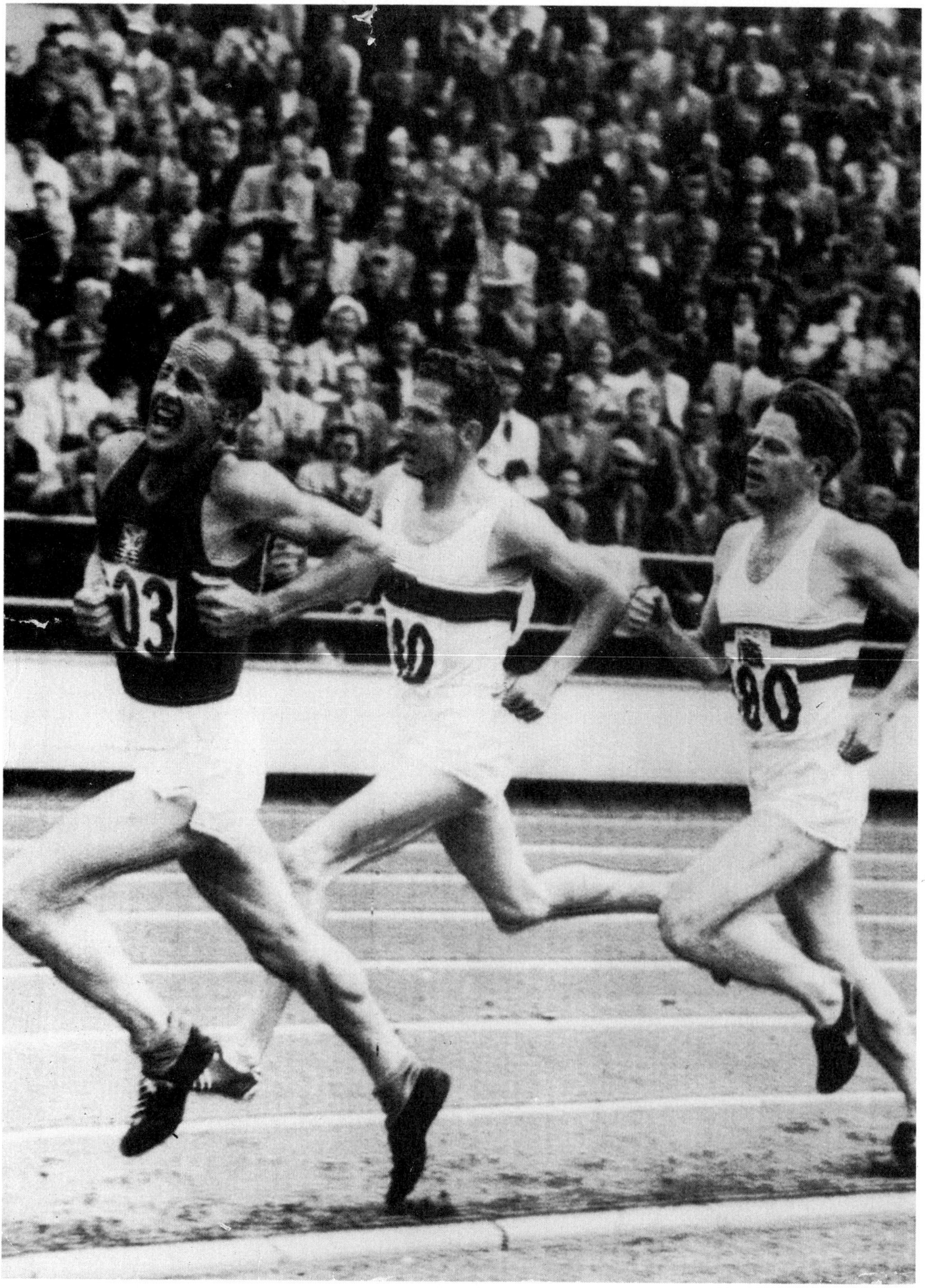
903
80
80

Zatopek set eighteen world records at distances ranging from 5000m to 30,000m during his career.

But he is still best remembered for his unique triple at the Helsinki Olympics. Within one week in late July he won the 10,000m by the length of the home straight, took the 5000m title after a four-man sprint around the final bend, and lined up for his first-ever marathon.

Determined to watch the experienced marathon men, like Britain's world record holder Jim Peters, Zatopek even introduced himself to Peters on the start line, to make sure it really was Peters.

After ten miles, and used to training at a much faster speed than their 5:25 a mile marathon racing pace, Zatopek asked Peters: 'Jim, the pace – it is too fast?' Peters jokingly replied, 'Emil, the pace – it is too slow.' But before the half-distance had been covered, Zatopek took him at his word and broke away. Peters himself dropped out with cramp at 33km, while Zatopek, despite tiring rapidly towards the end, held on to win by some 700m in 2hr 23min 4sec.

It was his third gold medal of the Games, and his third Olympic record, as the packed Olympic Stadium in the Finnish capital resounded to the chanting of his name. It really was the Zatopek Olympics, because on the same day as his 5000m victory, his wife, Dana, had won the women's javelin gold medal (and later had further successes, setting a world record in 1958 and taking the 1960 Olympic silver medal).

But Emil's own Olympic career ended on a sad, if courageous, note in Melbourne in 1956. Accepting that his era at 5000 and 10,000m might be over with the emergence of new names like Vladimir Kuts (USSR) and Britain's Gordon Pirie (who had idolized, copied and finally beaten Zatopek on the track), the Czech devoted his energy to defending his Olympic

Facing page: With his familiar agonized expression, the remarkable Emil Zatopek leads the Olympic 5000m final at Helsinki in 1952

Track progress

Born 19 September 1922.

	800m	*1500m*	*3000m*	*5000m*	*10,000m*
1941		4:20.3			
1942	2:02.8	4:13.9	9:12.2	16:25.0	
1943	1:58.7	4:01.6	8:56.0	15:26.6	
1944	1:59.8	3:59.5	8:34.8	14:55.0	
1945		4:01.4	8:33.4	14:50.8	
1946		3:57.6	8:21.0	14:25.8	
1947		3:52.8	8:08.8	14:08.2	
1948			8:07.8	14:10.0	29:37.0
1949				14:10.8	29:21.2
1950				14:03.0	29:02.6
1951				14:11.6	29:29.8
1952				14:06.4	29:17.0
1953				14:03.0	29:01.6
1954			8:19.0	13:57.0	28:54.2
1955				14:04.0	29:25.6
1956				14:14.8	29:33.4
1957				14:06.4	29:25.8

marathon title. As part of his search for new, harder training methods he started running while carrying his wife Dana on his back! The result, perhaps not surprisingly, was a hernia, which required an operation just six weeks before the Games. The doctors told Zatopek not to train for two months after the operation; instead, with characteristic stubborness, he went straight from the hospital to the training track.

His subsequent sixth place in the 1956 Olympic marathon, in a time of 2hr 29min 34sec, may, in the circumstances, have been one of his greatest performances. But he did not compete in major competitions again, with his last race being a cross-country event in 1957.

As a popular national figure in Czechoslovakia, he was still in the public eye after his retirement, and his support of Dubcek during the 'Prague Spring' of 1968, where the country briefly shook off some of the Soviet-backed restrictions, later landed him in trouble when Dubcek was replaced and the country occupied by Soviet tanks in August 1968. Going into hiding, Zatopek still severely criticized the Soviet control of his country, and in 1969 he was formally dismissed from his job as an army colonel in charge of sports training, and had to take menial labouring work.

But in the early seventies he renounced his earlier statements, which at least restored certain privileges, such as overseas travel. He was even able to travel as a guest to the 1978 New York City Marathon, where the sight of so many thousands of runners astonished him. And at home in Prague he was elevated to a post in the National Council of Sports documentation department.

While in New York he had reflected wryly on his early days of training experiments: 'I said, "Why should I practise running slow? I already know how to run slow. I want to learn to run fast." Everyone said, "Emil, you are a fool." But when I first won the European Championship, they said, "Emil, you are a genius!"' But he also revised his training beliefs later in his career, declaring, 'Quantity of kilometres is useless. Only to run 400m on the track is not the best. Training should be for everything – for speed, technique and power.' With the benefit of hindsight, it may be easy to find theoretical fault with his tortuous training. But, at the time, he was the one man who was prepared to test the untested. And without such pioneers, the sport would stand still.